PRAISE FOR *THE HEALING HOME AND GARDEN*

'Finally! A resource that addresses both the "visibles" and "invisibles" in our homes: how to create beautiful environments visually, but also ways to be sure the unseen energy there supports our personal well-being ... *The Healing Home and Garden* is a treasure trove of practical, step-by-step guidance from Paula's extensive body of knowledge about interior design, as well as offering a refreshingly intelligent sensitivity to the influence of the energy of our surroundings.'
Jean Haner, author of *Clear Home, Clear Heart*

'Every now and again, I come across a book like this, one that I wish I had found many years ago. This wonderful creation of Paula's is a solid, practical and beautiful guide to reimagining all parts of your home into a living, healing sanctuary. One where your heart, body and soul will long to spend time. This guide will make you want to restructure and re-imagine so many aspects of your living spaces in achievable and meaningful ways.'
Mary Reynolds, author of *We Are the ARK*

'Our homes should serve as secure sanctuaries, allowing us to escape the demands and pressures of the world, and to find solace in tranquillity amidst serene surroundings. *The Healing Home and Garden* is both creative and motivational, presenting cost-effective solutions to help you realise this heavenly sanctuary.'
Anita Moorjani, author of *Sensitive Is the New Strong*

'Paula Robinson urges us to step back from and reconsider our daily habitat, and to take comfort in the heart of our home.'
Richard Louv, author of *Last Child in the Woods*

'*The Healing Home and Garden* is an excellent guide for anyone motivated to transition their house into a home... Paula Robinson masterfully weaves scientific insights regarding the symphony between inanimate objects, plants, colours, music and household members. Beginning at the threshold, she walks through each living space and provides practical suggestions applicable to any home. As a physician, I am impressed by her suggestions which enhance the coordination of the left and right brain... Kudos for writing a book that provides guidance and useful references for a vibrant home.'
David MacDonald, DO, integrative family physician

'A must-read... Paula Robinson's *The Healing Home and Garden* teaches us how energy in our homes can influence our wellbeing, intuition, peace, joy and creativity... *The Healing Home and Garden* gives us the insights and tools to create an authentic home, true to our spirit. The world will change when we change ourselves. Start the change with your home!'
Carla Coulson, photographer and creativity coach

'I read this book during a very stressful time in my life, when I was riddled with debilitating headaches and living a very unhealthy lifestyle. Paula's advice on creating sanctuaries within the home really resonated with me... From uncluttering the entrance to walking barefoot at home in order to connect with the earth, this book has helped me at every step of my journey back to health. Not only therapeutic, this book is also impeccably researched and informative. Paula's advice helped me transform not just my life, but also my home, turning it from an unwelcoming box of sharp angles to a safe space where I can unwind and relax... Brimming with smart tips and advice, this should be required reading for anyone looking to redecorate or redesign their home, or indeed, their life.'
Awais Khan, author of *No Honour*

THE HEALING
HOME & GARDEN

In loving memory of my mother, Robbie Thomas,
who created healing homes and gardens wherever she lived.

THE HEALING
HOME & GARDEN

Reimagining spaces for optimal wellbeing

PAULA ROBINSON

First published in Great Britain in 2024 by Yellow Kite
An imprint of Hodder & Stoughton
An Hachette UK company

1

A CIP catalogue record for this title is available from the British Library
Illustrations © Philip Robinson 2024
onpointdesigns.co.uk@gmail.com
Cover photography: www.darrensetlow.com
A special thanks to Sonia Choquette for the Sonia Suggests boxes

Trade Paperback ISBN 9781399715447
ebook ISBN 9781399715454

Typeset in Celeste by Hewer Text UK Ltd, Edinburgh
Printed and bound in Great Britain by Clays Ltd, Elcograf S.p.A.

Hodder & Stoughton policy is to use papers that are natural, renewable
and recyclable products and made from wood grown in sustainable
forests. The logging and manufacturing processes are expected to
conform to the environmental regulations of the country of origin.

Yellow Kite
Hodder & Stoughton Ltd
Carmelite House
50 Victoria Embankment
London EC4Y 0DZ

www.yellowkitebooks.co.uk

CONTENTS

1

GETTING STARTED

'Imagination is more important than knowledge. Knowledge is limited. Imagination encircles the world.'

—Albert Einstein, *Saturday Evening Post*[1]

It's time to rethink how we're living in our homes, and question why we're doing things in certain ways, out of habit. Many of us are so inseparable from our devices that we end up working all hours and eating on-the-run. More often than not we're stressed, and we never seem to have enough hours in the day. To relax, we binge-watch television, and the majority of our time is spent indoors, disconnected from the healing qualities of nature. Our mental and physical health are suffering and our moments of joy seem all too fleeting.

For us to deeply relax, rest and heal, our homes should ideally be a sanctuary. Unfortunately, most aren't because they weren't designed to meet the demands of our 24/7/365 lifestyles, which have become dominated by technology. Many of us are living in formulaic spaces where form follows function, which can feel restrictive and outdated, and the latest interiors trends don't bring us lasting satisfaction or quality of life. These days, having a home designed to impress others seems rather empty and pointless, especially when it doesn't reflect who we truly are.

We're all in dire need of a space to breathe: a home that's a joy to live in, and feels comfortable and *real* to the people who really matter – the ones living there. Not the visitors. And certainly not the style police!

It's time to design our homes *intuitively*, not formulaically.

By rethinking the design of our homes, we can break unhealthy habits and form new ones that are right for us as individuals. But who has the energy or mental bandwidth for a major redesign at this point? The thought alone is exhausting!

In this book, we'll explore ways to transform your home, without major expense or upheaval, into a space that's nurturing and healing for you. When you listen to – and trust – your intuition, amazing things start to happen: you uncover your unique expression and surround yourself with what nourishes and soothes you. When your home mirrors who you really are you relax, which allows your body and mind to begin to heal. Inspiration soon flows and dreams seem possible again.

When home is healing to us, we thrive and feel able to contribute meaningfully in our global community. One of the greatest causes of unhappiness is the feeling of not belonging. Creating a home that mirrors who we are – and where we feel that we *do* belong – honours us. It's an incredibly powerful and healing experience. As Kahlil Gibran said: 'Your house is your larger body.'

To help you tap into your intuition, each chapter includes insights from Sonia Choquette, world-famous intuition coach and best-selling author of 28 books. Here's how Sonia defines intuition and her advice on how to listen to yours:

SONIA CHOQUETTE SUGGESTS

Intuition means inner learning. Inner guidance. Inner teacher.

There's an authentic spirit in all of us that is constantly communicating with us, not through intellect or language, but through vibrational, feeling sense. It's an inner frequency that gives you direction but is more than a compass to find your keys or locate a parking space. It's about keeping your spirit aligned with your soul's higher purpose. It's the guidance that keeps you connected to your authentic self. It keeps you associating with the energies that support you, and directs you away from engagements that will cause you to lose touch with who you are.

Intuition communicates through the emotional healing body, not the thinking body. More importantly, it isn't something you have to get; you already have it. You just need to drop into it. The best and most immediate way to get into your intuition is with your body because that's when you quiet your brain. Don't think on it, walk on it!

To get accurate feedback from your intuition you have to be truly available, so consider going for a walk, a bike ride or dancing. But if you can't find time for movement, breathing deeply will also help you access your intuition. Breathe deeply for 5–10 minutes, then put your hand on your heart and ask yourself the question you want an answer to. Say out loud: 'My heart says . . .' and you'll get an intuitive answer.

True intuition has a distinct effect on your body. It feels like your energy is opening and relaxing, whereas wishful thinking or any other kind of mind projection causes you to contract. Intuition brings you a sense of 'Aaah!' (relaxing), whereas a projection brings a sharp intake of breath (tensing). You have to feel what's going on in your body: do you feel more expanded, or more contracted?

Here's another tip to try on a daily basis: instead of saying, 'I know', say 'I wonder . . .' Wondering is about not needing to know the answer. When you say, 'I wonder . . .' you immediately go into your right (heart) brain. You're listening instead of talking and you're opening yourself up to new information. The heart is an intelligent organ, and intuition originates from the heart, which has been scientifically proven to be 5,000 times more perceptive to energy than your logical brain.

Intuition doesn't work in linear time. You have to give it space. It doesn't work in the space of true or false. It works in the space of 'What is true for me for right now.'

FIRST IMPRESSIONS

Albert Einstein once said 'I believe in intuitions and inspirations . . . I sometimes FEEL that I am right. I do not KNOW that I am.'[2]

When creating a healing home, intuition has to take the lead over logic. Unfortunately, if logic leads, the results can feel more stiff, formulaic and lacking in soul. But once intuition has had its say, logic is essential for working out all the minute details, problem-solving and turning the concept into a reality. The end result will be inspired but still practical.

Carla Coulson, photographer and creativity coach, says: 'Give yourself permission to do you! Creating our homes is a reflection of who we are, but it also adds to our wellbeing. The more pleasure we feel, the more wellbeing we have. The more beautiful your home is to *you*, the more wellbeing you'll have. Creativity is a marvellous elixir: in these quiet moments of mindfulness, you connect to your intuition. You can't create in the future or past, you're just present and, if you pay attention, you'll have an idea, insight or a little bit of information comes 'out of the blue'. We need more of these moments in our lives because they allow us to take a quantum leap forward with ideas, enthusiasm and heart-connection that all the logical thinking, planning and slaving-away never do.'

Everything is energy

How spaces make us feel is essential to our wellbeing. Do they uplift, calm and ground us? Or unsettle and irritate us? A space that doesn't feel good is like listening to music played off-key.

Everything is vibration and energy. Humans are energetically responsive, sensitive creatures who absorb information like sponges on many different levels – even if we're not consciously aware of it. Living and working in spaces that feel vibrationally off to our natural rhythm isn't conducive to physical, mental or spiritual health. It creates stress and ultimately can lead to disease.

Jean Haner is a leading authority on the spiritual side of Chinese medicine and the author of *Clear Home, Clear Heart*. Jean likens the energy of the people and places around us to invisible clutter. Unlike decluttering our homes of physical objects, we don't know how to clear energy because we can't perceive it with our eyes.

'Stagnation in your space can be part of why you feel stuck in life overall,' Jean says. 'Your feelings get imprinted in your surroundings. What space clearing is really about is you learning to be in touch with your feelings. We're all so stressed and distracted by everything, that most of us aren't even in our bodies anymore.

'Try walking through your home – or a room – and allow yourself to become quiet, take a breath, close your eyes or stare off into space. Notice how you're feeling in that spot. If there's a chair you never sit in, go and sit there. Tune in, see how you feel. It may take a moment because these feelings are very subtle: it won't be like being hit over the head! Stay quiet, stay put, and pay attention for the tiniest whisper of a feeling. Trust it when it comes, and explore it because it's actually based on something. This is new territory for most people, but whatever feelings come, remember they're not dangerous – they're just information. Don't worry about rules, and doing everything correctly. Your awareness makes a difference: just putting your attention on stressful energy eases it.'

When Jean does a space clearing, she looks at three different types of energy:

1. Old emotions

These get stuck in a space, whether they're from the current or previous occupants. The energy of stress, worry and anxiety expresses outward into our environment and – the more intense or frequent the feeling – the more likely that there's a little, invisible cloud hanging in a space. This continues to affect you every time you walk through that space: it can stress you even if you weren't stressed before you stepped into that spot! Typical areas include entrances, in front of the kitchen sink or cooker (stove), sofa, bed and desk chair.

2. The energy of the land

Just like the human body, the earth has meridians of energy running through it. These can become unhealthy for a variety of reasons. If the foundation of a nearby house cuts through a line of healthy earth energy, this can turn it into unhealthy energy, which runs through the land under your home, and ultimately can affect you.

3. The impact of technology

All our devices and gadgets emit electromagnetic fields. Everyone has a different sensitivity to EMFs; some aren't bothered at all, while others are extremely sensitive to the point of feeling faint or dizzy when around certain appliances or devices.

In space clearing, getting the overall balance of yin and yang energy right in the home is essential. Ideally, it should be around 40 per cent yin, and 60 per cent yang. Yin energy is the quieter, more still energy that we need in order to relax. It helps us to get a good night's sleep, and stay in touch with our feelings. Yang energy is more stimulating, helping us to get up in the morning, get things done and feel vital.

For the most part, emotions are yin. As we live our daily lives, we experience lots of different emotions, some positive, others negative. These can linger in our environment and affect us. Each time we have an emotion, we make a little deposit of yin energy in the space. Over time, the yin value rises – sometimes reaching as high as 90 per cent! If yin and yang are out of balance, this can be a contributing factor to tiredness, mood problems, difficulty with sleep or relationship issues.

Energy builds up over time, so having your home cleared once a year is very beneficial and is definitely worth considering whenever you move into a new property. While *Clear Home, Clear Heart* is an easy-to-follow, practical guide to the art of energy clearing, if you prefer to hire a professional I highly recommend Jean Haner for space clearing and Bruce Peters for personal energy clearing.

Budget tip

Here are some simple space-clearing methods recommended
by Jean:

- Devise your own ceremony, for example walk through your
  home with a candle and put some love into every room.
- Open the windows and let fresh air blow in.
- Play joyful or loud music – percussive sounds such as drumming are especially powerful.
- Try shamanic space-clearing techniques like clapping, pounding drums and ringing bells.
- Have a housewarming party with lots of people, noise, music
  and celebration.

EXPRESS YOURSELF

Chinese medicine is a 3,000-year-old goldmine of knowledge that can
help us to create a healing home. If we understand our unique nature
and needs, we free ourselves from the endless pressure to conform,
and our worry that others will judge us. This knowledge is not only
empowering but leads to a greater understanding and tolerance for
the needs of those who share our home. We stop taking things personally and reach a compromise that keeps everyone happy.

Jean Haner's latest book, *The Five-Element Solution,* examines the
five personality types and what they need to thrive.

'Chinese medicine is the original personalised holistic medicine,
but there's a psychological aspect to it that most people don't know
about,' Jean explains. 'It's about determining someone's personality
type and, based on that, understanding their unique needs in their
home environment.'

As you read through Jean's descriptions of the five main personality types, see which one you relate to most. While each of us has all

five energies present in our nature, there's always one that's our default setting and is how we move through life. Jean calls it our Home Base.

1. The Dreamer

Dreamers are highly intuitive, very creative and have a rich inner fantasy world. They do best in a quiet environment and need time alone. They thrive when they're in flow and not constrained by a schedule.

They're often drawn to a very romantic decor, love mood lighting, candles and areas of darkness in the home. They hate bright overhead lights and have a need for luxurious fabrics like silk and velvet. They love to retreat to a dark bedroom, with no light trickling in, or blinking lights from devices. Adding touches of black to their home is healing to them, along with water features and pictures of water scenes. They love baths and should never live in a home that only has a shower: the ability to close the bathroom door and have a long soak is wellness for them. The quality of their bedding is of utmost importance as they love to lounge in bed.

2. The Warrior

Warriors like to get things done and are very active and highly organised. They like structure and to have a place for everything, and everything in its place. They hate clutter and love to throw things away. They'll alphabetise their books rather than arrange them by height and tend to be highly scheduled and quite rigid in their schedule.

They hold a lot of inner tension and require a way to blow off steam daily. They need a workout room, or to live by a bike path or hiking trail. It's essential for them to get out into nature as they really shouldn't be inside all day. Having shades of green, plants and wood furniture in their home is healing to them, along with images of trees. DIY and making things with their hands appeals to them.

3. The Free Spirit

Free Spirits live from the heart and are very creative. They need a home that expresses who they are, and that is fun. Adding touches of red, bright colours and flowers is healing to them, along with candles and a fire. Having bird feeders outside windows or live-streaming birdsong makes them happy. They delight in walking into a room and seeing a favourite thing that brings them joy. They love the energy of original art – as opposed to prints – and anything quirky that makes them laugh. Sparkle thrills them, like crystals hanging in a window or a sequinned cushion (pillow). They need freedom to express themselves and are more avant-garde so others can often perceive them as eccentric.

They love to entertain and light up whenever they're around people; however, they're not necessarily extroverts and can be very shy. They tend to be emotionally sensitive and easily affected by how other people are feeling. A big kitchen, dining room and living room where they can celebrate with others are essential to their wellbeing.

4. The Nurturer

Nurturers need a certain level of clutter. They enjoy collecting and displaying things because of the fond memories the items bring up. They tend to be sentimental; home and mementos are very important to them. Their lives revolve around family and relationships, so comfort is essential: comfy sofas, big easy chairs and places to cuddle. They hate minimalism! A mantelpiece covered with family photos and trinkets on every table feels like a hug to them. But they can go overboard so they need plenty of storage to avoid having everything on display all the time. Shades of yellow and warm pastels are healing to them.

The kitchen is vital as they love to eat, cook or share meals with others. It feels very lonely to them to cook and eat on their own. This doesn't mean they can't live alone, but having people to eat with makes them happiest.

5. The Visionary

Visionaries have high ideals. They like to be surrounded by quality products and are very sensitive to the feel of things on their skin. They love minimalism and Zen interiors and can't stand small, cramped rooms, preferring big, open, well-lit spaces that make them feel as if they can take a deep breath. White, grey and metallics are soothing to them. They love big windows and distant views; being high up and seeing far feels wonderful to them. Equally, they love pictures of skies and expansive, uplifting views. They're very sensitive to visual clutter: empty worktops make them happy with everything put away, rather than immediately to hand.

They're the most physically affected by other people's energy, so they need space between themselves and others. They're brilliant entertainers, but can go a little overboard, typically making everything beautiful for everyone, then collapsing at the end of the night because they forgot to eat. Getting away from the rest of the world and recuperating from feeling others' energy is vital for them. They love their family but need a sacred space to retreat to – even if it's only for 10 minutes. Having their home space cleared is very beneficial for them, and they thrive with a room of their own for spiritual practices.

A collaborative creation

Combining two or more personality types in a home requires understanding and compromise. 'Our judgement of another person's clutter or minimalism comes from our own filter,' Jean Haner says. 'So many conflicts in relationships are just based on how someone else tries to arrange their environment. It's important to understand that the other person's needs are not wrong: they're just *different*.'

Creating a home as a family – or group if you're sharing an apartment or house – can be a bonding experience. First, spend time individually pondering the themes you'd like to see come to life. This can be a general theme for the home, or a room-by-room adventure.

When it's time to get together and share ideas, it's best to have one person who understands the creative design process in charge of discussions. This ensures that everyone is fully heard – including young children as they're often the most intuitive. The key to success is to avoid criticising others' ideas, listening carefully and asking lots of detailed, open questions. You'll end up building on each other's ideas and creating a home that's fun and inspiring for everyone.

Re-storying your home

Humans have always learned through story: we tell stories, read them and watch them on screen. A story touches us emotionally and resonates deeply when its arc is powerful, engaging us in ways that facts and figures don't.

Everything has an unfolding story. We're aware of it with people: their past, present and potential future. But we're not in the habit of focusing on the story of our homes and the objects that surround us – even though they too have a past, present and potential future. We typically view them only in terms of their aesthetics and practicalities. When we perceive them as also having their own story, we become more aware of their energy and less inclined to dispose of them without a second thought. A cracked mug that can't hold liquid any more can become an attractive pencil pot. A dresser with woodworm in its base can be repurposed as a kitchen wall cabinet. A disused grain sieve can become a striking wall light – the possibilities are endless. It's all about reimagining a piece's story and how it can continue rather than ending in landfill.

The interconnection of everything, both animate and inanimate, is energetic. We feel the energy of a hand-crafted piece, even if we're not aware of it consciously. This is because the love, energy and attention of the craftsperson went into the making of that unique piece (the Navajo believe that they weave part of their soul into their creations). If we engage our imagination and envisage a new future for a piece that has outlived its current use, our creative energy becomes entwined with it, providing a distinct energy signature and vibration that we connect with whenever we perceive the re-storied piece.

We can successfully re-story our homes by:

- Becoming aware of the energy of everything we have in them.
- Making conscious acquisitions – rather than impulse or convenience buying.
- Weaving our story into everything that's part of our home. This reaffirms the connectedness of all things and encourages us to live consciously rather than reactively or from a place of fear.

Author and teacher Sharon Blackie, whose work combines psychology, mythology and ecology, speaks of the importance of exercising our mythic imagination, and how our intuition is invaluable as we open ourselves to the possibility of re-storying our homes.

To do this successfully, we first have to delve a little into our own mystery and history and find what makes our heart sing.

Your Book of Inspiration

Before we begin this adventure, I suggest buying a blank notebook, the thicker the better, something beautiful and tactile for jotting down all your ideas and ideals for your home. Use it to let your intuition free-flow, and add doodle sketches and paste in images or anything else that takes your fancy.

Or consider getting a set of notebooks (matching or unmatched) to record different areas of focus. Whatever you choose, be sure it's something you're drawn to and will enjoy using. Flimsy exercise books have that 'back-to-school' feel and get dog-eared in no time.

To experiment with an alternative format, give hand scrolls a try, the ancient Egyptian and Chinese form of record keeping and art display. They're sold as ready-made sets or scrolls and can be customised as Xuan paper is inexpensive and comes in many lengths. Once completed, the scroll is meant to be a journey through a narrative.

Traditionally, it's unrolled from right to left, shoulder width by shoulder width, in order to study and appreciate each section's detail.

Creating an inspiration board on Pinterest is another option, but I love the tactile quality of paper; the scrapbook versatility of a notebook or scroll can't be recreated in the same way digitally.

Whatever format you choose, your Book of Inspiration will be an invaluable tool. It can help to reduce stress and create a state of mindfulness, much as adult colouring books do. You'll clearly identify what makes you feel at home, what nurtures you and makes your heart sing. As a touchstone for what's really *you*, it embodies the law of attraction: things begin to materialise in your life once you've defined them clearly.

Your Personal Blueprint

Each of us has a Personal Blueprint that's as unique as our fingerprints. From infancy through early childhood, the senses of sight, smell, touch, taste and sound are acutely experienced and absorbed, with emotional context intricately woven in. All of the feelings and associations that surround our early experiences – the sight of a dog; the smell of talcum powder; the feel of sand; the taste of apple sauce; the sound of a ticking clock – stay with us for life, for better or worse. We continually build on our Personal Blueprint during adulthood but, so often, it's our long-forgotten childhood impressions that guide our choices – even if we're blissfully unaware of the source.

Revisiting childhood as an adult tends to be an arm's length experience; it almost feels as if it happened to someone else. We look at snapshots, share anecdotes and smile at the memories, but the moment passes. Scratching under the surface of childhood memories is usually a therapist's remit, a journey we often undertake when life has pushed our buttons too hard. But childhood is a treasure trove if we choose to explore it, even just a little. Many of the signposts of who we are, what we love and loathe, what makes us thrive and what defeats us are all there for the reading. Following them leads to some fascinating and unexpected discoveries.

Creating your own Sensory Signposts to follow

The first step to creating a healing home is to trigger your childhood memories of likes and dislikes. This should be a fun journey, with lots of smiles and cringes along the way! But it's also reassuring as you'll often find that your strongest present-day likes and dislikes haven't changed all that much since childhood. Some of your memories may not seem to have an obvious connection to home, but experience whatever comes and jot each memory down. One word will do, as long as it will make sense to you later.

1. On five separate pages in your Book of Inspiration, doodle-sketch a signpost and label each with one of the five senses.
2. Begin with whichever Sensory Signpost draws you most. Jot down the first memory that comes.
3. Let your mind wander and write all the memories that follow the initial one. Maybe only a few will surface but, if you're lucky, they'll start to really flow.
4. When you feel inclined to move on, turn your attention to the next Sensory Signpost that beckons. Follow the same process.

You can work on one Sensory Signpost at a time until you feel it's completed, but it may be easier and more fun to chop and change between them. You can also do this exercise on a device but writing and doodling by hand helps you relax and encourages the return of memories.

PRACTICALITIES

Throughout the book, we'll be looking at how colours affect us and our personality type in Chinese medicine, along with the importance of soundproofing in creating a healing home. Here are some guide-lines on both to refer back to:

Colour

Colour is one of the most complex and intangible elements surrounding us. It's never exactly the same at any given moment of the day, depending on the light falling on it.

Colours have an amazing ability to alter our moods and perceptions. They give off their own electromagnetic field and – because our bodies are highly sensitive to the electromagnetic wavelength of light – we're physically affected by them. In tests, even subjects who are completely blind react to variations in colour! Schloss and Palmer's Ecological Valence Theory suggests that people 'like colours strongly associated with objects they like'.[3]

- **Blue** Has a sedative, relaxing influence, helping to focus the mind and intellect. It calms the central nervous system, reduces blood pressure and heart rate, and is excellent for alleviating stress. Blue reminds us of the sky and clear water.
- **Green** Known for its soothing, harmonious effects, green reminds us of nature and healthy vegetation and is the easiest colour on the eye. It's wonderful for calming all emotional states.
- **Creamy vellum** Stimulates the right brain and encourages creative work without tiring the mind. It creates a sunny but subdued atmosphere that's nurturing, but not intrusive.
- **Yellow** Like sunlight, yellow stimulates, rejuvenates and invigorates. It alleviates depression and mental tiredness. It acts on the left brain, encouraging logic and non-emotional thinking.
- **Orange** Associated with joy and exuberance, orange stimulates the appetite while easing fatigue. Therapists use it to treat depression, stimulate the immune system and reduce the perception of pain.
- **Indigo and violet** Linked with the healing of mind and spirit, purples create an aura of calm and retreat.
- **Black** Heightens emotional response and rivets our attention. Black is the absence of colour and absorbs everything else around it.

- **White** Known for its calming properties, white can also remind us of sunlight. As white light is the presence of all colours, it too can have the effect of absorbing everything around it.
- **Red** Associated with energy, passion, exuberance and vitality, red is wonderful for stimulating the nervous system and mind but can be oppressive.

Soundproofing

Noise affects us in profound ways that we're not always aware of. Whether it comes from the outside (traffic, neighbours etc.) or the home itself (electrical appliances, voices etc.), it can negatively impact our ability to concentrate, relax and sleep deeply, which all have long-term consequences for our wellbeing and health. Finding optimal soundproofing solutions is essential to creating a healing home. Options include:

- **Plants** create oxygen and are humidifiers, ionisers and odour-eaters, as well as sound absorbers. The more plants, the better!
- **Upholstered furniture** absorbs sound better than wood, metal or glass furniture. Acoustic furniture works even better.
- **Lined and interlined curtains** offer more soundproofing than unlined curtain panels. Be wary of 'soundproof' curtains as they're very bulky with multiple layers, and hang more like a blanket. All soundproof curtains are blackout curtains, but not all blackout curtains are soundproof – despite what some manufacturers claim! Lined and interlined roman blinds are also an option, but are less effective than curtains because there is less fabric. Unless you suffer from allergies, avoid wood, plastic or aluminium venetian blinds as they won't deaden sound on their own.
- **Carpet** made from 100 per cent wool fitted with a quality underlay feels soothing underfoot. But if you prefer hard flooring, avoid engineered, and opt for reclaimed or FSC wood flooring, and add rugs in natural materials to attenuate sound.

- Replace hollow-core doors with **solid-core doors**, and add **weatherstrip** around doorframes to prevent sound from travelling through any gaps.
- Floor-to-ceiling, wall-to-wall **cupboards** (closets) with solid doors are perfect for masking sounds from an adjacent room or neighbouring property. The same applies to a **wall of books**.
- Acoustic moveable **partitions** are worth considering, especially in a contemporary space. There are many options to choose from (please see Resources); some modular systems of stackable blocks can be built to any width, height or shape you want within minutes. They're easy to disassemble and reconfigure in a different position, making them ideal for seasonal changes. Others made from sustainably sourced paper in a range of colours can be shaped into a flowing configuration and then fold away to the width of a book when not in use. Some even offer high-backed seating integrated into the partition itself.
- **Acoustic panels** for walls and ceilings absorb sound waves well. They come in all manner of materials, shapes and sizes and can double as wall art. If you enjoy creative DIY, you can make your own panels from sustainable materials.
- **Upholstered walls** have a luxurious effect but require professional installation to create a wooden framework on the walls, fill it with an interliner or acoustic absorber, and then stretch your chosen face fabric (wool, velvet, suede or linen are ideal) taut. Or there are stretched fabric systems for walls and ceilings that are ideal for irregular shapes and uneven or curved surfaces (please see Resources).
- **Sound-deadening paint** reduces echo and high-frequency sounds but has a very different look and feel as it's textured.

A FINAL NOTE

This book includes many research studies, expert opinions, books that inspire me, and some of my whacky design ideas! At the end of each chapter, you'll find plans illustrating some of them, and a chapter-by-chapter guide to all products mentioned throughout in Resources on page 269. As a bonus, additional international resources can be downloaded on the book's website (thehealinghomeandgarden.com). If you're a DIY enthusiast, there are also PDF guides to the projects mentioned.

Take whatever resonates with you and discard the rest. If you just follow *your* intuition, you'll create a home that's perfect for *you*. I've spent years following my intuition and it's never let me down. I hope you have as much fun reading this book as I've had researching and writing it.

CHAPTER SUMMARY

- For us to relax, rest and heal, our homes should be a sanctuary designed intuitively – not formulaically.
- To access your intuition, practise saying daily, 'I wonder . . .' instead of, 'I know . . .'
- Consider a space clearing of your property to release old emotions, the energy of the land and the impact of technology.
- To understand your unique needs in your home, tune in to your personality type in Chinese medicine.
- Consider creating a Book of Inspiration to note all your ideas and ideals for your home.
- Become familiar with your Personal Blueprint using the Sensory Signposts exercise.
- Colours can alter our moods and perceptions because our bodies are sensitive to their electromagnetic fields.

- Good soundproofing is essential to a healing home and includes plants; upholstered and acoustic furniture; lined and interlined curtains and roman blinds; carpet; fitted cupboards; a wall of books; acoustic moveable partitions; acoustic panels; upholstered walls; and sound-deadening paint.

2

ENTERING

'I want to put the ever-rushing world on pause. Slow it down, so that I can breathe.'
—Lucy H. Pearce, *Medicine Woman:*
Reclaiming the Soul of Healing

All too often entrance areas get overlooked. They gradually become dumping grounds for everything from coats and footwear to bikes and prams (strollers). Or – at the other extreme – they are bare and lifeless with only a token print or two on a wall and an umbrella stand. Neither option is particularly welcoming.

When you return home, are you like most people who rush through their entrance area on automatic pilot, discarding everything as you go? If so, what if you paused for a moment instead?

When you walk through your door, you're leaving the outside world behind and entering a private inner sanctum where you can at last begin to unwind. This is a **threshold space**, an important transition area and an opportunity to take a breath and start to relax – even if you still have a million things to do!

Ideally when you come home, everything that you see, touch, smell and hear needs to engage your parasympathetic nervous system, the network of nerves that relaxes your body after periods of stress. The problem is that familiarity makes us overlook elements in our environment when we perceive them every day. Think about when you moved into your home: perhaps you grew accustomed to a stack of boxes waiting in a corner to be unpacked? At first, the boxes probably irked you; then, if left there long enough, you managed to turn a blind eye to them. But on a subliminal level you would still have been aware of their presence creating a low-grade sense of irritation within you. Remember the feeling of relief when those boxes were *finally* unpacked and cleared away? How the space changed – not just visually, but energetically?

The same principle applies to everything that you perceive in your entrance now. If there are elements subliminally stressing you, they need to be addressed in order to create a welcoming vibration when you return home, one that's cheerful, calming and grounded.

FIRST IMPRESSIONS

The best way to discern what's not working in your entrance is to conduct a 'viewing' – as if an estate agent (realtor) is showing you the property as a prospective place to live. On viewings, we tend to make impartial observations because we're experiencing a new space for the first time. We're immediately clear about what we do and don't like about the place because there's no attachment, and instinct and intuition are leading us.

To start your entrance viewing, grab a pen and your Book of Inspiration along with your keys. Unlock your front door and step into the entrance as if for the first time. What immediately strikes you? Jot down everything that comes to mind: smell, light levels, amount of space, colours etc.

Now close the front door behind you and make a detailed inventory of the entrance space. Walk around it. Touch things. Look up at the ceiling and down at the floor. Note everything – good and bad – that your senses perceive.

Afterwards, highlight your likes and dislikes. Apply the William Morris principle: 'Have nothing in your houses that you do not know to be beautiful or believe to be useful.' It's energetically very freeing.

Later we'll explore how some things can be transformed and re-storied. But if they can't be, they'll have to go. If they're objects rather than structural features, consider donating or recycling them – the aim is to avoid landfill at all costs.

The importance of smell and colour

Of all the senses, smell is the strongest memory trigger so how your entrance smells matters. If its scent is pleasant and reminds you of happy things, you relax. If it's malodorous – even slightly – you tense. Scent is highly personal; something that you dislike intensely might be lovely to someone else because it's associated with a happy memory.

Diffusing scent that you love in your entrance has an immediate, positive impact when you return home, but please don't be tempted to use air fresheners or scented plug-ins! Good-quality, pure essential oils are the healthy choice, and one of the best ways to diffuse them 24 hours a day is with an ultrasonic diffuser. Choose oils according to the scents you love and the way they make you feel rather than being a slave to expert recommendations. *The Healing Power of Essential Oils* by Eric Zielinski is a good introductory guide to using essential oils.

One oil to consider for energetically clearing any space – especially the entrance – is sage. Add 20–30 drops to filtered water in a small, glass spray bottle, shake well and spritz liberally. Sage also has antimicrobial and antibacterial properties and repels insects.

Colour can help to set a peaceful tone in your entrance. Which colours to choose depends on your personality type in Chinese medicine and what draws you (for colour associations, please see page 15) but remember that a little goes a long way. We feel the vibration and absorb the positive energy of colour, even in small quantities. Including an element of green to greet you when you return home reminds you to leave the energetic agitation of the day outside. All greens have a vibration that clears our energetic field and aura, soothes the nervous system and calms the spirit.

If you give a lot of your energy to others, or are stuck behind a computer all day, you may feel tired and drained when you return home. Seeing a splash of colour – like a photograph of poppies or sunflowers – gives an instant energy boost and makes you smile.

Budget tip

If you can't have fresh flowers, display a bouquet of brightly coloured felt ball flowers – you can even make them yourself.

If you work in customer service and are bombarded daily with people's complaints, you'll need something more soothing and calming to greet you when you return home: an image of a beautiful sunrise or sunset, or a photograph of fish in tropical waters can be very energetically balancing. Nothing beats the real thing though; an aquarium (no matter how small) will put you in a state of mindfulness. If budget allows, an aquarium wall can be spectacular and is *so* relaxing to come home to.

Discarding protections

When you enter your home, you're stepping into a safe space that protects you from the outside world. Home allows you to let your guard down, to go within and begin to relax on a very deep level.

SONIA CHOQUETTE SUGGESTS

Try this 20-second ritual that resets your nervous system and tells your mind that whatever is troubling you is left outside. You'll deal with it in a calmer, clearer space when you're ready. Before you enter your home:

1. Pause.
2. Take a deep breath in through your nose and exhale as if you're blowing out birthday candles. As you're doing this, set

the intention of emptying yourself of everything you've accumu-
lated throughout the day, including energy you're holding on to,
and energy from others.

3. Take in a second breath, imagining you're breathing in
through the bottoms of your feet. See the breath rise up your
legs into your heart space. Open your jaw wide, let out a deep
sigh 'ahhhhhhh!' and imagine yourself sliding out of your head
into your heart. As you exhale, imagine everything in your body
and energetic field being expelled and left outside: you're
emptying yourself of everything and coming home to your heart
space with your breath.

4. Smile. Now you can enter your home!

Try to do this ritual each time you come home. Introduce it to
the whole family – small children immediately take to it as a fun
game. The heart is your body's healing home: enter your heart
as you enter your home!

When you walk in the front door, try the Asian custom of removing your shoes and going barefoot at home. Not only will your floors
stay cleaner but, when your feet feel the ground, you reconnect to the
earth. Having contact with the earth is so important to the nervous
system; the soles of our feet have chakras, or energetic receptors, so
when we're barefoot, it's like plugging an electric wire into a grounding socket: the tension and stress drain from the body. Being connected
to the earth in the safety of your home allows you to energetically
unwind, and release anxiety. A 2007 study published in the podiatry
journal, *The Foot,* found that the more people wear shoes, the less
healthy their feet become.[1] The study compared the feet of Sotho,
Zulu and European people, and concluded that modern Europeans –
who wear shoes the most – have the unhealthiest feet of any group!
Going barefoot improves proprioception, the awareness of where we
are in relation to the space around us.

Budget tip

To avoid clutter in your entrance, resist the temptation to just
drop everything as you come in. Keeping this threshold space
clear and organised affects your ability to unwind and relax, and
sets the tone for the rest of your home. Having one or two large
baskets or attractive containers to temporarily put keys, hats,
gloves, bags etc. can be part of the ritual of leaving the world
behind, and stepping unguarded and unburdened into your
home. Having a system also means you can find things quickly
and easily when you need them later. No more panicked, last-
minute searches for car keys!

Adding built-in, floor-to-ceiling cupboards (closets) gives maximum storage space in your entrance, especially if you organise the
interior well. Have double rails for coats, making the lower rail accessible to children; cubbyholes to separate hats, gloves and scarves;
shoe/boot racks for storing seasonal footwear at the back of the
cupboard; and coat hooks on the inside of the doors so you can easily
grab anything you use daily. Doors with spring-loaded catches instead
of knobs or handles make the cupboards blend into the surrounding
walls rather than standing out like a sore thumb – especially if painted
to match the wall colour (although there will be finger marks to
contend with).

Instead of tripping over bikes in the entrance, consider suspending
them. Offset against a brightly coloured wall, they can even become
art!

Setting the right tone

Many consider the Divine Feminine energy to be the caretaker of
the home, representing all that protects, nourishes and loves
unconditionally. You might consider including one or more
symbols of the Divine Feminine in your entrance; these include
trees, water and bees.

- A tall plant or a living wall (panels of plants grown vertically) if daylight levels and space allow.
- A water feature or water weir (a wall of softly flowing water) is soothing and excellent for masking sound. It's an ideal feature in the summer, but be sure to warm the effect in the winter with subtle coloured lighting: smart lighting is ideal as you can adjust brightness, temperature and hue from any device.
- Indoor observation beehives are the perfect introduction to the fascinating and essential world of beekeeping – especially if you live in a city. Indoor beekeeping is simple, safe and much easier than outdoor beekeeping. The hives are smaller, and maintenance and extracting honey are straightforward. Beekeeping is therapeutic, rewarding and educational – especially for children. Invest in a well-researched and designed system that keeps you and your bees safe. It's important not to expose bees to white or blue light at night as it disrupts their circadian rhythm and can affect the health of the hive, so look for a system that includes an amber night-time cover.

EXPRESS YOURSELF

Surrounding yourself with the colours, textures and elements that you love is vital, but creating an entrance that's relaxing and inviting goes much deeper than that. It's also about daring to express an aspect of who you really are. This may sound scary as we perceive entrances as public spaces seen by anyone who visits. Why on earth would we let the world see who we really are? The thought makes us feel vulnerable, but as Brené Brown, researcher on shame and vulnerability, says: 'Vulnerability is the birthplace of innovation, creativity, and change.'[2]

There is power in being authentic and not concealing it. And it doesn't just make *us* feel better: it inspires others too. It starts conversations, sparks ideas and makes the world a more interesting place.

Now, where to begin in your entrance?

Creativity and fun

Don't start with the boring things, like what colour to paint the walls, which light fittings to choose or what flooring might be best. This is putting the cart before the horse.

We're all so programmed to rely on our left brain – to be logical and sensible – that our right brain, responsible for creativity and intu- ition, gets drowned out, or – worse still – never heard at all. To re- imagine and re-story our homes, we have to change this.

The first step is having fun and dreaming a little. (A lot, actually!)

Trust that the practical details will all fall into place easily and naturally once you've allowed your imagination and intuition to take the lead. As the quote loosely attributed to Goethe suggests: 'Whatever you can do, or dream you can do, begin it. Boldness has genius, power and magic in it. Begin it now.'

You may be surprised to find that being bold in the design of your entrance will have some wonderful knock-on effects in other areas of your life. Any form of authentic expression is empowering, and speak- ing your truth isn't confined to what you say or write. Your home is a blank canvas. Now is your chance to express yourself authentically within it and have fun in the process!

Bring a favourite theme to life

Delving into our dreams, aspirations and happy memories opens a world of possibilities to explore. Refer to your Sensory Signposts in your Book of Inspiration and pick a memory that makes you smile, or tap into an aspiration or dream. Find ways to bring this to life in your entrance. It doesn't have to take over the entire space: just seeing one wall or a corner with a token representation will give you an instant lift when you come home, and a chance to escape everyday reality for a moment.

Here are three ideas to kickstart your own creative flow:

1. Cinema

If you're a film buff, search for vintage cinema or theatre seating in architectural salvage yards. Vintage cinema seating is comfortable and practical in an entrance as the seats flip up when not in use, thus freeing up floorspace to move about easily. Reupholstering in an unexpected fabric – rather than the traditional red velvet – adds intrigue and edginess, especially if the fabric is contemporary.

2. Travel

If your entrance space is big enough, and you're hankering after a trip on the *Orient Express*, a vintage railroad train seat reupholstered in a plush material sets the scene. Team it with a vintage overhead luggage rack to store hats, scarves, gloves, umbrellas etc.

3. Seaside

If you're stuck with city living, but miss the ocean, enliven your entrance with playful and creative elements to remind you of seaside holidays: a portable striped changing tent (the contemporary version of traditional bathing tents) can easily become a coats cupboard; a felt stone rug that's soft underfoot but resembles pebbles on a beach; a sound conditioner playing wave sounds.

You may well be asking, why not just buy a framed photograph, print or painting that depicts your chosen theme, and be done with it? The answer is because it won't continue to draw your attention in quite the same way as something you've curated. The very act of going out and finding the right representations of your theme and dreaming up ways to transform them is where the magic lies. It fully engages your intuition and imagination and makes you happy in the process. That energy remains palpable for the long term and reignites a sense of joy every time you walk in your front door.

Getting inspired

The key is being in a state of relaxation, and not having an intended outcome in mind.

We're often afraid to let go, to allow ourselves to *feel*. It seems so unscientific, so out of step with society's norms. It isn't easy in our world of 24/7 connectivity, amid all the pressure to achieve and to be the best. We're forever competing with everyone else *and* ourselves. It's exhausting – mentally, physically and emotionally. We can be so obsessed with perfectionism and getting things right the first time around, that we become tense and rigid. And our intuition doesn't stand a chance under these conditions. It's forever being silenced by the mind, worrying about what others might think, or FOMO (fear of missing out).

If it's hard to still your mind's chatter, and you feel under pressure to be doing all sorts of other things, follow John Cleese's advice about creativity: schedule 1 hour and 15 minutes of uninterrupted time to reconnect with your imagination. According to Cleese, it takes 15 minutes to get into the zone and quiet the mind, then you can play with whatever comes in the remaining hour. In case you're worried that you're skiving, take note of what Glennon Doyle says in *Get Untamed:* 'Imagination is not where we go to escape reality but to remember it.'

Neuroscientist and author of *Mindwandering*, Dr Moshe Bar, recommends mindwandering (without the distraction of devices) for at least an hour a day to boost creativity and mood. The more you practise, the easier it gets, and the more comes to you.

Leaf through magazines and illustrated books. Go for a walk in nature. Sit outside a café and watch the world go by. It's important to put your phone on silent, and resist the urge to check emails, messages and social media. Allow yourself to unplug and notice what strikes you as you observe with an open mind. It could be a wrought-iron gate half-open; the bright colour of a passing beret; a bird soaring; the smell of warm croissants; the way sunlight catches the intricate patterns of a leaf. Sometimes it's the oddest thing that arrests your attention and leads to that 'aha!' moment, when the vision of what you'd like to create begins to become clear. In your Book of Inspiration, jot down any ideas that come and what triggered them – and take a photo to remind you.

There's no logic involved in this process, just intuition and trusting your gut. Remember that listening to your intuition not only supports your creativity but calms any anxiety or uncertainty you may be feeling. It helps you live a more harmonious life, so don't question what comes, just go with it! The more you do, the more your sense of security, confidence and courage will grow.

Building on the inspiration

Once you have a sense of your entrance's theme, build on it by researching ways to bring it to life. Our subconscious mind doesn't think in words, but in pictures and physical experiences. Doing something tactile and fun is the quest: you're gathering, intending and making choices. You're really contemplating: what do I *want*?

Start collating ideas and options in your Book of Inspiration (or a mood board if you want something larger). If you're doing online research, a Pinterest board is handy for when you're ready to make final choices and purchase items.

And don't forget to go on a treasure hunt at home, seeing everything with fresh eyes, including what's languishing in cupboards, the loft (attic), or the basement. We're creatures of habit and naturally resistant to change, so let your intuition be your guide as you roam from room to room. Just because a piece has always been in your living room or bedroom doesn't mean that it can't go somewhere else. If your intuition tells you it might work in your entrance, try it. If it's a flop, you can always put it back where you found it.

When you practise seeing things differently, you'll be amazed at the creative ideas that come. There's a real thrill to transforming and re-storying things; it becomes an expressive art form. Anything well-made can be given a new lease of life: think of how patchwork quilting brings together and extends the usefulness of old materials.

Mindfulness

If theming your entrance doesn't appeal, it's still important to have something that helps you enter a state of mindfulness when you come home. Mindfulness is achieved by concentrating on the present moment while calmly accepting the feelings and thoughts that come to you. It's used as a highly effective technique to induce relaxation.

Here are four mindfulness mediums to get you started:

1. Easel and canvas

If your entrance is spacious enough, have a blank canvas set on an artist's easel with a set of paints in proximity to the front door. Even if you haven't painted since you were a child, picking up a brush and adding just one stroke to the canvas is very liberating. You may even find that you linger and create something unexpected. The point isn't to create great art, but to allow your mind a moment to relax and express. This can turn into a household co-creation with everyone adding to the canvas when they come home. It takes no time at all, and will definitely make you laugh.

2. Whiteboard/blackboard

If paints are potentially too messy, consider a whiteboard hung in an attractive frame. Or paint one wall with blackboard or whiteboard paint and have chalks or markers in various colours handy.

3. Dress form

Another way to create mindfulness is to channel your inner Sarah Jessica Parker with the help of a dress form and a hamper full of fun clothing, costume jewellery, feather boas and outlandish hats in the entrance. Set a creative challenge to see who can assemble the most outrageous outfit. Regularly changing the hamper's offerings makes for fun treasure hunts, plus an opportunity to donate the pieces you're bored with to charity shops.

4. Mindfulness book

If the above suggestions feel a bit much, consider a mindfulness book and coloured pens or pencils by the front door – a welcome change from the dreaded visitors' book! Each time you come in, jot a word or two down in a colour that you're drawn to; doodle a picture; or just draw a line or shape. It's surprisingly calming and centring. The coloured pens or pencils are reminiscent of the creativity and freedom of childhood, and are much more fun than a black or blue Biro! Choose a book that appeals to your senses. To give your mindfulness book the requisite prominence, display it on a wooden music stand or anything that will catch your attention.

MAKING YOUR ENTRANCE WORK

Once you've let your creative juices flow, and you have a clear idea of what you'd love the story of your entrance to be, it's time to examine the space itself and consider some of the potential issues that need to be solved for the space to really work.

No entrance

If you live in a studio, or your front door opens directly into your living space, and you don't have a dedicated entrance area, it's important to create the impression of a transition space. This mitigates that uncanny feeling akin to opening a door and stumbling onto a stage mid-play. It's very subtle, but pervasive. To test the theory, watch how visitors react when they enter your home for the first time. Notice if they seem at a loss as to where to go. Without a proper threshold area to pause and acclimate to the interior, we're forced to take in the entire room at once, and our senses become overwhelmed. We feel uncomfortable rather than relaxed.

This 'door-onto-a-stage' feeling is also affecting you every time you come home – even if you aren't consciously aware of it. But, once you've demarcated an entrance space, you'll immediately notice the difference in the way you feel, and how you move around your home.

One of the easiest ways to define the entrance area's boundaries without closing it in is to play with clever furniture arrangement. This may sound counter-intuitive, especially if the room is small, but avoid the temptation to push sofas and chairs against the walls. Instead, use your furniture pieces creatively as building blocks as this fools the eye and creates the illusion of more space.

As you'll see in Plans 1 to 3 on pages 42–44, placing a long chest perpendicular to the wall opposite the front door creates the following: a boundary, storage space and a usable surface, where lamps illuminate the sofa backing onto the chest in the living area. To the right of the front door, a tall buffet set perpendicular to the wall can offer boot storage and a spot for keys, bags etc. while creating a visual division from the kitchen situated to the right of the entrance. The back of the buffet on the kitchen side can be used for hanging pots and pans. The entrance space is now clearly delineated by the chest and buffet, creating a small, but comfortable threshold space to pause in.

Tall plants are another great way of dividing space. Alternatively find an attractive, rectangular plant stand and add smaller plants like mother-in-law's tongue (variegated snake plant), which does best out of direct sunlight and is hardy; its sword-shaped, dark-green leaves also divide areas well.

Take a fresh look at all your furniture pieces, and try to see them in a new light. Imagine how they might be deployed to maximum creative and practical effect. The more willing you are to have fun and experiment, the better the results will be. Be open to playing – and failing. Try an arrangement and if it doesn't work, laugh and move on to your next inspiration.

Two or more entrances
If your home has more than one entrance, be sure that the secondary one is also appealing and practical, especially if you tend to favour it

for practical reasons (it's closer to the kitchen, or is the access point from the garage).

The suggestions for studios above apply here. Remember that subtle changes can have a big impact; even painting two parallel walls opening onto the main area in a contrasting colour creates the illusion of a separate space.

Small entrance

In many converted flats (apartments), it's obvious that the minimum required space has grudgingly been carved out of the rest of the property, giving the impression of being squeezed through a sausage maker every time you enter! While nothing short of major building work increases the actual size of the area, the illusion of space can be created relatively easily.

Let's start with the walls. Mirroring a wall from floor to ceiling opens the space up, reflects light and makes you feel less hemmed in. Reflections make us feel as if we're entering a different dimension. They create a sense of intrigue, of something beyond the predictable and everyday. A lack of daylight is also a frequent problem in many entrances. One solution is to fix floor-to-ceiling Shoji screens on a wall, backlit to give the impression of light and open space beyond them. Remember to keep all doors, colours and furnishings simple to blend with the screens and make them the focal point. An alternative is to use opaque acrylic sheets backlit with smart lighting to vary the entrance's colour and mood depending on the season and effect you want to create: Caribbean blue in the summer or an orange glow in the winter. It's amazing how the body instantly reacts, even though the actual temperature in the space hasn't changed.

In a small entrance, not only do the walls feel as if they're closing in on you, but so do the doors. There are a number of ways in which you can transform them:

• **Mirror** Mirrored doors create the impression of flowing, seamless space, and glass doorknobs complete the illusion (the only downside is occasional fingerprints on the mirror). Mirroring the entire surface of doors requires a glass company to measure and install.

> **Budget tip**
> The easiest and most cost-effective method is to buy bevelled, frameless wall mirrors from a DIY centre to create a large door panel on the face of each door.

- **Upholstered panels** This is a fun and easy project and can be quite spectacular depending on your choice of fabric. Upholstered panels provide soundproofing as they're made up of the face fabric plus one or more layers of batting for the padding. Opt for upholstery fabric that's easy to clean, like faux suede.
- **Glazed doors** To bring maximum light into the entrance, change doors to glazed doors – interior French doors for a more traditional look, multi or single lite Shaker doors for a clean, contemporary look. The glass can be clear or opaque, although the latter will filter the light coming into the entrance. While pre-finished doors are more expensive, they're worth considering, especially if you're opting for French doors as masking the glass and painting is very time-consuming. To comply with fire safety regulations in the UK, all doors that give onto a means of escape must be fire rated. Glazed fire doors tend to be more expensive.

Large entrance

A large entrance is often wasted space and can feel as impersonal as a hotel lobby. Consider adding the warmth and charm of a fire. An inset fire with gas or gel flame does the trick nicely and creates a reason to linger.

For an intriguing contemporary look, fit sheer, metallic floor-to-ceiling fabric to a wall – backlit by floor or skirting lights – and add a ceiling or table fan so the fabric sways in the breeze and light bounces off the fabric's metal fibres. Or opt for chain mail curtains if you're keen on a strong statement.

Most people walk through large entrances in straight lines, from point A to point B, because the centre of the space is empty. Altering this traffic pattern to a more flowing one slows everyone down and makes the area feel like a room in its own right, rather than Grand Central Station! Fill the yawning gap in the centre to create interest and make the space more convivial. A French love seat (small S-shaped sofa where two people sit facing opposite directions) looks wonderful and is an instant magnet for perching and chatting. A lobby sofa can comfortably seat four or more people. Vintage hotel lobby sofas are available in lots of styles and fabrics, including tufted leather. The contemporary versions offer cleaner lines and look more sculptural.

The energy of a large entrance changes if you use it for other activities too. Could it be a place to work with a small secretary or bureau that can be closed when you've finished for the day? Or what about a coffee bar or breakfast spot for the 'eat-and-run' members of the family? Alternatively, you could create an area for quieter games like chess, backgammon or cards.

In a large entrance, a wall of bookshelves (filled with books, not ornaments) absorbs sound and adds warmth and character. Don't be afraid to go rich when it comes to wall colour: aim for deep, warm colours that define the space. But do a large patch test first and observe it over a 24-hour period: it must look good as the light changes throughout the day. Keep the seasons in mind too – will your chosen colour feel oppressive in a heatwave? Chilling in the depths of winter? Be sure to choose paint that is non-toxic, zero VOC and environmentally friendly for you and the planet.

DRAWING THE EYE UP

Whatever type of entrance you have, don't neglect the ceiling. There's more to it than just picking the style of cornice and which light fittings to install. The entrance's ceiling is a wonderful area to draw the eye and engage the parasympathetic nervous system, especially if you get creative. Consider how colour, movement, sound and light can affect the space.

Colour

Consider painting the ceiling Haint Blue, the blue-green shades traditionally used to paint porch ceilings in the American South. They have a watery, soothing effect and immediately attract attention. The custom of using Haint Blue originated with the Gullah Geechee who believed it warded off evil spirits: 'haint' meant 'haunt', and the blue-green colour represented water, which spirits could not cross.

Movement

Seeing movement is important to our wellbeing: think of watching the ocean; tree leaves stirring in a breeze; a gust of wind creating a fishing net of light on a lake . . . Relaxing, isn't it? Introducing subtle movement to an entrance ceiling has a similar calming effect, perhaps because it reminds us of mobiles above our cots that mesmerised us as babies. Introduce kinetic art (made from materials like glass, acrylic, wire, metal, paper and feathers) that depends on motion for its effects, whether breeze, motor or perpetual motion. Some kinetic mobiles are Bluetooth-enabled, while the material of others is so light that walking past the piece elicits movement.

Budget tip

Creating your own kinetic ceiling art is fun, easy and inexpensive. Either hang multiple kinetic mobiles (that are similar or contrasting) in an interesting configuration or make your own using individual pieces of your preferred materials, and hang them in a non-linear formation, which is more intriguing and soothing on the eye. Spiral formations are especially restful. If you're feeling adventurous, create a sacred geometric pattern or a labyrinth on the ceiling with individual crystals suspended from invisible thread or fishing line, varying the lengths for added interest. The crystals will catch any available light and refract it in beautiful patterns on the walls to add an extra sparkle of magic. Or create a central ceiling sculpture by hanging your children's artwork from a fishing line in a circular or interesting shape that can be viewed from all sides. It gives their labours of love prominence and keeps the fridge door clear!

Sound

Wind chimes were originally used for sound healing in ancient China. Made from metal, wood or bamboo, the bells' different frequencies of sound are healing to our physical and emotional bodies and draw out negative energies from the spaces where they hang. Five-bell wind chimes are good at repelling negative energy, while six or eight bells attract positivity. There's an entire art of placement traditionally associated with wind chimes but keep it simple and hang one in a corner to catch a breeze, and your eye. Most importantly, choose one with a sound you love, and that makes you exhale and relax.

Light

If your entrance is very dark, consider adding one or more sun pipes. These small, round surfaces of light are relatively easy to install in the ceiling, and don't usually require planning permission. They'll transform the ceiling and create interesting pools of light on the floor.

Alternatively, play up a dark hallway – especially if the ceiling is low – with a bit of drama: paint the ceiling midnight blue and add starlight ceiling lighting; mirror one or more walls from floor to ceiling and keep the flooring dark and preferably slightly shiny. Your entrance will feel like a mini planetarium, and you won't be aware of the ceiling's actual height anymore.

HEALING TOOLS

Because entrances are such high-traffic areas, it's important to keep the energy clear so your entrance feels welcoming, but also calming and relaxing.

Scent
Have fresh flowers with scents you love. Some of the strongest floral scents include oriental lily, rose, gardenia, jasmine, freesia, lily of the valley, sweet pea.

Fresh air
Airing your entrance daily keeps the energy from stagnating. Opening any windows and the front door for as long as possible is ideal. This obviously applies to all rooms in your home.

Clean floors
Keeping the entrance floor clean and free from debris is important. If you dislike vacuuming, consider getting a robot vacuum and robot mop that can be programmed to run automatically.

A FINAL NOTE

Even if you're renting or don't feel that you're living in your 'forever home', don't be tempted to put up with things as they are in your entrance. It will sap your energy, and make you feel depressed every time you come home.

By changing the energy and creative expression of your current entrance, you'll hasten the changes you're longing for. Instead of stagnating, you'll start to really live and actually enjoy coming home. Spaces that reflect who you truly are and bring you joy always attract more of the same into your life!

CHAPTER SUMMARY

- Conduct a 'viewing' to take a fresh look at your entrance and determine what you do and don't like. Make notes in your Book of Inspiration about what will make your entrance more aesthetically and energetically welcoming. Pay close attention to smell and colour.
- Do an inventory of what's being dumped daily in your entrance. Plan proper organisation and storage solutions, whether that's baskets and containers or purpose-built storage.
- To nourish you, have a representation of the Divine Feminine in your entrance in the form of plants, water or bees.
- Dare to express an aspect of who you really are – even if it makes you feel vulnerable. Get creative and have fun choosing a theme. Treasure hunt for items to bring this theme to life both in the outside world *and* in your home.
- If theming is a step too far, find tools to create a state of mindfulness when you return home.
- Identify your entrance's issues and use practical solutions to overcome them, such as mirror, glazed doors (fire rated in the UK), coloured smart lighting, strategic furniture placement.
- Remember to draw the eye up to the ceiling by playing with colour, movement, sound and light.
- Keep the energy in your entrance clear with natural scent, fresh air and clean floors.
- Even if this isn't your forever home, change the energy and creative expression of your entrance to reflect *you*. It will pay dividends!

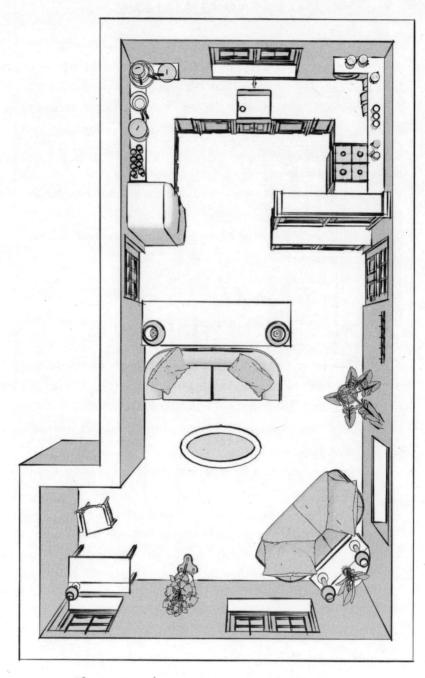

Plan 1: No entrance – creating a transition space

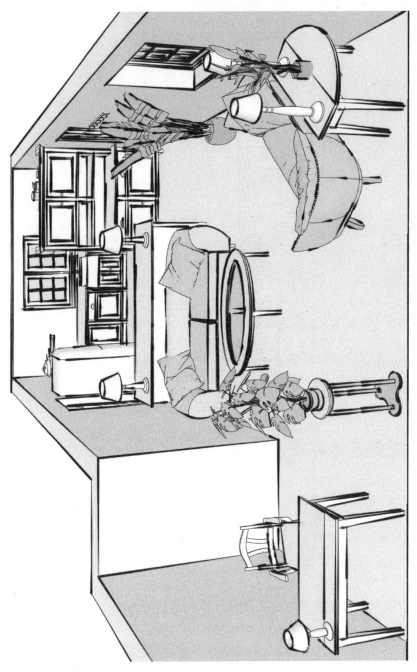

Plan 2: No entrance – creating a transition space

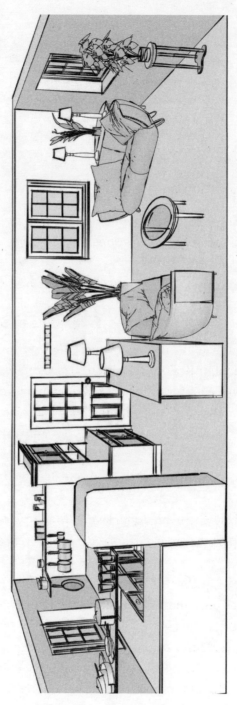

Plan 3: No entrance – creating a transition space

3

LIVING

'"Décor" and the conception of "interior design" have spread so widely, that very often people forget their instinct for the things they really want to keep around them.'
—Christopher Alexander, *A Pattern Language: Towns, Buildings, Construction*

When we contemplate furnishing a living room, our minds immediately turn to the requisite sofa, television, armchair/s, coffee and side tables. They're like a uniform that we pull on without thinking. As a result, living room layouts have – for the most part – become predictable and largely unimaginative. Tradition, design magazines, showrooms and other people's homes all reinforce the accepted model of the living room, and we don't dare colour outside the lines. But what if we did?

Let's first look at why living room layouts are the way they are and consider the impact they're having on our overall wellbeing.

Focal points

The fireplace was once the focal point of the living room, a place to gather for warmth, to talk, read, tell stories, do tasks, or relax. By the middle of the twentieth century, the television took over from the fireplace, and we have arranged our living rooms around it ever since, often turning our backs on spectacular views if the television is sited opposite a window. Since the arrival of the iPad and smartphone, our attention has become more scattered: everyone's focus shifts between the television and their individual device. It's like a symphony orchestra warming up: all dissonant sounds without cohesion between the players. This nightly scenario playing out in so many living rooms is detrimental to human connection, communication and bonding. Because our focus is on screens rather than each other, we make minimal eye contact – an essential part of non-verbal communication.

Television

We all love to binge-watch our favourite shows, and we consider this time our relaxation, and the chance to escape reality for a bit. Unfortunately, numerous studies worldwide have proved that watching several hours of television every day is bad for our physical and mental health. A 2019 study published in the National Library of Medicine even found that increased television watching is linked to cognitive decline over the age of 50.[1]

Far too many of us lead a sedentary lifestyle: we typically sit at desks all day, then – to relax and unwind – we sit for hours in front of the television. All this sitting increases our risk of developing a host of diseases, including obesity, diabetes and cardiovascular disease. Even if these adverse effects of prolonged, daily television viewing aren't immediately obvious to us, our eyes are a good barometer: when we stare at a screen, we forget to blink and our eyes become dry and tired, leading to eye strain.

So why do we keep watching? According to clinical psychologist, Dr Renee Carr, 'When engaged in an activity that's enjoyable such as binge-watching, your brain produces dopamine. This chemical gives the body a natural, internal reward of pleasure that reinforces continued engagement in that activity. It is the brain's signal that communicates to the body, "This feels good. You should keep doing this!" When binge watching your favourite show, your brain is continually producing dopamine, and your body experiences a drug-like high. You experience a pseudo-addiction to the show because you develop cravings for dopamine.'² I don't know about you but denying that dopamine rush when I have to know what happens in the next episode is tough! The *just a few more minutes* reasoning can easily turn into another hour, or more.

Dr Carr points out that the neuronal pathways that cause addiction to alcohol, drugs and sex are the same as for binge-watching. 'Your body does not discriminate against pleasure. It can become addicted to any activity or substance that consistently produces dopamine.' That's worrying enough, but if we examine the content that we're watching on a daily basis, the toll on our mental health becomes clear. Studies have demonstrated a correlation between exposure to violence on television and increased anxiety, depression, stress and other mental health issues. All too often, we expose ourselves to violence out of habit: we watch the news nightly before bed because we believe that we have to stay informed about current events at all times. But surely the question we should be asking ourselves is: *at what personal cost?*

Sofas

While we're riveted to the TV and our devices, we all want to be as comfortable as possible, so furniture design has responded accordingly with sprawling sofas and sectionals. Because of their size and bulk, sofas occupy a significant footprint in most living rooms (especially small rooms), so they tend to dominate the space. Many rooms have to be arranged around where the sofas fit. All too often they end up hugging the walls because people worry that other arrangements might make the room look smaller. Sofas tend to remain in the same spot for years because they're notoriously heavy and awkward to move. We grow accustomed to the arrangement and get bored – even if we're not consciously aware of it. Worse still, the energy becomes stuck.

Traffic patterns

Our furniture's placement steers us into traffic patterns: we walk from kitchen to sofa, from sofa to bedroom along well-trodden paths that become an ingrained habit. How we move around our home every day plays a big part in how we feel: subconsciously, these traffic patterns reinforce whatever is going on in our lives – good or bad. If you have a tendency to collapse onto your sofa after a long, stressful day, then binge-watch television until you finally drag yourself off to bed exhausted, this habit and the associated emotions stick. They're hard to shake, and affect your daily mood.

Underused space

We all have favourite spots – whether from comfort, habit or convenience. As a result, sections of a room can be underused, especially in a large living room. This contributes to energy build-up and stagnation in the overused spaces (like the sofa). We overlook the potential of other areas which could ultimately free us from the clutches of the television with the activities they offer: a cosy reading nook or a corner for creative activities. Ideally, all parts of the room should be used on a regular basis.

Shapes

Contemporary furniture and sofas are often angular, with sharp corners. While we may find them stylish, their shape is actually triggering a negative reaction in our brains! In a 1921 study, psychologist Helge Lundholm asked subjects to draw lines representing emotional adjectives: for words like 'hard' and 'cruel' they used angular lines, but for 'gentle' and 'mild' they drew curved lines.[3] And in 2007, cognitive psychologists Moshe Bar and Maital Neta proved that the amygdala – the region of the brain whose primary function is to process stimuli that induce anxiety, aggressiveness and fear – is more activated by sharp-cornered objects than rounded.[4] Think how many sharp-cornered objects we have in our homes – and what effect they're having on us! Conversely, 1920s architect Grace Cope proved that curves actually dispel irritability, depression and brain fatigue. She referred to the serpentine line as an 'exhilarating chase' and advocated its use: 'The eye is so delicately hung in its socket that it moves more easily and smoothly, and responds more quickly to a curve than to a hard, straight line.'

FIRST IMPRESSIONS

As suggested for your entrance (please see page 22), conduct an impartial 'viewing' of your living room. In your Book of Inspiration, write down everything that strikes your senses, what you like and dislike etc. Pay particular attention to the following:

1. Television
Observe and record your habits. Do you turn the television on in the morning or when you come home? Is it often on just in the background? How many hours of TV do you watch per day? What types of programmes (educational, uplifting, soap operas, crime etc.) do you watch? How do you feel when you switch the television off? What impact does watching TV have on your relationships? Do you bond with other household members over what you watch, or is it a means of escape?

2. Layout
How long have you had the current layout in your living room? How does it make you feel? Bored? Inspired? Happy? Depressed? Is the main focal point the television? What would you like to change about the layout?

3. Traffic patterns
Think about how you and your family move around your home and note any set traffic patterns. Do they trigger any particular emotions?

4. Underused space
Track where you spend the majority of your time in the living room. Note how many hours you're there each day. Highlight all the areas in

the room that you don't use and ask yourself why. Is it the feeling in that space? Or is it a more practical concern – like a chair or window seat that's uncomfortable?

5. Shapes

Take a look at any angular and sharp-cornered objects around you. How do they make you feel? What about curved, round-cornered objects?

In general, which shapes appeal to you most: circle, oval, rectangle, square, triangle, octagon, hexagon, rhombus etc? Doodle your favourites and note why they appeal to you. Do they remind you of something? Are they linked to a particular emotion?

SOLUTIONS

To reimagine your living room with your wellbeing as a priority, let's begin with some practicalities then move on to creative and intuitive solutions.

Television

If your analysis of your television viewing habits surprised you – especially the number of hours involved – you're not alone: most adults watch an average of 27 hours a week. That's over one full day and night – just think what you could be doing with that time!

In his book *Atomic Habits*, author James Clear says: 'What you repeatedly do ultimately forms the person you are, the things you believe, and the personality that you portray.' I doubt many of us want to portray Couch Potato!

While television watching isn't always an easy habit to break, the long-term gains are worth any short-term withdrawal symptoms. You'll end up with more time to pursue activities that inspire and excite you; your physical and mental health will improve (especially if you move your body); you'll have more energy and be happier as you're more likely to engage in social activities instead of isolating yourself in front of a screen. As philosopher and statesman, Francis Bacon, said: 'Friendship doubles joy and cuts grief in half.'

According to James Clear, the way to break a bad habit is to make it invisible, unattractive, difficult and unsatisfying. Start by taking your focus off the television: make it **invisible** and more difficult to instantly switch on. TV lift cabinets accomplish this as you have to press a button and wait for the concealed screen to rise out of the unit. If you're diligent about always retracting the screen when you switch off the TV, you'll minimise the temptation to start watching when you next walk into the room. When the television is off and its screen looms dark and blank on the wall, it can feel austere and look **unattractive**. (Unfortunately this can be motivation for switching it on to bring colour and life to it.) If budget allows, you can fit motorised moving panels to completely conceal the screen. A mirror TV (a mirror takes the place of the screen when you switch the TV off), or art TV (at the touch of a button, a canvas rolls back to reveal the screen) are other options to consider. To make your television habit **unsatisfying**, alter your living room's layout so that the television isn't the focal point, and you have to move chairs in order to view it. If you install the TV on a window wall, you can cover the entire wall with curtains: one pair opening onto the window, and another pair opening onto the TV. When it's off and the curtains are drawn to conceal it, the overall effect in the room is a stylish wall of full-length curtains. This also creates the illusion that there's more than one window.

Whenever you do watch television, remember to shift your gaze away from the screen frequently, and focus on something further away. This helps to ease eye strain and reduces headaches and fatigue.

If you're in the habit of turning on your TV for company and as background noise, try a wireless multi-room speaker system instead. Controlled by voice-enabled speakers, or through any smart device, you can play music, podcasts and other audio entertainment throughout your home or in specific rooms. You'll never be lonely again!

Budget tip

The Mayo Clinic offers 'Slim Your Screen Time' a free, at-home, self-guided programme designed to help you improve your health by reducing screen time.

Layout and traffic patterns

One way to prevent layout boredom *and* break traffic patterns is to rearrange furniture on a regular basis. It shifts and changes the energy, and allows new, positive associations to form. Famed twentieth-century architect Frank Lloyd Wright was known for rearranging the furniture in his home on a weekly basis!

For ease of movement, ball castors can be fitted on sofas and furniture and are available in antique and contemporary styles, in designer and budget ranges.

If you're good at visualising, play around with potential layouts in your mind, then roll your sleeves up and try them. If you prefer to plot everything to scale first, there are a number of 2D and 3D room visualisation apps listed in the Resources section (please see page 269).

A sense of humour and having fun are essential to rearranging furniture successfully. Being too serious can result in staid layouts, so have a light touch. Don't be afraid to try unusual configurations with sofas and furniture, and to experiment extensively with angles as the slightest variation can make all the difference. Small rooms often appear more spacious with the sofa perpendicular to a wall, or cater-corner (diagonally), as shown in Plans 1 to 3 (please see pages 42–44). Sometimes what looks good on paper, or in your mind's eye, doesn't work in reality; try not to become too fixated on a certain layout as this prevents spontaneity, and the ability to envision creative alternatives on the fly. If a configuration looks ridiculous, just try something else – and don't be tempted to put everything back where it started!

As the room becomes increasingly messy during the rearrangement process, it's easy to get overwhelmed. One solution is to remove all non-bulky items (lamps, side tables, rugs, occasional chairs, ornaments) to another room, and only reintroduce them once the major pieces have been arranged to your satisfaction. If you go to the extreme of clearing the room of all its contents, don't panic and wonder how you'll ever fit everything back: empty rooms always look much smaller than when they're furnished.

Humans are naturally resistant to change; we become so accustomed to things being in certain positions that it can look odd at first when everything in a room is rearranged. I always advise my clients to live with a new configuration for 24–48 hours to really get a feel for it.

Underused space

If your sofa held the highest score as the most used space, you're in good company!

With the underused areas of your living room, apply the same rule as for clothes in your wardrobe (closet): anything outdated or that hasn't been worn for a year has to go. In the case of spaces, I'd recommend 4–6 months as the maximum grace period before rethinking their use, especially if they're in prime locations near a window or fireplace.

Spend some time in each underused area to get a feel for the space. Move aside any furniture currently there to allow you to reimagine it. What might you enjoy doing there if the set-up were different? If you want to read more, look at ways to transform a space in front of the fireplace or window. Comfortable seating will entice you to spend time there.

Budget tip

If space and cost are an issue, consider bean bag chairs, available in a wide range of styles, colours and fabrics including leather, velvet and fleece.

If you need to divide one area from another, consider revamping a low or high back settle bench. They often include storage under the seat, and the solid back and side wings cut drafts and give a private feel. Originally designed to sit in front

– or on the side – of a fireplace in farmhouses and taverns, the settle has a utilitarian look, but can be made comfortable with a thick seat cushion and plump scatter cushions (pillows). If nothing else, your posture will be better on a settle than on a sofa! Paint the settle to blend with your wall colour, or turn it into a focal point with a statement colour. If it's dividing two areas, or creating a mini entrance by the door, mirror its entire back to increase light and make it appear less bulky.

Shapes

If during your living room viewing, your sofa fell into the angular, sharp-cornered category and brought up negative emotions, what can be done? If you've had it for a while, and aren't that attached, it might be time for a change. Consider donating it to people in need: a quick internet search should come up with a local charity that accepts unwanted furniture (or please see Resources). According to End Furniture Poverty, 9 per cent of adults and children in the UK are living in furniture poverty, without essential items.

When shopping for a new sofa, look for curved lines. There are many sustainable furniture companies offering cost-effective sofas made from recycled foam with washable covers that are interchangeable – perfect if you want to get creative with your living room's look. Look for poufs and footstools in different sizes, heights and colours, or furniture that can multitask as seating, footstool and rocker (please see Resources).

If you've invested a lot of money in your current sofa, and don't want to part with it yet, try to soften its angular lines by drawing attention away from them with unexpected, non-angular scatter cushions. Instead of the ubiquitous square cushions, experiment with unusual shapes like knots, waves, clouds, flowers etc. Their curved, round-cornered lines are guaranteed to make you smile, relax and forget your sofa's hard angles.

Other less expensive items in your living room can either be replaced or altered to soften their lines. Adding a round or oval top to a rectangular or square coffee or side tables helps. Tempered glass tops work well, but if the existing base is dark, your eye will still be drawn to its shape rather than the glass top's. Paint the base a light colour, or cover it with a thick, light-coloured material to soften the sharp corners. If there isn't space to add a top to your existing coffee table, camouflage its four corners (or two ends) with trailing plants in curved containers. Ivy works especially well as you can trail it around the table's legs. Or consider an all-glass coffee table – you can even find ones that can be configured into multiple shapes so you can change the look of your coffee table as often as you like!

Picture frames are usually angular, sharp-cornered, and often dark. As reframing is costly, consider removing canvases from their frames. Or, if you have light-coloured walls, soften the frames' appearance by spray painting them a light colour to blend with the background rather than contrasting to it. Conversely, if you have dark walls, tone frame colours with the walls. The upside is that art pieces stand out more when not competing with their frames. While there are plenty of oval and round frames, they may not suit art pieces, and can have a more old-fashioned look – especially if they're gilt and elaborate. For a more edgy, contemporary feel, consider spray painting them a funky colour – as long as it suits the picture.

EXPRESS YOURSELF

Think about what you most need from your living room. A sense of comfort that invites you to unwind and relax? A convivial place to reconnect with family and friends? Write down your personal wish list in your Book of Inspiration, then number the list in priority order – but try not to fixate on practicalities. Instead, focus on what would put you in a positive emotional state when you walk into your living room. So that you can take everyone's wishes into account, get other household members to make their own lists, as outlined in Chapter 1 (please see page 11).

Next, revisit the list of the shapes you like. If your current living room's furniture layout is the typical square, rectangle, or L-shape, but your favourite shape is the circle, you're not alone. Humans are universally drawn to the circle, as designer Manuel Lima explores in his fascinating book, *The Book of Circles*.

Ancient and tribal cultures see the circle as the most powerful of shapes, and it has deep ritualistic and ceremonial significance. In *Black Elk Speaks* by John Neihardt, Black Elk, Medicine Man of the Oglala Sioux Nation, said: 'Everything the Power of the World does is in a circle. The sky is round, and I have heard that the earth is round like a ball, and so are all the stars. The wind, in its greatest power, whirls. Birds make their nests in circles, for theirs is the same religion as ours. The sun comes forth and goes down again in a circle. The moon does the same, and both are round. Even the seasons form a great circle in their changing, and always come back again to where they were. The life of a man is a circle from childhood to childhood, and so it is in everything where power moves. Our tepees were round like the nests of birds, and these were always set in a circle, the nation's hoop, a nest of many nests, where the Great Spirit meant for us to hatch our children.

'But the Wasichus have put us in these square boxes. Our power is gone and we are dying, for the power is not in us any more.'

This is enough to give us pause, as most of us live our lives in square boxes! However, the overall shape of your living room's layout can be softened – even if most of the furniture pieces are angular. Try turning a rectangular or square arrangement into a circular one: instead of having all seating facing forward, and parallel to the walls, try angling each piece towards a central point until you achieve the semblance of a circle. With straight-backed sofas and chairs, it may be more of an octagon or hexagon, but the configuration is easier on the eye, and feels inviting.

Alternatively, start small and build up from there. Two chairs facing forward with their backs parallel to a wall always look more formal, and conjure up a waiting room. If you angle them both slightly towards each other, they immediately feel more inviting. Try it, and see how you *feel* – both viewing each arrangement, and sitting in each chair.

Once you know what isn't working in your current living room and you have your personal wish list, it's time to give your intuition free rein and reimagine the room. Have a light touch and have some fun! Here are three ideas – albeit somewhat aspirational – to get you started:

1. Fire circle

Instead of the TV, make the centre of the room the focal point, and build out from there in a circular configuration. One of the best focal points is a central fire that everyone can gather around. Sitting around a fire is comforting, convivial and part of our DNA; it's also very healing. A 2014 study led by anthropologist, Christopher Lynn, found that watching a fire *with* sound decreased blood pressure in participants.[5] The longer they watched, the more relaxed they became – particularly those who scored higher in prosocial behaviours like empathy and altruism. Lynn's hypothesis was that when we sit by a fire, all of our senses become absorbed. Having this calming focus of attention could help to reduce anxiety: 'Hearth and campfires induce relaxation as part of a multi-sensory, absorptive, and social experience.'

While wood burning or gas fireplaces require a flue or chimney, bioethanol fireplaces don't. Bioethanol is a renewable liquid fuel produced from agricultural by-products which burns clean. It's a decent heat source (up to 3kW – comparable to most flueless gas fires) and does less damage to air quality than other fires. Indoor fire-pits and fire tables (which double as coffee tables) are now available and are perfect for gathering around. They are usually easy to move and can be used outdoors during the summer.

Unfortunately a bioethanol fire isn't a multi-sensory experience: the scent and sound we associate with a real fire are missing (Lynn's study found that sound is all-important). To make a bioethanol fire multi-sensory, try burning wood smoke incense sticks and downloading the sound of a crackling log fire.

> **Budget tip**
>
> Create your own fire table on a smaller scale with a bioethanol tabletop burner placed in the centre of your coffee table as the focal point. It will give off around 1 kW of heat and is particularly eye-catching on a glass coffee table that reflects the flames. Magnify the effect by encircling the burner with pillar candles – real flame, not battery-operated.

2. Dance space

Consider turning an underused space in your living room into an area to dance – no matter how small. Dance has a range of proven health benefits, including increasing endorphins and dopamine (the feel-good hormone) production; lowering the risk of cardiovascular disease and osteoporosis; reducing pain perception; and it may prevent dementia. Prabha Siddarth's 2021 health study at UCLA involving participants with depression, anxiety, or a history of trauma found that conscious, free-flowing dance produced positive mental health benefits.[6] Ninety-eight per cent of participants reported that conscious dance improved their mood, and many said it gave them more confidence and compassion.

Quite apart from what science has discovered, dance *feels* good – whether you're rocking out to your favourite song solo, or dancing with a partner, or as a group. For inspiration and pure feel-good factor, watch 'Matt Harding Dancing Around the World' on YouTube. As he says: 'And when we dance together, we will save ourselves.'

Dancing also helps to clear a space's energy, along with your own. You don't need a large area for free-flow dance: an unencumbered corner will do. Decide how much space you want to move freely, and keep the area clear – if you have to move furniture to dance, chances are you won't.

Consider buying a portable dance floor made from Marley, acknowledged as one of the safest surfaces to dance on because it offers support and helps avoid slipping and injuries. Available in sizes from 41cm (16 inches), it can be placed on any floor surface without damaging it.

If you're hankering after a disco ball or two to really get you in the mood but are worried they'll clash with the rest of the room, opt for disco ball planters suspended from the ceiling. By day, they'll green your living space and reflect light, and add that extra sparkle by night.

3. Window on Africa

I used to live in Africa so the continent holds a special place in my heart. I was therefore delighted to discover the live-stream Africam (africam.com) with 16 African bush locations to choose from. The game viewing is fascinating, and the background sounds make for a much more relaxing option if you can't break the habit of keeping your television on for company throughout the day.

If you have your own links to the continent you can enhance the experience by creating an African corner: site your TV on a window wall (please see page 51) and add some African flavour – while avoiding kitsch choices! Green your corner with plants native to Africa such as fiddle leaf fig, giant bird of paradise, mother-in-law's tongue and spider plant.

If the African bush doesn't appeal, there are plenty of other live-streamed nature options from around the world.

To help you tune into your intuition and successfully reimagine your living room, try this great exercise from Sonia. It's a terrific aerobic workout, and really shifts your perspective!

SONIA CHOQUETTE SUGGESTS

If you do this fun, short neuroplasticity exercise for 30 days, you'll completely rewire your brain and create new neuronal pathways! To help you, I wrote a song that you can download from soniachoquette.com. You can do this exercise solo, but having a partner really helps as it forces you both to keep going.

1. Begin by raising your arms above your head and opening your mouth like a baby bird waiting for a morning worm. As you do, release the sound 'Ah'. Then pull your arms down quickly and, as you do, exhale fully by letting out the sound 'Ha!'. Repeat this movement: with each raise of the arms, say 'Ah'; and each exhale with movement, say 'Ha!'.

2. Once your basic move is established, begin to move your arms in a different way each time you inhale with 'Ah', and exhale with 'Ha!'. Continue this for 3 minutes and 40 seconds.

The exercise coordinates breath and movement, which is what changes the energy, quiets mind chatter and awakens your spirit.

What to expect:

- **1st minute:** It's a novelty, and you're willing to go with it. Your left brain – which is where most of us live – begins to talk to your right brain. Soon, these two brains are communicating again the way they were designed to.
- **2nd minute:** You'll start getting bored and bumping up against resistance. This is where you have to push yourself because *this* is when you're starting to change your brain. Just keep going, keep breathing. When you breathe the energy of the breath into your body, your whole brain lights up – it's actually been scientifically measured.
- **3rd minute:** When you keep pushing through the resistance, something miraculous happens: your brain flips, and starts talking to your heart, which is your first brain and your highest intelligence. Pretty soon, you start rewiring yourself in the way that you were born and are designed to live! All of a sudden, the intelligence and brain in every cell of your body comes alive.

If you start your day with this exercise, you'll not only bring your vitality back, but you'll actually physiologically change the energy in your body. Remarkably, this will stop the ageing process when your spirit is *fully* embodied!

MAKING YOUR LIVING ROOM WORK

Taking all your creative ideas and making them work in your current living room can feel like a logistical challenge, especially if space is tight. The first thing to consider – if your home has multiple rooms – is whether you're using the right one for *you*. In most houses, the living room is typically on the ground (first) floor – but it doesn't have to be! Much depends on your personality type in Chinese medicine (please see page 8). If you're the Nurturer, you'll want your living room close to – if not part of – the kitchen. If you're the Visionary, you prefer being higher up, with plenty of light and views, so the first (second) floor may appeal more for your living room. With this in mind, conduct a 'viewing' of your home, and consider possible alternatives to your current living room.

Let's delve into ways to make different size living rooms work.

Studio living

We'll explore how to successfully combine a living room and bedroom into one space in Chapter 6.

Open-plan living space

The ideal of the late twentieth and early twenty-first centuries lost some of its appeal during Covid-19, when the open-plan living space had to accommodate multiple people doing disparate activities day-in, and day-out. The sound of other people going about their daily business increased everyone's stress levels. Movable acoustic partitions are an excellent solution to this issue. They make an open-plan living space flexible, letting you alter it to suit your mood and needs of the moment. They're perfect for dividing a large space from open plan for entertaining to cosy and intimate, for screening off a kitchen, and for sequestering an area for a home office, cinema or games zone.

Budget tip

To absorb sound waves without investing in movable partitions, try adding acoustic panels to walls and ceilings.

To create a sense of visual separation between areas, try tall plants in box planters on castors so you can easily move them, or ceiling-hung sheer curtains mounted on discreet tracks. These can be curved or straight, and hand/rod drawn, corded or electric.

If a major traffic corridor runs beside the living area of your open-plan space, it can feel less than relaxing to sit there. Movable acoustic partitions are a great solution as they give a sense of visual and auditory separation but, if you love large, open-plan spaces, you may feel hemmed in. Another solution is to install a glass wall. It's significantly more soundproof than a partition wall and maintains the sense of open space. When you need privacy, you could consider 'smart' glass, which changes from transparent to varying degrees of opaque on demand. A glass wall is effective, minimalist and stunning, but it's an expensive option requiring professional installation.

Small living room

One of the biggest issues with a small living room is how aware you are of the size of the space. The walls and door tend to close in – especially if the ceiling is high. If the space is cluttered and/or has lots of busy fabrics, it can feel stifling.

Painting the walls and ceiling a shade of white or cream helps to push them back, and choosing a palette of whites and creams for curtains and upholstery makes the room feel more spacious. If this palette feels too stark for you, create variety and interest with lots of different textures (chenille, velvet, bouclé, wool etc.) and add the occasional splash of colour or pattern with scatter cushions (pillows), ornaments and art to draw the eye without being overpowering.

Changing the living room's door to a glazed door brings in more light and camouflages one of the overpowering elements. A multi-pane French door, or single-pane glass door does the trick. If you have a busy household, opaque glass gives a sense of privacy, but clear glass makes the living room feel part of the adjoining space – typically a hallway – while still maintaining a sense of separation. If you prefer a solid door, consider replacing your current one with a pair of doors. They take up less floorspace, and don't feel as bulky because each door can be positioned at a different angle when open. Paint wood doors to match the walls so they blend in rather than stand out. If the wood is anything other than pine, this can be a difficult choice, but the feeling of spaciousness gained is worth the sacrifice. As mentioned earlier, to comply with fire safety regulations in the UK, all doors that give on to a means of escape must be fire rated. Glazed fire doors tend to be more expensive.

Creating a focal point diverts attention away from the size of a small living room. If you have a large window – or more than one window – draw the eye to it. If the view is good, position comfortable seating by the window facing the view instead of the room: this creates the illusion that the outside space is part of the living room. If the view isn't pleasant, but you can still see the sky, have a window box planter on the inside of the window that spans its entire width; the plants help to obscure the unsightly portion of the view, and draw the eye skyward. Opt for a planter that blends seamlessly with your wall and window frame colour. If the windowsill isn't deep enough, hang the planter with unobtrusive brackets – although scroll brackets can also work if their colour matches the planter and walls. To prevent water leakage, have a waterproof liner inside the planter. A plain roman blind provides a good backdrop for an indoor window box. Install it high enough above the window frame so it doesn't cover any part of the sky when the blind is open. If you want to frame the window, consider a pair of louvered exterior shutters: they're light-weight and fix easily to the wall.

If your small living room is dark, mirroring an entire wall from floor to ceiling is one of the best ways to reflect more light and create the illusion of space. A mirrored wall must be professionally installed by a glass company, which can be expensive, depending on the wall size, and number of cut-outs needed for sockets and light switches.

Budget tip

If you can't justify the cost of mirroring a wall, hang window garden mirrors to mimic a wall of arched windows. They're available in a variety of shapes, styles and sizes in wood or metal. Use the same size and style for all window mirrors as a mix and match draws too much attention and breaks the illusion of a wall of windows. To create an outdoor feel and conserve floorspace, intersperse the window mirrors with hanging plants.

Introducing an outdoor theme to a small living room offers a peaceful and relaxing escape from the outside world. Play to the sense of being confined by four walls by creating an indoor secret garden, walled garden, or inner courtyard (please see Plans 4 and 5 on pages 71–2).

Create the impression of open sky overhead with a translucent ceiling or light panel. 3-D stretch ceilings (suspended fabric ceilings) are cost-effective and recyclable and come in different sizes, shapes, textures and colours, or can be printed to look like a sky – or any other effect you choose.

Have as many plants as the space allows or consider a living wall (plants grown vertically) if the room is very small. To mimic outdoor lighting at night, have concealed uplighters shining up into the foliage, floor lanterns and plenty of candles. Luminous, wireless furniture can multitask as mood lighting, seating and side tables.

Budget tip

Instead of a sofa, which may look incongruous with your inner courtyard theme, find a vintage French-style wrought-iron daybed at an architectural salvage yard. Add plush seat and back cushions. Have plenty of floor cushions for lounging.

Keep surfaces transparent: all-glass or acrylic pieces blend seamlessly while still reflecting light. Alternatively, add glass tops to interesting pots in keeping with the indoor garden theme – but make sure they're stable and can't easily topple. Instead of a coffee table, save on space with a low nest of tables in glass or acrylic that are easy to move and can double as extra seating, or footrests. We associate the sound of water with inner courtyards, so include a water feature if possible (wall-mounted saves on space).

Large living room

Large living rooms are wonderful for entertaining but can feel cavernous when you're on your own. While you can create more than one seating area, be wary of the hotel lobby effect: coordinated sofas and chairs arranged in square and L-shapes can look very uninteresting.

Try to make each area of the room inviting and intriguing. Double-sided sofas are an option: they're available in many styles, from traditional Chesterfields through to contemporary models with lovely, flowing lines, although the latter work best because traditional versions can be rather heavy and imposing. Play with different heights to add interest to a large living room: high-backed sofas and chairs help to delineate different seating areas, while Arabic-style majlis floor sofas create the illusion of a sunken floor area. Sitting in the lotus position on floor sofas aids digestion, increases energy levels and lessens food cravings. Majlis are great for kids, but not the elderly.

Get creative with the corners of your large living room. A contemporary upholstered corner chair fills a wall corner nicely and offers flexible seating: you can face three different angles without ever having to move the chair! Or soften the angle of the corner and make the room convivial by placing a chest *across* the corner (rather than against a wall), then conceal a floor lamp or smart lighting behind it to cast an unexpected, moody light behind objects displayed on the chest.

Movable acoustic partitions (please see Chapter 1, page 17) are worth considering for a large living room, especially when you want to make the space feel cosier in the winter. For a truly luxurious effect that absorbs sound well, consider upholstering your walls!

Budget tip

If you're a book lover and want to divide your large living room without investing in movable acoustic partitions, create additional 'walls' by securely fixing tall bookcases perpendicular to your existing walls and filling them with books, which are excellent sound absorbers. Use the backs of the bookcases like walls to display art above a console table or seating. Experiment with potential shapes and configurations to create private nooks, like a reading corner by a window with a small table and a couple of chairs, or a chaise-longue. Having mobile seating (on castors), upholstered cubes and plush floor cushions lets you choose your ideal spot depending on your mood of the moment.

For a more see-through partition, use tall, open bookshelves instead of bookcases and display ornaments, plants and books – but be sure that the arrangements look good on both sides. The only downside is that open bookshelves absorb less sound than bookcases lined with books.

Using a central feature to divide seating areas breaks a large living room up cleverly: a central fireplace or water feature (proportional to the room's size); an inner courtyard (please see page 72); or an indoor garden. The latter is a great option if you don't have good views. It's also very uplifting to see lush greenery and life during the cold, drab winter months. Form a circle of indoor trees and greenery in the centre of a large living room and have seating arrangements face this indoor view. Leafy trees to consider include weeping fig, majesty palm, kumquat, guava and rubber tree. Make your indoor garden distinct from the rest of the room with outdoor-style seating to lounge in: vintage wrought-iron rocking chairs are eye-catching and relaxing – the French nineteenth-century versions are plain and elegant.

PRACTICALITIES

1. Ball castors
Choose ball castors that can take the weight of your furniture and ensure the balls are plastic or rubber so they won't damage wood floors. Adding castors increases the height of the piece, and you may need to choose ones with a locking mechanism so furniture won't move.

2. Bioethanol fires
These don't need a fireplace, but they have large, naked flames. Choose indoor models with protective glass to avoid accidents. Take great care around curtains, soft furnishings, children, pets etc.

3. Movable partitions
These need to be in proportion to the overall size of the room other-wise they'll either dominate it or look out of place. If they're not a permanent fixture, make sure you have adequate space for storing them when not in use.

4. Glass wall
If you have a suspended timber – rather than concrete – floor, it will require localised strengthening to take the weight of glass, and you'll have to contract a structural engineer. In the UK, fire-rated glass is required if the wall gives onto a means of escape or is part of a kitchen. To make a glass wall inconspicuous, its retaining channel should be mill-finish aluminium, painted to match the colour of the

surrounding walls and ceiling – not shiny, powder-coated strips seen in corporate offices.

A FINAL NOTE

We change our wardrobe seasonally, so why not make seasonal changes in the living room? Minor details can make all the difference.

Summer

The aim is for a cooling and relaxing effect in the living room – no matter how hot it gets. Ideally what you see should be light and bright; what you touch, cool and smooth. Natural fabrics like cotton, linen and silk work best, especially if your skin comes into contact with them. Leather upholstery heats up and becomes sticky and unpleasant to sit on. Use throws to cover dark winter sofas or have slipcovers in creams and whites. Change cushion covers to summer accent colours.

Summer colours should recede, reflect light and inspire you from a distance; use bright colours as accent – not main – colours. If softer colours are more your style, make sure they're uplifting rather than drab and dense.

Let daylight flood the room, while keeping out direct midday sun. White or cream sheers or curtains without interlining are ideal for framing windows without arresting your attention as you look out. Curtains in bright, summer colours will interrupt your view, and won't create a feeling of light and space.

Move furniture into an open, spacious configuration; creating a sense of maximum floorspace decreases the feeling of being hemmed in. Bare tiles and floorboards work well. If your carpet is dark, consider a large, plain rug – or one with a contemporary, minimalist pattern.

Transparent pieces are ideal for warm summers: glass and acrylic coffee, side and console tables, as well as chairs and stools, reflect light and increase the sense of space.

Bringing the outdoors in is vital if you're stuck indoors for long periods of time. Window boxes planted with bright, native plants draw the eye outside, while tall, light indoor plants are healthy and refreshing on the senses.

Winter

Conjure a sense of warmth and cosiness by playing to the senses – especially sight and touch. If you have wood, stone or tile floors, have a large rug that's soft underfoot – but avoid lots of small rugs as this can look bitty. Soft furnishings need to look *and* feel inviting and soft – especially sofas. Muffle stark lines with throws in chenille, faux fur and mohair. Change scatter cushion covers to velvet, suede, wool or heavy weave cotton. Avoid silk, polyester and anything that looks shiny and feels cold to the touch. You may also want to cover a glass coffee table. Consider alternating your curtains seasonally: light-weight/light colour in the summer, heavier weight/darker colour in the winter.

For winter colours, choose from ranges of warm tones that appeal to your personality type in Chinese medicine (please see page 8).

Budget tip

Ready-to-hang curtain panels with concealed tab tops don't hang as well as lined and interlined curtains, but they're cost-effective and easy to clean and store. Faux suede in a rich colour looks plush and helps block drafts.

CHAPTER SUMMARY

- Record how many hours of television you're watching per week and decide if it's a habit that needs breaking for improved mental and physical health.

- If the television is the focal point, consider the following options: alternate layouts; TV-lift cabinet; motorised moving panels; mirror or art TV; a wall of curtains; home sound system for company instead of the television.
- To break set traffic patterns, rearrange furniture (ideally on castors) regularly. Try unusual configurations and use angles to avoid the waiting room effect.
- Rethink underused spaces for activities you might enjoy.
- Curves dispel irritability, depression and brain fatigue, while angular, sharp-cornered objects can induce anxiety, aggressiveness and fear. If you can't change the furniture, soften lines and shapes with oval or round glass, trailing plants, fabric and paint. Try circular arrangements instead of rectangular and L-shaped.
- Consider creating: a fire circle, a dance space or a window on Africa.
- Divide an open-plan living room with movable, acoustic partitions.
- Disguise small living rooms with neutral colours or a glazed door (fire rated in the UK), and make the window the focal point with an indoor window box.
- Mirror a wall in a dark room or hang window garden mirrors.
- An outdoor theme works well in small living rooms.
- Make large living rooms interesting with double-sided, high-backed or majlis floor sofas and corner chairs.
- Cosy up large living rooms with movable, acoustic partitions, upholstered walls or bookcases set perpendicular to a wall.
- Divide seating areas with a central feature: fireplace, water feature or indoor garden.
- Make seasonal changes with colour, texture and lighting.

Plan 4: Small living room – creating an outdoor theme

Plan 5: Small living room – creating an outdoor theme

4

RELAXING & WELLNESS

'Noticing what feels good and what doesn't is radical these days,
because it is wisdom that can only be unlocked from within.'
—Wendy Havlir Cherry, *The Mistress of Longing*

A PERSONAL SANCTUARY

Most homes offer activity-specific rooms, but what about sanctuaries and relaxation spaces? Given the way that most of us are living, we really need to prioritise relaxation spaces if we want to achieve mental and physical wellness!

The dictionary defines relaxing as: 'To become less active, and more calm and happy', but our 24/7/365 lifestyles aren't exactly conducive to that, are they? How many of us *really* relax on a regular basis? Even on weekends and holidays, we're constantly connected to everything and everyone, so how can our minds and bodies get the break they desperately need to heal?

As authority on the spiritual side of Chinese medicine, Jean Haner, says: 'Our Western culture doesn't value just *being*, and that's a real problem. Instead we're taught to value *doing*: constantly busy working, chasing more money, or racing towards the next goal. When you ask someone what they do during their downtime, they'll probably laugh and say: "Downtime? What's *that*?" But it shouldn't be a mark of pride to always be busy. We need to balance time spent "doing" with time devoted to "being": regular downtime for periods of deep replenishment.' Unfortunately, zoning out in front of the television at the end of a long day is all too often our definition of relaxing.

Bernadette Pleasant, somatic healer and founder of The Emotional Institute, recommends having a space in your home that's yours alone. Somewhere you can go to truly relax and be yourself. It doesn't matter how small it is – it's the knowing that it's *your* space – to do as you please in – that counts. Bernadette points out that men have always claimed a space in the home that's uniquely theirs: whether a study, man cave or Dad's chair. Everyone in the household understands that the man's space is to be respected, and not disturbed.

'Batman has a Bat Cave. Superman a phone booth,' Bernadette says. 'But Cat Woman – or any other female superhero – I can't think of a room for her! Similarly, I don't know that women *claim* a space of their own – a Mom's room or chair – a place that's just *her* sanctuary. Even if she has a space that's carved out for herself – like a sewing room – it's often perceived as more of a utility room where everyone can come and go as they please. But how can you take care of others and *not* have a space for you to just *be* as a woman? The ability to close a door, and have that boundary respected by the family is essential. A woman has to say "yes" to herself and claim the alone time she needs to refuel and get nourished personally, in private.

'Women in particular need ritual to ground, and remind them of who they are – even if it's only 10 minutes a day. Having a sanctuary allows them to drop into the feminine body, become still and quiet (even if they have to use headphones). It's important that they're very clear with other household members that they need this time in their sanctuary, and it's non-negotiable. With time and practice, others will learn to accept it.

'Your private space needs to be a creative space, a womb where you can *grow*, and learn to create internal safety. If you don't feel at home within yourself, then you can't feel truly at home anywhere.' Bernadette emphasises that people of colour have a very strong need to feel safe at home because they don't always feel safe in the outside world.

EMOTIONAL OVERLOAD

Most of us are running on emotional overload, which plays havoc with our hormones, and consequently our health. Grief and stress are two of the biggest issues that we deal with on a regular basis, and our homes need to offer us safe harbour to process.

Grief

We often associate grief with bereavement, but there are many other losses throughout life that cause us to grieve, including infidelity, divorce, job or home loss, relocating, retirement, empty nest, health challenges etc. These 'little griefs' can be just as crippling as the death of a loved one – often because we grieve in silence.

In her book, *It's Grief*, therapist Edy Nathan says: 'The disappointments carried within our souls are all part of a grief phenomena. We are grieving all of the time. Depression, anxiety, and even obesity can be in response to a loss, and at the same time can cause a grief reaction. The funny thing is that no one talks about how present grief is in our daily lives. The silence occurs because few people know how to talk about the life cycle of grief. The subject of grief is taboo! Much like the conversation about mental illness. Avoidance seems to be the best coping mechanism. It is the inherent need to deny that prevents this important conversation. The disappointments and rejections are the little "g's" (griefs), while the loss of a limb and the death of a loved one is a big "G".[1]

Stress

According to the World Health Organization (WHO), stress is the health epidemic of the twenty-first century. Living with stress – or dealing with stressful life events – can cause a drop in our body's dopamine and serotonin production. This can have a negative impact on our health and mood, which makes it even harder to deal with stress. Research has shown that experiencing stress over an extended period of time can turn into chronic stress, which negatively affects our physical and mental health. In *The Body Keeps the Score*, Bessel van der Kolk shows how traumatic stress literally rearranges our brain's wiring (particularly the areas dedicated to pleasure, engagement, control and trust). He explores some of the many ways to deal effectively with traumatic stress, including neurofeedback, mindfulness techniques, play and yoga.

Stress throws the body out of balance, increases cortisol levels, and keeps us in fight or flight mode. In this state, the body's natural healing mechanism isn't switched on, which makes it vulnerable to germs that can – if the body remains out of balance – lead to disease. This is why it's so important to create a space where you feel comfortable enough to really rest and do nothing.

Because our lives are so fast-paced, we mistakenly believe that, if we just relax or catch up on sleep, we will instantly feel better. Instead we often feel worse after relaxing, but we need to ride it out and trust our body's innate wisdom, which knows how to heal – *if* we allow it to. It's a process, not the flip of a switch. The symptoms we may experience are just the toxicity leaving our system.

'Allow stuff to come up, and don't resist it,' Davyd Farrell, co-founder of Quantum Plant Healing, says. 'It might be anger, grief, exhaustion – just go with it. It's your body processing and releasing. Surround yourself with plants that are going to assist in the process. Plants show us how to listen to our own inner physician. A large part of my work as a plant alchemist is encouraging people to work with plants, letting them show us what's going on in our energetic and physical fields.'

Davyd recommends paying close attention to what we call resting. Ask yourself: am I really resting when I'm watching TV? Or when I'm watching TV *and* reading a book, or playing a game? How often do I sit and do nothing, and don't feel pressured to go and *do* something?

STRESS MANAGEMENT

Our homes can help with stress management – especially if we have a sanctuary of our own to retreat to.

Sensory thresholds

We're all different in terms of what stresses us because we have different thresholds for sensory input: we each sit somewhere on the spectrum between hypersensitive and hyposensitive. Hypersensitive people have a strong reaction to sensory input and startle easily at loud noises or unexpected touch. Hyposensitive people have minimal reaction to sensory input, don't hear when their name is called, don't react when touched, and crave stimulation. Knowing our sensitivity to sensory input and how best to manage it – along with understanding the sensitivities of others who share our home – helps to make life much easier for everyone.

Empowerment and relationship expert, Terri Cole, recommends discovering and sharing your soothing language: 'Dive into the enquiry of what soothes you. It can be so helpful to share your soothing preferences with your loved ones, partner and friends, and to ask them to share with you in return! We are all so different, and what soothes you might not soothe another. Think of it almost like the five love languages. Each of us has a unique way of feeling and receiving love, and I find it to be the same with soothing. Have these conversations when you are both in a calm state, so, when things get rough, you will know how to help soothe one another.'[2]

Watchful stillness

In an age where we're constantly bombarded with information, and feel driven to connect and be productive 24/7, slowing down and just observing – without the need to *do* – is essential to our mental and physical health. As Jenny Odell says in *How to Do Nothing*: 'To do nothing is to hold yourself still so that you can perceive what is actually there.' Being still is difficult for most of us. Practising stillness is akin to first going to the gym when we're out of shape: we instantly want to quit because it feels so hard and uncomfortable. Plus we feel guilty because everyone else is so busy, and we automatically think that we're shirking if we're not keeping pace. But the more we practise, the easier it gets. Finding an activity that allows us to slow down and observe – like birdwatching or field sketching – can be helpful in honing our watchful stillness skills. It's highly effective at making us relax and unwind.

Octavia F. Raheem's *Pause, Rest, Be* offers a fresh take on being rather than doing all of the time. The book includes yoga practices but, even if you're not a yoga fan, Octavia's wisdom and advice are restorative and empowering.

Me time

Photographer and creative coach, Carla Coulson believes that creating time for yourself is possibly one of the most valuable uses of your time. 'When you're relaxed, happy and rested, you have the energy and enthusiasm you need to be able to create what you want in life. Exhaustion is the killer of creativity, joy and enthusiasm. If you're procrastinating, or not getting things done, the best thing you can do is look at how you can rest and recuperate. As women, we've been taught that if we do the things we love, we're selfish – but it's actually the opposite. When you're in a vibration of enthusiasm is when you're creating from a place of pure alignment with your soul, and that's where the magic happens.'

Retreating to a sanctuary where you can regenerate, create, meditate, play and connect to your inner desires allows you to be in the present moment – no matter what's happening in the world outside.

SONIA CHOQUETTE SUGGESTS

Do you feel as if you're *expected* to take care of everybody else first, and you last? Are you exhausted and resentful because of it? Taking care of you isn't wrong or selfish! It's your responsibility to address your needs with the same love as you do anyone else's. Here's how:

1. Let others know that you have a need and ask for their support. Get comfortable with saying: 'I need to do this for me. This is really important to me.'

2. Practise being okay with their disappointment. When you start changing your behaviour, people get insecure and think you don't love them anymore because they equate you prioritising them as love. So end your request for support with: 'I love you. I'm doing this for me.'

3. Learn *not* to volunteer to help all the time. Just breathe through it. Don't offer or do more for others than they're willing to do for themselves. If someone comes to you with a problem, respond differently: listen with interest and compassion, keep breathing, then ask: 'Have you thought how *you're* going to handle that?' Put the responsibility back into their hands. Affirm your trust and confidence that they'll come up with a good solution.

4. If others refuse to hear and honour your needs, say: 'I'm not going to change you, but I'm going to respond to the choices you're making. If your choice lets me know that what's important to me doesn't matter, I'll bear that in mind when I'm making my choices about *our* relationship.' Don't say about 'you' (that's mean-spirited) and don't try to get the other person to be different: *you* be different.

You're going to be tested, but don't be pushed into getting angry. As soon as you start yelling, you've lost your power. Instead remain calm and remove yourself. Screaming matches hurt and exhaust everyone and achieve nothing. When we're in an ego vibration, we try to control one another and it never succeeds. Instead, go to a higher frequency, and be sure you breathe. People are used to a certain behaviour from you and, when you change it by treating yourself better, there'll be an adjustment period. So you can also end by saying: 'You'll get used to this. I know it's a change and disruptive but, in the long run, we'll both be happier.'

These techniques get easier the more you practise them!

FIRST IMPRESSIONS

Finding your sanctuary

According to geographer Jay Appleton's prospect-refuge theory, outlined in his 1975 book *The Experience of Landscape*, we all have an inborn desire for opportunity (prospect), and safety (refuge). And as biophilic architectural and interior designer Oliver Heath explains: 'We usually feel the sense of refuge in places that are sheltered, covered from behind and have a view. We feel most relaxed when we can observe our surroundings without being seen by others.'

Where in your current home can you create a safe space that you can retreat to whenever you want – without being interrupted?

Few have the luxury of allocating an entire room to their sanctuary, so thinking outside the box may be necessary: a bathroom not shared with others; a balcony that nobody else uses (although this can have seasonal drawbacks); a window seat that can be screened off to give a sense of privacy.

- Wander around your home with your Book of Inspiration and jot down the areas where you feel most relaxed and safe. Add notes as to what inspires this feeling. Chances are these are spaces where no one else spends much time.
- Choose the space that feels the very best to you, inspires and makes you feel hopeful.

- Decide what might make it feel even safer and more relaxing: screening it off with plants, fabric panels, sheers or a screen? Adding somewhere to sit comfortably? Including a sound conditioner to block out household noise? Adding music?
- Having natural elements in your sanctuary is very calming: plants; a water feature; fire; candles; pebbles to hold; a container of beach sand to dig your fingers into or trace patterns on the surface.
- Make it clear to other family members that it's *your* safe space and has to be respected. If you keep being interrupted, you won't feel safe, and relax. Maintaining boundaries can be challenging if you live with a narcissist. If your sanctuary is a yoga mat, or anywhere that doesn't have a door to close (and, ideally, lock!), intrusions are almost inevitable, which can be very stressful. Unfortunately, many empaths and highly sensitive people (HSPs) are drawn to narcissists – energy vampires, as Dr Christiane Northrup, calls them. In her book, *Dodging Energy Vampires*, she gives excellent advice on how to handle the emotional and mental health consequences – not to mention inevitable health challenges – if the exposure is ongoing.

What you do in your sanctuary should be what feels right to you in the moment: napping; daydreaming; reading for pleasure (not work); meditating; creative activity; dancing, etc. Unlike the rest of your life, there's no set agenda: it's a mini holiday where daily concerns and responsibilities are left outside and you get to do what you want without feeling guilty – which takes some getting used to, I'll admit!

Even if you live alone, it's important – from an energetic standpoint – to have a space in your home that's just for you, where nobody else goes. Try to keep your space free from electronic devices if possible – or have them on silent – and don't be tempted to check social media, emails and messages when you're in your safe space.

The importance of movement

Moving your body daily in your sanctuary is healing. I highly recommend the Non-Linear Movement Method (NLMM), a powerful somatic release modality which requires minimal space (a mat or blanket) and can be practised at any age, fitness level and mobility. NLMM was developed by Michaela Boehm, clinical counsellor and author of *The Wild Woman's Way*, which explores how to free your body from stress and trauma and tap into your inherent creativity.

'The key in NLMM,' Michaela explains, 'is that it "unfreezes" you, and with that, the body's natural genius can release and attend to whatever needs to be let go. Stress, tension, overwhelm and trauma of all kinds tend to put us into fight, flight, or freeze mode. Of those three responses, freeze is the hardest to detect and work with, as you are frozen, which creates a numbness that makes you "feel fine". With this gentle, non-forcing method, stored tension and emotion – as well as programmed coping patterns – can be loosened; and as the body moves it can facilitate its own release and restoration.'[3]

The movements are designed to be self-regulating and can be done in any position, including lying down, although NLMM is traditionally done on hands and knees as it's the most grounding. You practise with your eyes closed, and keep one part of your body moving at all times as this is what breaks up trauma into flow. There's a comprehensive, 17-minute 'Non-Linear Movement Method Introduction' on YouTube, and live online classes are offered four times a month (michaelaboehm.com).

An expert on intimacy and relationships, Michaela also advocates that couples should have separate spaces to retreat to where they can surround themselves with things they love. This has a positive effect on the relationship because a shared life and all its incumbent responsibilities can kill the spark between two people. Not being together 24/7 is important for the health of the relationship and recreates some of the essential tension present at the beginning when you were first dating.

Music and sound

Einstein said: 'If I were not a physicist, I would probably be a musician. I often think in music. I live my daydreams in music. I see my life in terms of music.'[4] Consider including music in your sanctuary, whether it's through a home sound system, portable speaker, headphones, or ear pods: play whatever makes you happy!

Music is one of the best healing tools for our physical and mental health. Research has shown that dopamine (the happy hormone) is released in the brain when we listen to music, while cortisol (the stress hormone) levels drop.[5] Studies have found that music therapy reduces stress and anxiety in critically ill patients in intensive care; positively affects depression symptoms (classical, jazz and upbeat songs are the most effective); lowers blood pressure; and helps reduce acute and chronic pain post-operatively and for conditions like fibromyalgia.[6]

Another wonderful option that we'll explore in depth in Chapter 8 is listening to the Schumann Resonances (SR), a set of spectrum peaks in the extremely low frequency portion of the earth's electromagnetic field spectrum. When you tune in to SR, your nervous system and body synchronises with the frequency of the earth and you move out of the beta brain waves associated with stress. Your breathing becomes more relaxed, your heart rate slows, and you enter the alpha brain wave state associated with relaxation. If I'm stuck indoors, my quick fix is listening to 'Pure Schumann Resonance' by Biosfera Relax; there's no music, just SR. It resets my nervous system in 10 minutes!

Light, texture and scent

Harsh, bright lighting doesn't belong in a sanctuary. Natural light, soft mood lighting and candles all enhance relaxation and create ambiance.

Surround yourself with as many natural elements as possible: these reminders of being in nature are calming to the nervous system.

Plants, stones, crystals and driftwood introduce soothing textures and natural fractals, which have a restorative effect and can reduce stress by 60 per cent. Make sure soft furnishings are pleasing to touch and invite you to linger. Have a luxurious blanket or throw in case you get chilly.

A view of nature is always restorative, whether watching birds at a window feeder, or looking out on trees or the sky. Non-rhythmic sensory stimuli (NRSS) improve relaxation, restore energy and reduce anger, aggressiveness and fear.

Diffuse pure essential oils in your sanctuary to bring calm and serenity (please see Chapter 6, page 141) and have flowers you love around you.

EXPRESS YOURSELF

If space is tight in your home and you're having trouble finding an ideal location for your sanctuary, you may have to think laterally! Here are three suggestions to get you started:

1. Hiding in plain sight

If silence and being able to close a door are essential for you in a sanctuary, but you can't have a room of your own, consider investing in a soundproof pod (also known as a telephone booth). Granted, it's a micro space, but it shuts out all noise and distractions. Furnish your pod to *your* taste with things that inspire you. Sheers offer additional privacy while still allowing daylight through. Ideally, try to site your pod in a lower traffic area, like your bedroom. While a pod can dominate a room, you can transform it into an intriguing focal point, especially with clever mood lighting.

Budget tip

A cost-effective alternative to the soundproof pod is to turn a corner in a quiet room into your sanctuary with a cotton or muslin bed canopy, suspended from the ceiling and draped around a comfy chair or pile of floor cushions (pillows). It's amazing how fabric that can be pulled closed not only makes you feel safer, but deters intrusions. Bed canopies are available in a wide range of colours and dimensions and can range from plain to decorative. Furnishing the space inside your canopy depends on how you plan to use your sanctuary (a space for gentle movement, reading or daydreaming in comfort). Making it soundproof requires noise-cancelling ear pods or headphones. However, a bed canopy is more of a boho-chic look, so it may not work with all interiors.

2. Repurposing a cupboard (closet)

A home filled with more people and activities than we could stand was the norm during the pandemic, and many of us were so desperate for peace and quiet that we resorted to extreme measures: a large, underused cupboard suddenly became *very* appealing! My sanctuary was my shoe cupboard: a long, narrow space that was surprisingly peaceful once I'd made it cosy (please see Plan 6, page 91). One of my Jack Russells agreed, so his bed had to be added to the set-up! From a historical point of view, closets in large houses in seventeenth-century England were small rooms reserved for the exclusive use of the master or mistress to retreat to for solitude and prayer. How things come full circle!

Look for an underused cupboard that could be reinvented. Ideally, it needs to be one that nobody else in the household uses, and offering enough space for you to stand up and move reasonably freely (hanging garments are a potential issue if you can't push them aside). If it's currently used as a broom cupboard, consider relocating its contents to another area of your home as being surrounded by cleaning tools and products isn't conducive to relaxation!

If the cupboard has an overhead light, you may need to either change it, or add a fitting that appeals to you – a bare lightbulb casts a harsh light. Alternatively, consider a wireless, portable light, many of which are dimmable, colour-changing and offer a diffused lighting effect. A wireless speaker with good sound quality makes a great addition.

While a repurposed cupboard's lack of daylight and cramped space won't appeal to the Visionary or Warrior personality types (please see page 8), the Free Spirit will probably enjoy its quirky aspect, and the Nurturer will find it cosy – especially if a furry companion joins them.

3. A shamanic retreat

Using a room solely as a sanctuary (playing music, drumming, carrying out spiritual practices etc. and never arguing in the space) contributes to the build-up of positive energy over time. Whenever you step into the room, you'll instantly feel the higher frequency vibration. Author and speaker Anita Moorjani says that she often goes into her sanctuary room at home to recharge for a few minutes when she's having a stressful moment.

Caitlín Matthews, renowned shamanic teacher and author of over 80 books (including *Singing the Soul Back Home*), has a small studio at the bottom of her garden in Oxford which takes your breath away when you cross the threshold. While it's a cosy and very comfortable space with plenty of light, the energy that greets you is palpably different: it's like stepping into another world!

If you have an outdoor space, consider converting – or adding – a shed as your sanctuary. Or if you're hankering after a circular space, invest in a small yurt. When it comes to furnishing your sanctuary, *African Nomadic Architecture* by architect and scholar Labelle Prussin is worth reading. It explores how the nomadic tent's interior space is organised around human need, not objects and appearance; is crafted emotively, not logically; and is rich in colour, pattern, texture and symbolism.

MAKING YOUR SANCTUARY WORK

No sanctuary

You can create a space of your own in a room shared with others as long as you have ear pods or headphones, and good boundaries that are respected by others. If you're struggling with interruptions, try bringing the Japanese custom of *kuuki wo yomu*, 'reading the air', into your household. It requires that people be situationally aware, and attentive to the needs and feelings of others around them – without having to verbally communicate it.

The amount of space required for your sanctuary depends on how you plan to use it:

- Doing yoga, NLMM or creative projects requires more room to move without restriction. Make sure you prioritise your comfort, and that the allotted space – however small – is reserved for your use only. Having some form of screen gives you a sense of privacy and safety: create your perfect nook in a corner with the help of a movable partition; folding screen; curtains; plants; a bookcase set perpendicular to a wall etc.
- For meditating, reading and daydreaming, consider upholstered seating with high back and sides to attenuate noise, comfortably cocoon you and give you a sense of privacy. Position it where nobody is likely to walk in front of you and angle it away from doors and natural corridors. Siting it close to a window not only gives you a view but creates the sense of being in a separate space from the rest of the room.

Small sanctuary

It doesn't matter if the room is a complete contrast to the rest of your home, as long as it feels like a sanctuary to you, and you can completely unwind there. Play to your personality type in Chinese medicine (please see page 8) with furnishings, colours and layout; for example, flowing lines, water, luxurious fabrics and touches of black for the Dreamer, and no clutter, plants, plenty of green and wood for the Warrior.

For mindfulness, try a tabletop Zen sand garden. If you miss being barefoot on the beach, consider a shaped adult sandbox to ground you. While sunken sandpits are more streamline, you can still create the illusion by gathering low seating or deep floor cushions around the edges. Fill the box with play sand that's 100 per cent dust and silica free.

Soundproofing a small sanctuary makes it feel cosy and safe. (Please see Chapter 1, page 16.)

Large sanctuary

For the Visionary personality type – who'll love having a spacious sanctuary all to themselves – the room should ideally be light-filled, minimalist, with lots of white and metallics, and have a good view. Consider a labyrinth rug for walking meditations – these can calm the mind, relieve stress, anxiety and PTSD.

The Free Spirit wants to share with others, so having a sanctuary that doubles as a music room for instance – with splashes of red and lots of fun, quirky touches – will bring them joy. The Nurturer might love a creative project room with a central 'work island' unit with a generous sized worksurface and a base made up of maximum practical storage – perfect for craft making. If the room is brightened with yellows or warm pastels; has very comfortable seating, and showcases the Nurturer's collections, it will be a wonderful sanctuary.

A movable acoustic partition to divide a large sanctuary whenever you need is handy – especially if it can be folded away to free the room up for other activities.

A FINAL NOTE

You'll always find a sanctuary in nature; sitting under a tree and just 'being' is one of the most grounding, relaxing and healing things you can do – as we'll discover in Chapter 8.

If, like me, you dislike going to the gym, consider volunteering with an organisation like The Conservation Volunteers: you get to work out in nature, *and* contribute to its protection.

CHAPTER SUMMARY

- Having a personal sanctuary or relaxation space – no matter how small – in your home to just 'be' rather than 'do' is vital to mental and physical health.
- Women need to claim a space of their own where the boundary is respected and they have private time for ritual and to recharge – even if it's on a yoga mat.
- Home needs to be safe harbour from grief and stress, which negatively affect our mental and physical health, and make us vulnerable to disease.
- Pay close attention to what you call resting: zoning out in front of the TV doesn't facilitate the healing mechanism. Allowing yourself to do nothing in a space where you feel comfortable lets your body process and release.
- Identify your sensitivity threshold and soothing preferences. Share these with other household members.
- Practise watchful stillness: slow down and observe.
- Have 'me time' in your sanctuary without feeling guilty and do whatever makes you happy there.
- Be sure your sanctuary caters to your innate need for prospect and refuge. Think laterally to find the optimal place – even if it's a bath, balcony, window seat etc.

- Incorporate movement (like the Non-Linear Movement Method); music; healing sound (like the Schumann Resonances); soothing lighting and textures; non-rhythmic sensory stimuli (NRSS); aromatherapy.
- For privacy, consider a soundproof pod or bed canopy, or repurpose a cupboard or outdoor space.
- Create a private nook in a shared room with the following: a movable partition; folding screen; curtains; plants; a bookcase set perpendicular to a wall.
- Take into account your personality type in Chinese medicine when choosing and furnishing your sanctuary.
- To instantly restore: go outside, sit under a tree and just *be*!

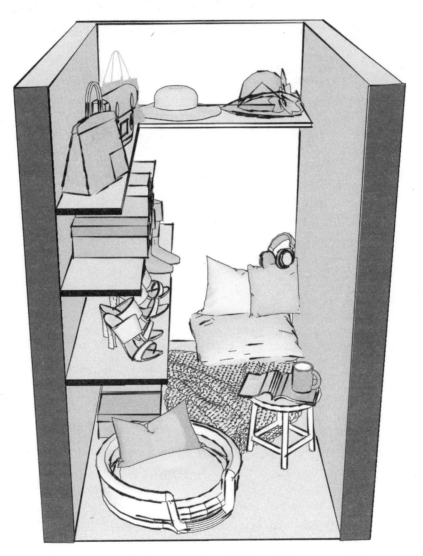

Plan 6: Re-purposing a cupboard (closet) into a sanctuary

5

COOKING & DINING

'When you reach the end of what you should know, you will be at the beginning of what you should sense.'

—Kahlil Gibran

COOKING

The central theme behind the look and layout of most built-in kitchens dates back to the beginning of the last century. It's based on the industrial efficiency model, which sought the best and shortest way to perform any task done by hand, and then standardised it. The industrial efficiency model swept through factories, shops and offices, saving time and increasing company profits dramatically. When Christine Frederick, a middle-class housewife struggling to successfully manage her home, children and husband, heard about the industrial efficiency model, she challenged herself to adapt Harrington Emerson's 12 principles of efficiency to her home. To her delight, the model saved her time and helped her to perform tasks better. In 1912, she wrote *The New Housekeeping*, outlining how housewives could structure and run their homes – the kitchen in particular – based on an adaptation of the public factory model. From then on, kitchen design and layout were based on these principles. Each decade brought style changes, and new and improved appliances, but we're still fundamentally cooking on a factory line!

In the quest to identify the best and shortest methods, the industrial efficiency model heralded the advent of TV dinners, fast food, takeaways and frozen and non-perishable foods. It fundamentally changed the way we shop for, prepare and eat food – often with dire health consequences as these highly processed foods proved to be hugely addictive.

OUR IDEALS

While the industrial efficiency model was based on the ideals of the twentieth century, our ideals and lives have changed significantly, and today the model has lost much of its shine. We see companies like Apple, LinkedIn, Google and Zillow shunning those rigid models and redesigning their corporate offices in innovative, playful ways that prioritise their employees' mental and physical wellbeing over corporate identity and profit. So isn't it time to re-evaluate our kitchens in the same light, and check how much the efficiency model is subliminally affecting what, and how we eat? Our twenty-first-century ideals include looking after our physical and mental health, so designing our kitchens around our nutritional and emotional needs is an important step in achieving this goal.

There's little point in having a large, statement kitchen that impresses everyone, but doesn't inspire you to cook, or linger. How you *feel* in your kitchen really matters because your energy affects the food you're preparing. When Jean Haner does space clearings, she typically finds lots of stuck energy around the cooker (stove) and sink because people tend to ruminate about their problems while they're standing in these areas. Over time, the energy builds up and can affect your mood – even when you're happy. Jean has many stories of how clients worried about their problems while cooking, and later their families suffered indigestion after eating the food!

Neuroscientist, researcher and author Dr Joe Dispenza says: 'We are bound and connected by an invisible field of energy, and this energy field can affect everyone's behaviours, emotional states, and conscious and unconscious thoughts.'[1] When you're happy and experiencing elevated emotions, you're in a heart-centred place, and there's coherence in your body. The frequency you emit into the field around you is much higher and faster. But when you're angry or frustrated, and the hormones of stress are running rampant in your body, there's a lot of incoherence. Your frequency is slower, lower and more chaotic, and this radiates out into the field, affecting everyone and everything around you. 'When an individual's heart is in a state of coherence or harmonious rhythm,' Dispenza writes in his book *Becoming Supernatural*, 'it radiates a more coherent electromagnetic signal into the environment – and this signal can be detected by the nervous systems of other people.'

To see how our frequency can affect our environment, it's worth reading Dr Masaru Emoto's *Messages from Water and the Universe*. He studied how the molecular structure in water transforms when it's exposed to different words, thoughts, sounds and intentions. After freezing the exposed water, he examined the aesthetic properties of the ice crystals with microscopic photography. He concluded that water exposed to positive words and thoughts created 'visually pleasing' ice crystals, while water exposed to negative words and thoughts created 'ugly' formations – the photographs are fascinating.

Many people have the television on while cooking. Even if they're not paying close attention, it's still a distraction that takes them out of the present moment, and the state of mindfulness and relaxation that cooking can induce – not to mention the fact that the content will subliminally affect their energy.

Since everything is connected, our environment affects us – especially empaths and highly sensitive people (HSPs). It's helpful to cook in an environment that's optimal for you, so spend some time thinking about your ideals, and what would make you feel good in your kitchen. Revisit the shapes, textures, colours and elements that appeal to you and your personality type (please see page 8). While a minimalist, linear, built-in kitchen may appeal to the Visionary, it probably feels boring and predictable to the Free Spirit, and too stark for the Nurturer, who would both doubtless prefer an unfitted kitchen.

FIRST IMPRESSIONS

Conduct an impartial 'viewing' of your current kitchen and jot down any impressions that come in your Book of Inspiration. Does your kitchen make you feel creative and inspired? Are you excited to be there? Or is it somewhere that you want to get in and out of as quickly as possible? Do you have fun preparing meals? Or does your kitchen remind you of an industrial assembly line? What would you change about it? What would engender the kind of feeling you want?

The fixed nature of a kitchen means that changing it can be a challenge – not to mention expensive and disruptive if you opt to remodel. If remodelling is your only choice, check first with organisations that accept donations and recycle kitchen units and furniture before gutting it. While donating your kitchen requires careful uninstalling rather than ripping everything out, it's more than worth the extra effort: not only are you being environmentally conscious by keeping it out of landfill, but someone else may really need and appreciate it!

As we examine the different components of a kitchen, have a close look at yours to see if you might be able to transform them.

Kitchen cabinets

Cabinets are the number one attention-grabber and set the tone of any kitchen, especially if they're outdated or unattractive. Matching wall and base cabinets can feel oppressive – especially in wood and dark colours. For an instant makeover, replace doors and drawer fronts and choose eye-catching, unusual knobs or handles to complement your new doors. Glazed doors add interest and depth to a kitchen – clear glass calls for tidy shelves and interesting displays of crockery and food, whereas opaque glass conceals the contents. Glazed doors are less conspicuous than solid doors because they reflect light, and won't close a space in.

Consider replacing a section of cabinets with attractive open shelving to display unusual storage containers in enamel, earthenware and glass. Open shelves are practical, decorative and break the monotony of a fitted kitchen nicely, but you need good extraction and ventilation, or the shelves and their contents will need constant de-greasing! Introduce some curves to a linear kitchen with floating, wave-patterned wood shelves.

Budget tip

If you're yearning for a completely new look, but can't replace your cabinets, painting them is a cost-effective – if time-consuming – solution. Provided the surfaces will take paint and you use an appropriate primer and top coat, let your imagination run wild: fluorescent, metallic or hammered finishes are just some of the many choices available. For best results, spray paint cabinets, and make sure the finish is wipeable – emulsion is not an option!

Worktops (countertops)

Dated or unattractive worktops aren't an easy fix, unfortunately. While you can paint them, the surface won't stand up to normal wear and tear without chipping. Tiling is possible, but you'll need to use an epoxy grout to ensure a bacteria-free environment.

Budget tip

If you're dreaming of a natural stone worktop, but can't justify the cost or upheaval, consider a worktop overlay, a slab of man-made material that's only 8mm (1/3 inch) thick which slides over your existing worktop – including the edge. It requires professional installation and, given its thickness, is not as hardy as real stone, but it beats a laminate worktop!

For a unique and environmentally friendly splashback or worktop, a number of companies make products from 100 per cent recycled and recyclable waste plastic; these often have no VOC off-gassing, are waterproof, mould-resistant and easy to work with and maintain.

Splashbacks

Splashbacks always draw the eye when they contrast with the cabinets. Replacing an unattractive splashback can be messy and fiddly but, if you're lucky enough to have bare wall, consider a splash-back that adds depth and reflects light. Mirror does this beautifully – whether professionally installed panels or mirror tiles. Polished edge mirror tiles give a more uniform look than bevelled mirror tiles. They're also available in mosaic sheets.

Instead of a straight, horizontal line, consider giving your splash-back a curved silhouette. This is easier to achieve with marble and stone than tile – unless you use a round mosaic or tiles in alternative shapes.

Lighting

Overhead lighting on its own is insufficient, both in terms of practi-cality and ambience. Having multiple sources of dimmable lighting really transforms the feel of a kitchen. Ideally, you need task, mood and feature lighting. Task lighting is bright and essential over the hob (stovetop), sink and food preparation areas, whereas mood lighting is soft and creates atmosphere. Feature lighting is achieved through statement light fittings, coloured lighting or plinth lighting.

> ### Budget tip
> If you want to light your worksurfaces without hiring an electrician, plug-in under cabinet lights are a cost-effective solution and can be bought individually or in sets. For the best overall lighting effect and most versatility, opt for dimmable batten lights, and avoid battery-operated versions. Also, most types of light bulbs or strip lights are available with Bluetooth connectivity: by replac-ing bulbs in existing fittings, you can programme lights to change colour, or be dimmed through an app, or by using voice-activated smart assistants.

Flooring

To limit the amount of chemically treated items in your home, opt for natural materials (unpainted wood or stone) as much as possible for their health benefits, but remember to seal them after installation – you can find natural and environmentally friendly finishing products for wood, terracotta and stone that give excellent protection. Reclaimed terracotta floor tiles always look good, as do reclaimed wood floors – although the installation can be costly and messy when sanded.

While synthetic flooring made to look like natural materials is cost-effective, it will emit chemicals.

Budget tip

If you can't justify the cost of real wood or stone, consider flooring tiles that emulate natural materials. Italian tile companies do an impressive job with the reclaimed, distressed wood look – some even have realistic wormwood holes, stains and scratches! Elegant wooden parquet tiles are also an option, as well as 100 per cent plastic-free floor tiles that resemble natural stone, made using corn crops, rice straw, coffee grounds, discarded seaweed and clam shells!

QUICK FIXES

If you can't make any structural changes to a built-in kitchen, there are numerous ways to transform its look and feel.

Decorative elements

Anything that speaks to you and adds character to the space: a vintage butcher's sausage drying rack is perfect for hanging mugs and kitchen utensils; an old ladder suspended from the ceiling (or wall) for hanging pots and pans, dried herbs, strings of garlic etc.; round, wooden baker's boards make perfect chopping boards; vintage grain sieves make interesting wall lights.

Display

Displaying food attractively tickles our taste buds and inspires us to experiment. It can also limit food waste as nothing is out of sight, out of mind – plus it's far more appealing than soulless packaging!

The Nurturer personality type in particular loves seeing fruit, vegetables, nuts etc. displayed in decorative containers because it elicits a feeling of wellbeing and abundance for them. Consider:

- Vintage wine strainers as they're eye-catching and unexpected. Suspend them from the ceiling, or place on the worktop if space allows.
- Decanting nuts and dry goods into glass storage jars, and displaying these on worktops, shelves or in a pantry keeps them fresher than leaving in unsealed packaging after opening.
- A large, attractive jug full of wooden spoons set close to the hob (stove top) is practical and decorative.

Edible walls and towers

Nothing brings life and soul to a room like living plants. So why not bring the outdoors into your kitchen with a vertical indoor garden that doubles as a living edible wall? It's worth considering indoor hydroponics (soilless gardening) where plants are grown in water mixed with solutions containing all of the ingredients required for plants' development. There are many options available – including worktop versions – in which you can grow a range of herbs, vegetables, leafy greens and fruits. For an in-depth understanding of hydroponics, *Home Hydroponics* by Tyler Baras is worth reading.

A very useful item to have – especially if you live in a flat (apartment) – is an odourless kitchen waste disposal unit and composter that sits on the worktop. There are compact models that break down everything from fruit peels and meat scraps to paper and degradable plastics and then turn them into fertiliser for your indoor plants or your garden. They save your pocket *and* reduce landfill.

Budget tip

If you have green fingers and enjoy container gardening, but don't have a wide enough windowsill, install a toughened glass shelf in front of the kitchen window on which to grow herbs and vegetables. If your view isn't good, this has the added benefit of creating a fresh and inspiring focal point.

EXPRESS YOURSELF

For food preparation and cooking to be enjoyable, you ideally need to like your kitchen, otherwise you'll want to get in and out as quickly as possible – which makes unhealthy food choices more of a temptation. Thinking laterally and exploring ideas intuitively opens up fresh possibilities. Here are three suggestions to get you started:

1. Pop-up art

If you don't have a space in your home to fully explore your creative streak, and your kitchen feels static and boring to you, why not paint the cabinet doors with blackboard paint? It's available in a range of colours and can provide the perfect backdrop to channel your inner Banksy! This works well on flush cabinet doors – especially if you need a broader 'canvas' for art pieces to spread across several doors rather than being confined to one or two. Create something new each day, or add touches to a more complex creation. Convey a message that's important to you, or just have fun doodling; beyond exploring your creativity, it puts you in a state of mindfulness, which is good for relaxing. On a practical level, use the cabinets to make lists, write yourself notes or jot down recipes you've come up with. Other options include whiteboard, magnetic and glow paints.

If you like the concept, but don't want to paint your cabinet doors, you could paint one or more of the walls instead. You may get stiff competition from your kids, who'll relish the freedom to draw on cabinets or walls! This arty, quirky kitchen will probably appeal most to the Free Spirit and Nurturer personality types.

2. On the move

We've explored the advantages of moving furniture regularly in the home to keep the energy flowing, and break up traffic patterns, but the kitchen is a very static space due to its fixed services and cabinetry. What if you could make it more mobile, and change up the positions of pieces when you felt like it?

An unfitted/freestanding kitchen offers more flexibility and character than a fitted one. In countries like France where properties are often rented without a kitchen, investing in a freestanding kitchen makes sense as you can easily take it with you when you move.

Create your own original, unfitted kitchen with pieces that express your personality and ideas. For character and interest, opt for a cohesive look rather than one that matches perfectly. Adding castors to units that don't house services (plumbing, gas, electricity) allows you to vary a larger kitchen's configuration: a freestanding unit can be placed flat against a wall, perpendicular to it, or at any angle you choose. Altering its position brings novelty, changes the way you move around your kitchen, and two or more people can work opposite each other which is more convivial. A mobile chef's table or butcher's trolley is always a handy addition. They come in a variety of sizes and styles and create extra worksurfaces and storage. Vintage 'work in progress' trolleys – originally used in factories – are perfect for mobile storage: they're on wheels, very sturdy, and have at least three fixed trays. Have fun and turn them into works of art with different paint colours that transmute their industrial efficiency model origins.

3. Go green

For a walk on the wild side, create an architectural salvage kitchen. It's environmentally friendly and oozes character and charm. Any little glitches and imperfections in the pieces are all part of the appeal rather than glaringly obvious errors.

Architectural salvage yards and flea markets are usually brimming with options to choose from: team old glass-fronted cabinets with a spice cupboard; an open shelf or two; several hanging racks; a wire mesh larder, a vintage butcher's block (carefully restored but complete with undulating surface from years of hard service); a small cupboard announcing the contents of each compartment; old brass luggage racks to store kitchen essentials, fixed in either a stepped formation, one above another, or in a row (train style).

For a striking look, offset salvage pieces with contemporary details. Paint a wall a bright colour you love – be bold with lime green, fuchsia or tangerine – and add a minimalist glass or acrylic table, brushed steel fridge/freezer, or anything that highlights the contrast between old and new. Add a fun note with brightly coloured accessories.

MAKING YOUR KITCHEN WORK

Let's look at some of the things you can do with different kitchen types – with a nod to your personality type (please see page 8).

Kitchen wall in a studio

Many studios are dominated by the kitchen wall – especially if the cabinets are wood, or a dark colour. Camouflage is the best way to deal with this issue: painting the units the same colour as the walls makes them blend in and recede. An even better solution is to create a seamless bank of floor-to-ceiling, wall-to-wall cabinets with flush doors framing a large, central opening housing the hob, oven and sink. The configuration shown on Plans 7 to 9 (please see pages 127–9) shows a pair of full height doors on either side of the central opening which conceal a fridge/freezer, pantry and crockery storage. The smaller overhead cupboards require a ladder to access them, and are reserved for items not needed every day. All doors are meant to look like decorative wall panels, so spring-loaded catches – or door and drawer tops profiled for fingertips – instead of cabinet knobs are the best choice. To reflect light, create additional views and conjure the illusion of space, mirror the cabinet doors – discreet all-glass knobs or finger edge pulls keep fingerprints to a minimum.

Make the central opening a statement feature with a contrasting finish on all internal surfaces: eye-catching wood, stone or metal. Or, if you prefer an understated look, tone it to blend with the cabinets with toughened, sandblasted glass. The Visionary personality type will doubt-less appreciate the ultra-minimalism of technology which transforms a worktop into a visual panel from which all kitchen appliances – includ-ing an interactive induction hob – can be managed from one central point (please see Resources). The lack of knobs and buttons is futuristic to say the least!

A central island in front of the kitchen wall multitasks as an addi-tional kitchen worktop, dining space, work desk and room divider and can be fixed or mobile, depending on your preference.

Budget tip

If you like the idea of a floor-to-ceiling, wall-to-wall seamless bank of cabinets but can't justify the cost, improvise! Ideally, remove all cabinet knobs, install spring-loaded catches, and paint your existing cabinets to match the wall colour so they blend in. In front of the kitchen wall, hang curtains, or fabric panels from a ceiling-mounted track that runs from wall to wall. Plain fabric in a neutral shade that tones with the wall colour is unobtrusive and won't close the space in, whereas patterned fabric makes a strong statement and can feel overpowering in a small space. Unlined, washable fabric works best. If your sleep-ing area is on the opposite wall to the kitchen (as illustrated in Plan 7, page 127), matching floor-to-ceiling, wall-to-wall curtains or fabric panels in front of the bed creates symmetry and an interesting effect in the room.

Open-plan kitchen

Much like the kitchen wall in a studio, an open-plan kitchen can call too much attention to itself – especially in a smaller space. A good solution is the seamless bank of floor-to-ceiling, wall-to-wall cabinets with flush doors teamed with a central island. Playing with the latter's shape takes the focus away from the linear lines of the kitchen – especially if you light the island cleverly. Many models now have rounded edges, and some have a flowing base; both are easier on the eye and more convivial for family and friends to gather around.

Budget tip

Find a vintage restaurant bar in an architectural salvage yard to transform into your central island. Many bars have wonderful lines and curves and are always very solidly built. You may need a carpenter to adapt it to your space, but it's worth the time and cost: vintage bars typically have plenty of practical storage on one side, while being visually appealing on the other.

Having the hob on the central island is perfect for the Free Spirit personality type because they can cook and entertain at the same time. Experimenting with new recipes and types of cuisine and using the hob more than the oven or microwave are very healing for them. It doesn't matter if the hob is gas, electric or induction.

A central island is also a plus for the Warrior personality type who enjoys cooking with – or for – friends. Having a place to sit down to eat is important for the Warrior as, in their eagerness to get on with the next task, they have a tendency to stand to eat in the kitchen or eat on the run. A breakfast bar or dedicated area on the central island with comfortable seating gives them an easy solution that doesn't involve trekking to a dining table. A wooden central island appeals to them, and is conducive to savouring meals and relaxing, which is important for the Warrior's health.

An open-plan kitchen may not be ideal for the Visionary personality type as they need lots of alone time. Being creative and experimenting in the kitchen with new ingredients without following a recipe is very healing for them. Having a sense of separation from the living space is important too. Glazed partitioning in the form of a glass wall, or a reclaimed period shop front creates an air of spaciousness and light (which are vital to Visionaries) while making the kitchen feel more private.

Budget tip

Installing a glass wall or period shopfront is expensive, so consider a partition of freestanding glass bookcases to maintain the light, airy feel while creating additional decorative storage – albeit minimalist for the Visionary! Freestanding acrylic bookcases are cheaper, and there are many vintage models from the 1970s, although the Visionary will doubtless prefer the feel and quality of glass.

Small kitchen

A fitted kitchen with matching wall and base units tends to accentuate the size of the space and make you feel hemmed in – especially if the wall units don't extend to the ceiling. By changing the doors to taller ones that reach the ceiling, you'll create a more seamless look, and add storage.

Painting the walls and cabinets in a matching rich, dark colour creates a moody feel, and camouflages the size of the kitchen – but good task, mood and feature lighting are essential to make the overall look intriguing rather than gloomy. Alternatively, using bright, fun colours can be uplifting and inspirational. A coloured glass splashback adds depth and interest to a contemporary look.

If you have one or more large windows, make them the focal point, and draw the eye out to increase the sense of space. Shades of white or cream for cabinets, worktops and splashbacks achieve this objective, whereas wood or coloured units narrow the focus and draw attention away from the windows. If the views aren't good, create an indoor greenscape with window boxes, glass window shelves with pots of fresh herbs, and, if you have space, a living wall. Glazed cabinet doors (clear or opaque) complement this look perfectly. Add dimmable lighting inside the cabinets for an interesting night-time effect.

Windowless kitchens can feel very claustrophobic. Mirroring walls and/or splashbacks creates the illusion of depth and space and reflects more light. Even mirroring a small section of wall works well.

Sometimes the best way to deal with a small, windowless kitchen is to up the drama in terms of colour and overall look. If you have a high ceiling, paint it black or a dark colour to confuse the eye on proportions – it sounds scary, but it really works! Create an unexpected and eclectic theme with vintage glass-fronted shop units, display cases and/or bookcases that a skilful carpenter can adapt as wall units (please see Plans 10 to 11, pages 130–1). Apart from their charm and character, they're usually sturdily built with plenty of shelving, and their height is a distinct advantage: the taller the units, the more storage you'll get. Granted, you'll need a ladder to reach the top shelves, but you can store items not in daily use. A sliding library ladder on a rail is another option, but this only works for two layers of cabinets with the rail running between them. Suspend a stylish pot rack from a high ceiling – but be sure cabinet doors open without bumping into it.

Budget tip

To save on the cost of base units, try the French look: mounting slim café curtain rods (in brushed steel, wrought iron or brass) to the edge or underside of worktops, and hanging unlined curtains in a decorative, washable fabric to conceal storage and white goods. Depending on your choice of fabric, this can add colour, pattern and a clear style statement. Plan your base storage carefully with pull-out units and a butcher's block on wheels to provide an extra worktop plus storage.

Large kitchen

While a large kitchen is a luxury that many of us only dream of, it can feel cavernous if the cabinets hug the walls, with an empty space in the centre.

A large room is perfect for an unfitted kitchen with mobile units so you can alter the kitchen's layout and look regularly and with ease (please see On the Move, page 104). If you prefer things fixed, free-standing open shelving set perpendicular to a wall is perfect for breaking the space up while preserving its airy feel.

Large kitchens are the perfect place for a pantry. While there are many freestanding pantry cupboards on the market, they tend to be bulky and draw attention to themselves – plus they're not always the best use of space.

The pantry has always been about efficient food storage and making the harvest of each season abundantly available year round – especially if you have a vegetable garden, or allotment. In *The Modern Preserver's Kitchen*, Kylee Newton shows how to make and use preserves in innovative, delicious recipes. If you are lucky enough to have a big pantry, get your creative juices flowing by displaying produce with a nod to food preservation tricks from the past: store vegetables in tubs of sand; eggs and apples in straw; cheese wrapped in muslin; bread in earthenware crocks; and hang strings of onions, garlic and drying herbs from hooks. With modern staples and luxuries, decant anything that's unattractively packaged into decorative storage containers. Glass is ideal so you can quickly find what you're looking for without having to rummage.

Large kitchens are often perfect for an edible/living wall, or tower and can break up the space creatively.

Budget tip

If you have an underused alcove, cupboard (closet) or corner, create your own pantry. Install shelves from floor to ceiling for maximum storage, then hang a pair of full-height doors. The cheapest option are flush doors painted to match the wall colour so the pantry blends seamlessly. Glazed doors are more expensive but will turn the pantry into a feature; use clear glass if you want to display its contents, opaque glass if you don't. Mesh doors promote clean air flow between spaces. Opt for a pair of large, interesting door pulls that make a statement, especially on flush doors. Vintage often work best as they're solid and have more character. Lighting each pantry shelf makes all the contents visible, plus it creates mood lighting through glass or mesh doors.

PRACTICALITIES

1. Extractor fan
A good extractor over your hob that removes airborne grease as well as smells and steam is essential, particularly if you have open shelves.

2. Painting kitchen cabinets
Most cabinets require sanding to remove any finish. While time-consuming, it's an essential step otherwise the paint peels off in time. Spray painting gives a smooth, professional finish with no tell-tale brushstrokes.

3. Ball castors
Castors must be able to carry the weight of units – bear in mind that they will increase their height. Choose castors with a locking mechanism for safety.

4. Adapting architectural salvage
Advanced DIY skills, or the help of a good carpenter are essential. Check pieces carefully before purchasing for signs of woodworm, and factor in the additional cost of any restoration. Be sure pieces have sufficient depth to accommodate dinner plates and any bulky items you plan to store.

5. Pantry
Site it well away from the oven, fridge-freezer, or any heat-generating white goods.

DINING

In our endless busyness these days, we sometimes kid ourselves that eating on the run, in the car, at our desk or in front of the television is successfully multitasking. But at what cost?

To many Americans, consuming food is like refuelling their vehicle: a necessity done on automatic pilot, as quickly as possible. The fact that it's bad for digestion and often involves poor food choices is overlooked in favour of expediency. To the French, eating is one of life's great pleasures, and is treated as a respected ritual. Whether it's breakfast, lunch or dinner, they take the time to sit down and enjoy their food, in good company. Even when not entertaining, they'll use their best china, glass, cutlery and linen daily, and food is arranged attractively on plates, not piled high.

While this ideal of aesthetic dining appeals to many of us, it can sometimes be hard to implement, especially when we're exhausted, and it feels like yet another 'to do'. If nothing else, choose one thing that brings you pleasure and do it regularly – even if you're dining alone. For me it's lighting candles: it settles my nervous system and helps me enjoy the meal – I even light candles at breakfast when the weather's cold and dreary! Battery-operated candles don't have the same energy as real flame, but if they're easier for you, go for it!

SHARING

Eating together around a table without devices or watching television builds relationships, keeps us in the present moment and pauses our constant need to 'do'. It allows the body and mind to relax, especially if the meal isn't rushed. Research at the University of Oxford into the benefits of social eating found that: 'Those who eat socially more often feel happier and are more satisfied with life, are more trusting of others, are more engaged with their local communities, and have more friends they can depend on for support.'[2]

Gathering people you care about together to share at least one meal a day can be very healing, especially if laughter is involved. Laughter helps to relieve anxiety and stress, and improves a low mood by boosting dopamine and endorphin levels. To the Free Spirit personality type, throwing a party for people with whom they can be their authentic self – and express their *true* feelings – is very healing. Having fun and enjoying each other's company is as important to the Free Spirit as the creativity of cooking and entertaining, especially if what they create expresses what's in their heart. To the Nurturer, sitting down to dinner every night as a family is a bonding experience and brings them joy.

Letting children pick a meal each week and then helping them to create it can be a fun – if messy! – experience that boosts oxytocin levels. Research shows that kids who help prepare meals tend to have healthier diets and learn responsibility. Eating around a table with their families has significant benefits for children of all ages, including better mental health, self-esteem and confidence; a broader vocabulary; better academic performance; and a lower risk of eating disorders and engaging in high-risk behaviours. Clinical professor at Harvard Medical School, Anne Fishel, explores the many benefits of dining as a family in her book *Home for Dinner*.

Round tables are ideal for connection as everyone can make eye contact. Chairs are slightly angled towards each other which feels more convivial and intimate than when they're directly facing at a rectangular or square table. The circle is a powerful shape without hierarchy that dispels irritability, depression and brain fatigue, so it's no wonder eating at a round table feels relaxing and encourages lively group discussions!

Unfortunately, a meal can sometimes become a challenge when there's tension, an argument, or you're sitting next to someone who's draining your energy, and you can't escape. Energy clearer Bruce Peters recommends the grounding cable visualisation, a quick-fix that releases unwanted emotions – yours, and other people's that you've taken on. It's easy to do, and nobody knows you're doing it! Bruce says: 'Sit quietly, and imagine a cable running from your perineum all the way down to the earth's centre, grounding you to her core, and letting her take all the stuff you can't handle. Some people like to allow the earth's grounding energy to come back up the cable into their body. Start practicing alone, at home. Eventually, when you're out in the world, and get flustered or overwhelmed by other people's energy, you'll be able to do the visualisation, and feel better within 1 minute. I'm not a big fan of putting up energetic shields or barriers. Instead, I do the grounding cable practice all the time – especially when I'm in a mall, and feel exhausted from all the energy. I run the cable and, within 30–60 seconds, I'm no longer overwhelmed, even though I'm still aware of the energy around me.'

Sonia's recommended practice below really works – especially if you're stuck alone over a meal with a partner or pal who's determined to dump.

SONIA CHOQUETTE SUGGESTS

Toxic relationships are when you try to help someone, but their goal is to take your energy. They have no intention of taking responsibility for themselves, so you get robbed of your energy – voluntarily. When someone is venting, and draining your energy – whether they're someone you live with, a family member, a dinner guest or a colleague – here's how to deal with them:

1. Get back in your own energy, and mind your own business! This means focusing on what you care about, and what matters to you in your life.
2. Don't be available to other people's drama. My teacher said: 'Never work harder for someone else than they're willing to work for themselves.' When someone dumps on you, say to yourself: 'That's their business. Frankly, I'm more interested in my own right now!' The more you mind your own business, the more your aura fills with your own vitality and life force. This becomes your protection from toxic people who want to zap your energy.

Take a breath, then subtly cross your arms over your chest, turn your body away from them, and exhale. See your heart flooding your body with a beautiful, bright light that's so uncon-ditionally self-loving that nothing negative can come in. If they ask: 'What are you doing?' Smile, and answer: 'I'm breathing more. Listening.' If they carry on dumping, say: 'I'm not going to give you any advice because I have confidence that you'll work it out when you're ready.' This vote of confidence is the last thing they're expecting! It's affirming of their spirit instead of feeding their victim ego.
3. If you are asked to do something you don't want to do, say: 'I wish I could do that, but it won't work for me.' And then smile. You don't have to explain why it won't work – that's what's so empowering! There's nothing noble about sacrificing yourself by throwing yourself into the abyss of someone else's nightmare! Don't fool yourself that if you love them enough they'll be different. Only when they love themselves enough will they be different. Nothing *you* do in the meantime is going to change their

behaviour. Love them, and be neutral about their behaviour. The more neutral you are, the more your own life can work.

4. Learn to say: 'Excuse me, I have to get back to my business.' And do just that! That's how you can co-exist with toxic people. Minding your own business is the most loving, grounded, healthy way forward. Don't be surprised if, in doing so, you create more healthy space and neutrality around these people.

Prepare to get pushback at first. They'll guilt-trip and shame you to try to get you into submission, but just breathe and say: 'I'm sorry you feel that way, but I still have to mind my own business.'

When toxic people realise you mean it – and they test you, and you *still* mean it – they stop because you've just put a boundary in place. All the drama stops.

Keep practising. Minding your own business instead of every-one else's leaves you a lot more time for pleasure, fun, joy and to create the life *you* really want!

FIRST IMPRESSIONS

Where we eat is an important and highly personal choice. While some prefer to eat in the kitchen, others enjoy a separate space where the washing-up (dishes) is out of sight!

Traditionally, the dining room was formal and spacious, with a large table that could seat anywhere from 6–12 people. These days, our more informal lifestyles mean that it can be proportional to the number of people who use it on a regular basis. If you're a couple who only entertains once or twice a year, is it worth sacrificing a large room to the dining room? Could you make do with something smaller, and improvise when you entertain?

Many dining rooms now multi-task as home offices – which we'll explore in greater depth in Chapter 7. One downside to this practical use of space is the effort required to transform it back into a dining room. You can either clear the table, and have a 'take us as you find us' attitude, or have sufficient storage and camouflage solutions for office paraphernalia, such as built-in cupboards and/or attractive storage containers.

Choosing the right space in your home for your dining space should centre around your needs and preferences. Do you like eating in – or close to – the kitchen? Is it important to catch the morning sun at breakfast? Does having different meals in different spaces appeal to you?

Dining style

Before picking the ideal space for your dining area, decide which dining style appeals to you most. Here are four of many options:

1. Cosy

For a relaxed, intimate atmosphere, place a round table in a corner or by a window and arrange the rest of the room cosily with a small sofa, and additional seating that doubles as dining chairs for extra guests.

As Oscar Wilde said: 'Comfort is the only thing our civilisation can give us.' While armless, straight-back dining chairs are the norm and offer good support for many – including the elderly – one of the best ways to get people to linger over a meal is to seat them comfortably. Upholstered chairs are more relaxing than hard surfaces, like wood or metal.

2. Vignette

A rectangular table set against a wall with a sculpture and a pair of lamps or some striking candlesticks creates a focal point without being an obvious dining table. Two people can dine side by side, and four can be accommodated without having to move the table away from the wall. Or have a living table with a central sunken container for growing herbs.

The 'vignette' dining area arrangement frees the rest of the room to be used as a library, quiet sitting room etc.

> **Budget tip**
> With good DIY skills, you can create your own living table by adapting a sturdily built wooden table (farmhouse tables are ideal). The project involves cutting a central opening the length of the table, and installing a waterproof trough for herbs and plants. (Please see the book's website for project details.)

3. Chameleon

If you're tired of traditional dining, rise to new heights then sink to new lows with a vintage, height-adjustable geometer's or architect's table, or an industrial drafting table. Team the table with bar-height chairs for a fun, high dining experience. Next day, lower it to coffee table height, draw up a chaise-longue and floor cushions (pillows), and lounge Roman-style over your meal.

Another good option is a narrow, drop leaf, or gate leg table placed behind an angled sofa. It serves as both a sofa table for lamps, and as a dining table for two when one leaf is opened, or four when both leaves are opened.

4. Informal

Built-in banquette seating in a corner with a rectangular or oval table offers plenty of compact seating in a small space – especially if you run the banquette along two walls. If you have lots of people seated, getting in and out means others have to move, but it creates a nice, informal atmosphere.

> **Budget tip**
> Look for reclaimed antique church pews which are perfect for banquette seating, beautifully crafted, very durable and usually cost-effective.

Identify *your* ideal dining style/s and see how they could fit into your home so that it's effortless and enjoyable to use on a daily basis. I like having more than one spot – to indulge the mood of the moment!

EXPRESS YOURSELF

Your dining space is a wonderful area to express your creativity and conjure the kind of atmosphere you want. Here are three suggestions to get you started:

1. Say it with flowers

The Victorians used flowers to convey secret messages and express their feelings – good and bad. Jessica Roux's beautiful *Floriography* is a perfect guide to the meaning and origin of each flower and herb, and what to pair it with for different meanings. Mint paired with cornflower tells a friend they're thought of and loved during a difficult time; heather paired with cattail for good health for someone awaiting a diagnosis; fern paired with foxglove for a secret love.

Make a dinner unique and express your feelings with flowers. If a guest is celebrating something, create a 'bouquet for new beginnings' and display it as a centrepiece: crocus for youthful glee; daisy for innocence and childhood purity; lilac for first love; baby's breath for purity and innocence; wheat for riches. Take it a step further and have one or two flower cards at each guest's place setting to convey a message unique to them.

Or look into *ikebana*, the Japanese art of flower arranging: a meditative practice done in silence which allows you to slow down as you see and connect to the arrangement as a living thing. Shozo Sato's illustrated *Ikebana* has everything you need to know about this fascinating art form.

2. Escape reality

Create a special dining spot that evokes something you love and that inspires you. If space is tight, have a folding set of nineteenth-century-style wooden or metal bistro table and chairs by a window to enjoy your *petit déjeuner* while watching the world go by. Or add a splash of Mediterranean fun with Greek taverna chairs painted in eye-catching blue with rush seats, and a checked tablecloth for authenticity.

Having a special spot that has symbolic meaning for you to escape to – either solo or with friends – gives you something to look forward to when you're stressed.

3. Fire circle

As we explored in Chapter 3, gathering around a fire is healing on many levels. Communal eating around a fire is a primal experience, so try dining on plush floor cushions around a low level fire table. It's convivial, relaxing and ideal for informal meals of tapas, sushi or fondue. Or create your own fire table with a burner placed in the centre with a circle of real candles around it.

If you need good back support, Japanese zaisu or tatami chairs are legless and armless. There are many options, ranging from thin to well-padded, and some of the most stylish are made from hardwood, and can easily be stacked and stored when not in use. If you're able to, sitting on the floor is better for your circulation, and aids digestion.

If you don't feel like dining around a coffee table, try picnic style! Throw a colourful tablecloth on the floor with lots of cushions, add hurricane oil lamps – the glass is temperature resistant and shatter-proof – and enjoy your meal on handmade stoneware.

MAKING YOUR DINING AREA WORK

No dining room

If you live in a studio, having two tables that can multitask as dining and working surfaces is ideal (please see Plan 12, page 168). One table can seat 1–2 people and, if it has a removable leaf that can be stored in a cupboard, its seating capacity can increase to 4–6. Alternatively, if the sofas, ottoman and tables are on castors and can easily be rearranged, the two tables can be placed back to back in a central position to accommodate more people – although the tables must be the same height. If you don't want to clutter the studio with additional seating, and there's plenty of storage, folding chairs are a good choice.

Budget tip

If space is tight, a pull-down table that's concealed when not in use behind a decorative shutter, panel or painting is a great solution and seats up to five people in a cosy huddle. Team it with upholstered, stackable cubes that can be arranged as an eye-catching modern sculpture, or dispersed as occasional tables, foot rests and additional seating. (Please see the book's website for project details.)

Budget tip

Sometimes the only option in a studio is to create a novel breakfast bar for two. Source an eye-catching and unusual base that can be mounted to a wall – like a solid piece of driftwood, or a vintage grape harvester's basket. Top it with a shaped sheet of tempered glass firmly fixed to the wall. Add concealed lighting, and you have art and dining in one! Choose upholstered bar stools with low, comfortable backs to relax and enjoy a leisurely meal. (Please see the book's website for project details.)

Small dining room

When space is at a premium, even the smallest dining table can appear bulky. A tempered glass table is often the best solution, especially if you need to seat more than four. All-glass tables typically consist of three separate pieces: a glass top (available in multiple shapes and sizes), and two bent glass bases that can be configured into multiple shapes. The look is contemporary, reflects light and fools the eye as to the actual size of the table. Round tables are more practical for a small dining room as they occupy a smaller footprint, and more people can squeeze around them.

Create a dual-purpose table: a stand-alone base with separate top that can double as wall art! Use a lightweight table top, or have a sheet of wood made up and edged, then paint it a single striking colour, or create your own colourful masterpiece (sealed to avoid wear and tear). Hang it on a wall where it can easily be removed when needed as a table top. Depending on the overall table size you need, select a single or pair of intriguing bases: columns work well, but be sure they're sturdy while still being easy to move (you may need lockable castors). Alternatively, use a small table as the base, and add your 'artwork' top when needed for extra guests.

Large dining room

A large dining room needs to be used regularly, otherwise it feels uninviting because the energy becomes stagnant. Unless you have a big family that dines together daily, this is the perfect multi-functioning space as clever storage can easily be included to conceal work and creative projects, as needed. A floor-to-ceiling, wall-to-wall, built-in unit offers maximum storage while being unobtrusive. Flush doors painted to match the wall colour give a contemporary look, while tall, reclaimed glazed doors make a style statement. To conceal the unit's contents, give the glass an opaque effect with frosted window film.

Budget tip

A vintage breakfront bookcase (often found in architectural salvage yards) makes a perfect storage unit because it's very sturdy and offers plenty of shelving and storage. Don't worry if it is too tall for your ceiling height as the glazed top section and base are typically separate and can be used as two freestanding units in a large dining room.

While the glazed section will easily stand on the floor without support, for aesthetics you may want to build a wooden plinth and finish it with veneer stained to match the wood.

The bookcase's base will have an unfinished top where it previously held the glazed section. Finish this by sanding and staining, or adding a top of your choice – marble or stone always look good but are expensive when custom cut; opaque glass or mirror are more cost-effective, look stunning and are perfect for a bar. (Please see the book's website for project details.)

A large dining room is an ideal space to grow fresh herbs and vegetables in living walls and towers. Try creating a serpentine line of freestanding hydroponic towers: their sculptural form makes them perfect area dividers. You'll also need LED indoor grow lamps.

A FINAL NOTE

If you're struggling to slow down enough to enjoy cooking and eating meals, start small.

Make a list of your favourite foods and tastes from childhood or foods that remind you of people you love. Choose something simple from your list that brings back fond memories, such as a cake, fruit, or a snack. Allow yourself time away from all devices and commitments, and just savour it. Take at least 10 minutes out of your day and linger. Close your eyes, and really smell and taste the food – don't rush to get to your next task. Taking time and allowing your senses free rein yields surprising results when you're not distracted by other things (talking to people, browsing social media, watching television). You slow down, and your body relaxes because it's being infused with happy memories and positive associations. The taste of something may make you sad and nostalgic – or even cry – but this is healing too. It's like a hug from someone you love when you let your guard down and allow your true feelings to surface. Trust what comes, but remember it's not about bingeing on a favourite food! The more you do this practice with simple favourites from childhood, the easier you'll find it to slow down and actually take time to enjoy cooking and savouring your meals.

CHAPTER SUMMARY

COOKING

- Contemporary kitchens are based on a 1912 adaption of the industrial efficiency model which doesn't reflect our twenty-first-century physical and mental health ideals.
- Consider what makes you feel good in a kitchen, and which shapes, textures, colours and elements appeal to your personality type in Chinese medicine.
- Revive cabinets: change doors to ceiling height; replace sections with open-shelves; or paint them.
- Transform worktops with tiles, a worktop overlay or another environmentally friendly material.
- Splashbacks can be mirrored or transformed with a curvaceous silhouette.
- Have dimmable task, mood and feature lighting.
- Choose natural materials for flooring – stone, terracotta, reclaimed wood – or tiles and recycled materials that resemble natural materials.
- Add character with vintage elements: butcher's drying racks; baker's boards; grain sieves; ladders.
- Display produce and dry goods in wine strainers, glass storage jars, jugs etc.
- Consider edible walls and towers to grow food with hydroponics.
- Blackboard paint creates a pop-up art kitchen. Castors make an unfitted kitchen mobile. Visit an architectural salvage yard for eco-friendly kitchen alternatives.

- In a studio, consider a seamless wall of floor-to-ceiling, wall-to-wall cabinets with flush doors framing a central opening.
- Divide the kitchen from the living room with a glass wall, vintage shopfront, or glass or vintage acrylic open-shelving.
- Make small kitchens dramatic with dark colours and excellent lighting. Give them a spacious feel with neutral colours through-out; add plants and maximise any views. Mirror walls and/or splashbacks in small, windowless kitchens and paint ceilings black to confuse the eye, or give them an eclectic, vintage look.
- Large kitchens are well-suited to an unfitted look with mobile units and benefit from a pantry.

DINING

- To make eating pleasurable, create one simple ritual that you enjoy and do it regularly.
- Build good relationships by sitting down and eating together at least once a day. It especially benefits children of all ages.
- Know where you most enjoy eating – but not in front of the TV! Work out what your dining style is, whether cosy, vignette, chameleon or informal.
- Get creative when you dine: say it with flowers, escape to a foreign destination, or create a fire circle or picnic feel.
- In a studio, two tables can multitask as dining and working surfaces. If space is tight, try a pull-down table with cube seating or a breakfast bar for two with an unusual base and glass top.
- All-glass, round tables work best in small dining rooms.
- Large dining rooms need to multitask and will benefit from floor-to-ceiling, wall-to-wall, built-in storage.

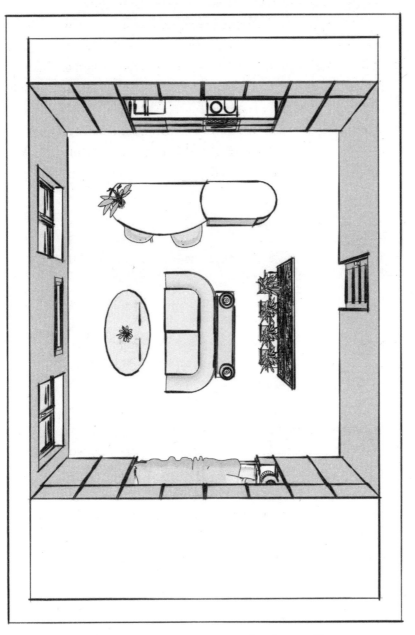

Plan 7: Studio – creating a kitchen wall

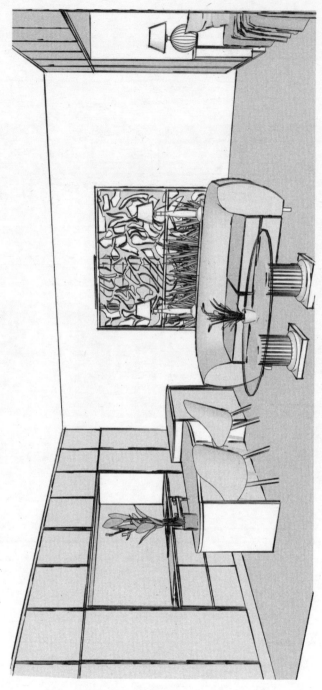

Plan 8: Studio – creating a kitchen wall

Plan 9: Studio – creating a kitchen wall

Plan 10: Small kitchen – using architectural salvage

Plan 11: Small kitchen – using architectural salvage

6

BATHING & SLEEPING

'Whenever you are creating beauty around you, you are restoring your own soul.'

— Attributed to Alice Walker

BATHING

In the West, streamlined, rational bathrooms are coveted, but –
beyond aesthetics and ease of maintenance – are they relaxing to
our bodies and minds? We seem to be prioritising looks and practi-
cality over the more subtle aspects that would actually make us feel
at ease. Often our bathrooms are akin to car washes, where getting
clean as quickly and efficiently as possible is the primary objective!
Isn't it time to rethink our bathrooms with wellness as a priority?
Achieving wellness is all about relieving stress and relaxing, especially at the end of a long day when getting a good night's sleep is
essential.

When it comes to relaxing body and mind, the Japanese have bathing down to a fine art. Water is associated with spirituality in Japan,
and *ofuro* is a pleasurable ritual that's part of everyday life. It involves
soaking in a deep tub of hot water – often heated to 45°C (110°F) –
after washing outside the bathtub. Traditionally, an *isu* stool and *oke*
basin set were used, but contemporary Japanese bathrooms have a
hand-held shower beside the tub. The bathroom is essentially a wet
room that the toilet isn't part of.

When we immerse ourselves in a warm bath, blood flow increases to
the skin (our largest organ), endorphins are released and our nervous
system settles. Our muscles relax, releasing pent-up stress from the day.
Other benefits include pain relief and reduced inflammation; improved
breathing and oxygen intake; lower blood pressure and reduced risk of
heart attack; more balanced blood sugar levels; and reduced stress and

anxiety. Research has shown that a 30-minute bath at 40°C (104°F) improves depression.

Budget tip

Adding 2 cups of Epsom salts (magnesium sulphate) to a warm bath is a cost-effective and natural way to ease stress and aching muscles, although it's important to soak for at least 15 minutes.

For anyone struggling with sleep issues, The University of Texas concluded that having a bath at 40–43°C (104–109°F) 1–2 hours (ideally 90 minutes) before going to bed helped people achieve the best quality sleep – plus they fell asleep an average of 10 minutes more quickly than normal.[1] The hot water changes your body's core temperature, so you go to bed with a lower temperature, which aids sleep.

It's worth noting that, in the US, the Environmental Working Group (EWG) warns that we may absorb more chlorine and other contaminants from bath and shower water than from drinking polluted water with the same toxic chemicals! According to the Drinking Water Inspectorate (DWI), levels of chlorine in UK drinking water are well below the guidelines set by the World Health Organisation (WHO); however, this isn't the case in many countries. Do check your water quality with your supplier and consider investing in a whole house water filter system or, if that's impossible, a water filter on your shower head. To neutralise chlorine in bath water, add 1 teaspoon of vitamin C crystals and wait 5 minutes, or try adding a dechlorination tablet.

ENGAGING THE SENSES

What surrounds you while you're relaxing and rejuvenating matters. If your bathroom engages all your senses, you're more likely to want to spend time there, and look forward to the experience rather than rushing in and out as quickly as possible.

Texture

We experience texture not only through how it feels when we touch it, but how it looks. As biophilic architectural and interior designer, and author of *Design a Healthy Home*, Oliver Heath, explains: 'If a texture looks inviting, we take this as a "haptic invitation": an appeal to our sense of touch to have a positive tactile experience. We feel more comfortable if we're surrounded by appealing textures. If a space lacks texture, our wellbeing is negatively impacted, and we can experience tactile deprivation and "touch hunger".'

SANITARY WARE

It's no wonder we don't want to linger in bathrooms with a preponderance of ceramic or fibreglass, because everything looks and feels the same. While matched bathroom suites are utilitarian and lack haptic invitations, replacing them with more appealing options can be costly. A wood, copper, natural stone or glass bath has immediate impact, but a price tag to match – even a countertop basin in these materials doesn't come cheap. If you do have the budget, create intriguing contrasts between fittings: a wooden basin with a glass bath, a copper bath with a stone basin. If you do opt for a wooden basin or bath, make sure it's FSC rated and consider cypress and cedar woods for their aromatic qualities.

> **Budget tip**
> If you dream of a copper bath but can't afford it, introduce its warmth and burnish with a vintage double-handled copper pan, or French Charlotte mould, repurposed to display bath accessories.

WALLS AND FLOORS

Ceramic tiles are an automatic go-to in bathrooms because they're easy to maintain and offer endless variety in terms of style, colour, pattern and texture. Unfortunately, tile makes bathrooms echo, and can feel cold and clinical. The most environmentally friendly choice are glass tiles which are often made from recycled materials, and require less energy to produce than ceramic tiles.

Pebbles add a natural, less-regimented feel to a bathroom. A floor tiled with pebbles stimulates the reflex points in the feet and balances the body's energy. A 2005 study found that older adults who walked on stones had lower blood pressure, and better overall mental and physical fitness![2] Tiling a shower's floor *and* walls with pebble can be a bit overpowering, especially if the bathroom is small so limit pebbles to one surface, either the bathroom and shower floors, or one wall.

Concrete has been a favourite of architects and bathroom designers for a while, but it can feel austere, and isn't conducive to relaxation. It's also not an environmentally friendly choice: cement production is the largest single manufacturing source of greenhouse gases. Instead, look into clay plasters, which come in a variety of wonderful textures and colours. They're non-toxic, have zero emissions, are heat and moisture regulating, anti-fungal and environmentally friendly. But if you want the concrete look, consider its environmentally friendly alternative: plant-derived resin floor and wall coverings.

One of the best ways to add warmth, character and soundproofing to a bathroom is by introducing wood, whether it's on the floor, walls or vanity unit. With a good extractor fan, there shouldn't be any issues. Reclaimed wood flooring, or sustainably harvested bamboo, work well on the floor. Bevelled siding can look amazing on an accent wall but – like pebble – don't overdo it!

Sight

When you can't change your sanitary ware, wall and floor coverings, camouflage them by introducing haptic invitations to transform your bathroom into an inviting space.

PLANTS

Plants generate oxygen, draw the eye and help to absorb sound. As Oliver Heath points out: 'Thanks to our evolutionary development, we're hard-wired to feel more comfortable with greenery nearby, and feel a strong association between plants and health. High planting recreates what we would experience in a jungle, or forest habitat.'

Bathrooms are ideal for high planting with hanging baskets, or glass shelves for trailing plants. Pothos, spider plant, philodendron, fern, English ivy and baby's tear all do well in bathroom humidity, but do check their individual requirements for light levels and exposure to direct sun. For a splash of colour, add azalea and begonia, or consider air plants like tillandsia which bring an exotic, colourful feel.

Create an instant sound absorber in your bathroom with a living wall or for the ultimate luxury, step onto the welcome softness of a live moss bath mat.

WOOD

Wooden accessories like towel ladders, mirrors or shower benches are a cost-effective way of adding warmth and character to a bathroom. Consider also changing cabinet pulls and knobs to driftwood as they feel wonderful and remind us of nature. There are many options including sanded and polished versions if you prefer a less rustic look.

Budget tip

Create your own wall art and focal point with driftwood. If you're far from the beach, Etsy has lots of driftwood pieces sold by the pound, or to specific sizes. Or repurpose your wine corks to create original wall art; cork is also excellent at absorbing sound.

PEBBLES

Pebbles remind us of the beach and rivers and are soothing to the eye and touch. To create a spa-like feel, and draw attention away from an unattractive bath panel, fix a strip of wood to the floor, parallel to the bath, and fill the gap between the wooden strip and the bath panel with pebbles. Larger ones work best, and you won't need many to create this eye-catching effect. Reaching down to touch them during a luxurious soak is very heal-ing! A thin layer of sand under the pebbles conceals the floor, but remem-ber to seal the base and sides of the wood strip with silicone.

NATURAL FABRICS

Cotton, linen and natural fibres absorb sound, add texture and invite touch. Spoil yourself when it comes to towels, facecloths (washcloths), bathmats and bathrobes: opt for plush and soft – organic Turkish cotton and bamboo are ideal – and don't skimp on quantity. For extra relaxation, have a bath pillow to sink back on. There's nothing worse than stepping onto a cold bathroom floor in the winter so cover tile or stone floors with a large, wash-able cotton rug, or any natural material that's pleasant to walk on.

NATURAL STORAGE JARS

Try to avoid plastic wherever possible and choose accessories in natural materials that look and feel more inviting. For a relaxing, spa-like bathroom, decant products into attractive containers: it's worth the extra effort. Pouring Epsom salts into the bath from a glass jar is so much nicer than from its plastic packaging! Glass offers an intrigu-ing haptic invitation as it reflects light, reveals the colours and textures of products, and looks less bulky than non-transparent containers. For intriguing contrasts, group glass containers together.

Budget tip

Sets of glass storage jars with flat bamboo lids (typically sold for kitchen storage), work well in bathroom cupboards as they're stackable. Mason jars with hinged lids are leak-proof, very sturdy and are also stackable.

Scent

Of all the senses, smell is the strongest memory trigger. Use it in the bathroom to create positive, uplifting associations.

ESSENTIAL OILS

Quality essential oils are part of the healing experience in the bathroom: they're antiseptic, anti-fungal and antimicrobial, and steam inhalation gets the oils' phytoncides deep into the body. Phytoncides reduce stress hormones; improve mood; lower blood pressure; increase hours of sleep and have anti-cancer proteins. Douglas fir and cedar are wonderful for relaxation, and cedar is very calming. Pine eases itchy skin and relieves pain and congestion from colds, flu and seasonal allergies – as do spruce and fir. *A Scented Life* by Pat Princi-Jones is a great guide to the many ways to use essential oils (inhaling, bathing, massaging), and includes recipes of the best combinations to improve emotions and health at different stages of life. Try a self-care ritual inspired by Japan's bathing traditions and an oil diffuser to maintain your favourite scents consistently in the bathroom.

SOAPS

Indulge yourself with soaps that smell wonderful to *you*. Don't limit yourself to one bar in the bath or shower: have a decorative display of different soaps (removed from packaging for added scent and appeal) to choose from. This will create a feeling of luxury and plenty in a bathroom. I love soaps made with organic virgin coconut oil and soaps that look like pebbles.

CANDLES

Real flame candles – not battery operated – are deeply soothing and relaxing. Candles made from 100 per cent beeswax smell wonderful, burn clean and last for a long time.

When choosing scented candles, avoid artificial scents and opt for aromatherapy candles which contain only essential oils. Studies have shown that lavender essential oil reduces anxiety;[3] clary sage reduces cortisol levels which trigger stress;[4] bergamot reduces negative emotions and stress;[5] and ylang-ylang can increase self-esteem.[6]

NATURAL CLEANING PRODUCTS

Reduce your exposure to toxic chemicals by buying all-natural cleaning products and room sprays (check the labels carefully) or make your own. A bathroom that smells of bleach or other strong chemicals isn't relaxing – not to mention chlorine is corrosive to the lungs, skin and eyes, and can cause headaches and other ailments.

Sound

Sound insulation is so important in a bathroom; you won't fully relax if you can hear household or outdoor noise. An added benefit of an extractor fan is that it creates white noise and drowns out external sounds well.

Consider changing the door to a solid-core (please see Chapter 1, page 17) and, if you're renovating your bathroom, add insulation to walls, floors and ceilings and choose your surfaces carefully: ceramic tiled walls and floors echo, whereas wood absorbs sound.

Bathroom speakers are wonderful for relaxing and unwinding in the evening or getting your groove on in the morning. Stream your favourite music or podcasts with wireless bathroom speakers: the sound is excellent and they're moisture and humidity resistant. While soaking in the bath, listening to water sounds (waves, waterfalls, streams, rain, thunderstorms) enhances the experience, and is healing and relaxing.

> **Budget tip**
> If you can't make major changes to your bathroom, add fabric wherever possible. Rolling or folding extra towels, and displaying them on open shelves not only absorbs sound, but looks luxurious.

FIRST IMPRESSIONS

Changing bathroom fittings can be a challenge – not to mention expensive and disruptive. If you opt for a partial, or full remodel, consider donating your old fittings to organisations that will recycle and repurpose them. You'll help the environment by keeping fittings out of landfill, and someone may really need and appreciate them! Ceramic, porcelain and stone tiles can be reused by others if removed carefully rather than hacked off. Or look for a tile recycling programme.

Take an objective look at your bathroom by conducting a 'viewing' and making notes in your Book of Inspiration about what is and isn't working. Focus on how your bathroom makes you *feel* – the practicalities can come later. Do you feel relaxed when you walk in? Is it an inviting space where you want to linger? Or does it make you want to run? Pay close attention to whether your bathroom has haptic invitations.

Natural light

A window or skylight opens a bathroom up, and makes it feel more inviting. Even a small window can appear larger if you mirror the wall around it or have mirror on the opposite wall to reflect light and the view. Windowless bathrooms can feel claustrophobic, and definitely benefit from adding one or more sun pipes. These small, round surfaces of daylight are relatively easy to install, and don't usually require planning permission. They'll transform your bathroom ceiling, create interesting pools of light on the floor, and break up the gloom.

Shapes

Most contemporary bathrooms are modular with lots of straight lines and sharp corners, which – as we saw in Chapter 3 – activates the amygdala, whose primary function is to process stimuli that induce anxiety, aggressiveness and fear.

As bathroom renovations are costly, messy and disruptive, making do is sometimes the only solution. Camouflage and playing with optical illusion are key to solving the problem – especially if you're renting.

- Wave patterns remind us of flowing water, and make us relax. Introduce them to break up straight lines with subtle pattern in fabrics, texture in towels and floor coverings, and imagery in art. There are also lots of stunning 3-D tiles and panels with textured wave patterns to choose from.

Budget tip

If you can't tile the walls, create a freestanding wave art piece with either tiles or panels, and hang it like a picture. Panels are usually made from plaster or plant resin and can be painted, so you can get quite creative!

- Humans are universally drawn to the circle, and ancient and tribal cultures see it as the most powerful of shapes. Help to offset and draw attention away from straight lines by choosing cylindrical containers for bathroom accessories – think soap dispensers, storage containers, laundry bins, plants holders. Opt for round towel rings over straight towel rails, and round mirrors over rectangular or square ones. Bring in art and imagery that depict circles and spirals. Add a round stool.
- Conceal an unattractive bath or shower cubicle with a pair of ceiling-hung, washable curtain panels to create a cosy alcove: muslin, linen, unlined cotton or any see-through fabric will allow the passage of light and won't close the space in. Instead of a straight track, try a curved track to create a gentle wave of fabric. This also works if you have a shower curtain instead of a shower screen: hang the fabric panels on a separate pole or track in front of the shower curtain rod. If your ceiling is high, you may need an extra-long shower curtain. Alternatively, hang plants at varying heights in front of an unattractive screen to draw the eye.

Lighting

Having multiple sources of dimmable lighting lets you set the ambiance in a bathroom. Ideally, you need task, mood and feature lighting. Bright task lighting is essential around the basin and over the bath or shower areas; mood lighting is soft and creates atmosphere; feature lighting is achieved through statement light fittings, coloured lighting, or plinth lighting, which washes the floor and ceiling with light from fittings concealed at the base and top of built-in units.

Budget tip

If your bathroom lights aren't on a dimmer switch, resort to the soothing charm of candlelight to unwind, whether from tea lights, pillar candles, wall sconces or chandeliers. Play with colour, shape, texture, scent and arrangement to create variety and intrigue and to calm your nervous system.

For windowless bathrooms, consider circadian lighting – or human-centric lighting (HCL) – which mimics the natural progression of sunlight throughout the day in colour, temperature and brightness. HCL is designed to have a biological impact on our circadian system to achieve better sleep and overall wellness. Circadian bulbs adjust the light according to the time of day: high in blue spectrum and bright to energise us in the morning, and warmer and dimmer with no blue spectrum to unwind in the evenings and prepare for sleep.

Colour

If you can't stand the colour of your sanitary ware and/or tiles, but can't make changes, you can either camouflage it or highlight it.

Camouflage by introducing harmonious colours that sit together on the colour wheel so your eye shifts easily from one colour to the other. An avocado-green bathroom suite is less of an eyesore if you introduce yellows or blues to the bathroom. Playing with other shades of green also works as it simulates the variety of greens that we're used to seeing in nature.

Highlight and go for dramatic effect by adding pops of complementary colours. Reds and purples complement greens, but – unless you want a striking contrast that's energising – aim for colours in the same hue and saturation. Pairing burnt sienna, terracotta and clay with avocado is gentler on the senses than vermillion red or violet.

EXPRESS YOURSELF

We can be too fixated on design 'rules' and worry that everything has to match and coordinate in bathrooms. Unfortunately, this can create cold, uninviting spaces – even if all the taps (faucets) and accessories are a perfect match. To be healing, your bathroom has to feel right to *you* – not the style police!

A good starting point is to recall the bathrooms you've instantly loved, felt relaxed in, and wanted to linger in, whether that's hotel bathrooms, or other people's. Write down in your Book of Inspiration what about these spaces appealed to you. Go into as much detail as possible: size; layout; fittings; lighting; flooring; colours; accessories etc. Contrast this with a list of bathrooms that made you want to leave as quickly as possible and note the reasons why.

When considering your perfect bathroom, do take into account your personality type (please see page 8):

- **The Dreamer** likes a bathtub; images and sounds of water; flow-ing fabrics; candles; a hint of black – even in a single hand towel. Bright overhead lights are stressful to them. Alone time to relax in the bathroom is very healing to them.
- **The Warrior** thrives around wood; plants; images of trees and water; the sound of thunderstorms and waves; tall objects remin-iscent of the height of trees; green. Surfaces need to be devoid of clutter for the Warrior to relax.
- **The Free Spirit** needs quirky or fun art (preferably original) to make them laugh; anything with sparkle, including hanging crys-tals and prisms; birdsong; flowers; candles; bright, cheerful light-ing; red or any vivid colour, including bright orange, hot pink and rich purple.

- **The Nurturer** enjoys pictures of landscapes, mountains and pastures; collections of mementos; baskets of shells, pebbles etc.; yellow – although beige, brown gold, soft pink, peach or warm pastels also appeal to them. They like a cosy atmosphere in the bathroom, and a little clutter is comforting to them.
- **The Visionary** thrives around imagery of big skies and expansive views; quality products; non-scratchy materials; a window with a view; clean surfaces devoid of all clutter; essential oils; candles; white, grey and metallic. They prefer large, well-lit bathrooms and don't like to be overstimulated by too many elements when they walk in.

To create the optimal bathroom for you, play with some themes. Here are three suggestions to get you started:

1. Escape to nature

To reduce stress, lower heart rate and blood pressure, and revitalise your senses and mind, consider a nature theme for your bathroom (beach, woodlands, mountains) – whatever feels restorative to you, and where you would go for a much-needed break.

If you have a high ceiling, consider installing a freestanding outdoor shower indoors, and fit out the shower area as if it were *en plein air*. Opt for simple, cost-effective materials like marine-ply wood slats for walls and flooring, or try an all-natural, striking look with rough-hewn stone. Have a rustic bench for shower accessories, and for relaxing on. Create the impression of lush vegetation with lots of plants – especially high planting – and a moss bathmat. A window is ideal, but you can still create the illusion of natural, dappled light with concealed lighting behind resin or wood screens with leaf cut-outs.

2. Hammam

Create your own hammam (Turkish bath with humid heat) at home. There are typically three steps to this spa experience: an extra-hot steam to relax you and open your pores, followed by lathering in olive oil-based black soap and scrubbing with the traditional *kessa* glove to remove dead skin, then finally immersing yourself in cold water.

If your budget allows, your shower cubicle could do double duty as a hammam with the installation of a steam generator, insulation kit and door. However, if installing a steam room isn't possible, create the feel of a hammam with tadelakt, a shiny, lime-based plaster historically used in Moroccan hammams. The final effect looks surprisingly contemporary and striking, and feels wonderful to touch. Tadelakt is environmentally friendly, extremely hard-wearing, water-resistant, heat and moisture regulating, and anti-fungal.

Don't forget to add the classic, flat-woven peshtemals towels with hand-knotted fringe to your hammam and, finally, a Moroccan lantern or two with candles creates a moody, relaxing atmosphere with dappled, patterned light from the multiple perforations in the metal.

3. Reading room

If you're a bookworm, there's nothing more luxurious than relaxing in the bath with a book. Add a bath caddy with a reading rack, and all you have to do is turn the pages! There are caddies to suit all bathrooms, from bamboo and hardwoods to various metal finishes. If you're reading in the bath at night, keep the lighting soft and moody, but have a portable, rechargeable LED book light with an amber setting to support your circadian rhythm and eye health. If you're reading on a device, have the screen on night mode to avoid exposure to blue light.

If space allows, have your own mini library in the bathroom with a bookshelf, or book chest within easy reach. Books are wonderful sound absorbers, but a good extractor fan is essential to reduce humidity.

MAKING YOUR BATHROOM WORK

Each type of bathroom presents different challenges to overcome.

Open-plan bathroom

Having the bathroom as a living space that's part of the primary bedroom is popular in larger, contemporary homes. It's reminiscent of when royalty and nobility used their bedchambers to sleep, bathe, dress and receive visitors.

While there are some stunning layouts and designs, open-plan bathrooms can be impractical if a couple have different routines and needs. If one partner likes to unwind in the bath at night, they won't relax if the other is watching television, especially if their personality type is the Dreamer: they'll yearn for a bathroom door to close! If one partner is a night owl, but the other goes to bed early and is a light sleeper, an open-plan bathroom isn't ideal.

Consider screening the bathroom area with plants and tall trees, or a curved bookcase – especially if you like the reading room theme. For ultimate flexibility, try moveable acoustic partitions (please see Chapter 1, page 17).

Japanese *ofuro* soaking tubs are perfect for open-plan bathrooms as they usually accommodate more than one person. Traditionally made from hinoki wood – a cypress with a citrus/ginger aroma – they're the ultimate spa experience as their depth lets you almost float, surrounded by the healing aromatherapy of the wood.

Small bathroom

Small bathrooms often lack storage space, making them cluttered, difficult to clean and far from relaxing. Pedestal and wall-mounted basins – no matter how stylish – waste useful space as they don't have worktop (countertop) space or storage. Replacing them with a vanity unit is worth the expense.

Budget tip

If you have advanced DIY skills, consider converting a sturdily built, vintage chest of drawers or small cupboard into a statement piece with either an undermount or countertop basin. It's best to add a stone or glass top to avoid water issues.

Create the illusion of space with a seamless shower screen, and mirror one wall to reflect light. Better still, build a floor-to-ceiling storage unit with flush doors that can be mirrored. Or paint the doors to match the walls and add a pair of towel rings to double as door pulls, and camouflage doors.

> **Budget tip**
> If you only have a shower, but hanker for a long, hot soak, you could consider a portable, inflatable bathtub. Please see Resources for a suggestion.

Most small bathrooms don't have space for seating, so the toilet is the only place to sit for beauty regimes, or if someone comes to chat while you're in the bath. A toilet cover is hard and uncomfortable, so keep a seat cushion handy: U-shaped outdoor cushions work best – the thicker, the better.

A white or neutral colour scheme gives small bathrooms an airy feel, but vary shades and textures to create interest and warmth. Or opt for drama and impact with a dark colour scheme to confuse the eye as to the bathroom's size. So it doesn't feel gloomy, have good task and mood lighting: washing the floor and ceiling with light maximises the impact of dark colours.

Large bathroom

Large bathrooms can feel cold and uninviting if all the fittings hug the walls with an empty gap in the centre. If you're renovating, cosy up your bathroom fittings and use them to divide the room cleverly. Have a vanity unit perpendicular to a wall, and/or the toilet's built-in housing perpendicular to a wall. Set an infinity-edge bathtub in the middle of the room (or a sunken bath to give an air of opulence) and create a wet area instead of a corner shower.

If you can't reposition sanitary ware, draw attention away from the bathroom's waiting room layout. If the toilet is in the middle of a wall and feels exposed, make a privacy wall with a long planter planted with bamboo, or a planter set on either side of the toilet to create a low-walled cubicle. Bamboo is easy to care for, loves humidity and grows rapidly. Snake plants are another good choice as they offer good cover and thrive in bathrooms. If you need storage, use mid-height or low open bookshelves to display towels, plants, books and bathroom accessories – preferably in attractive containers.

Built-in, floor-to-ceiling storage looks great with glazed doors and interior lights for practicality and additional mood lighting. A vintage apothecary cabinet or other wall-mounted cabinet with shelving and small drawers creates interest too.

Make a large bathroom cosy and intimate with a comfortable chair, chaise longue or upholstered bench to relax on – the bench can even double as a laundry bin. Add a fireplace, and you'll never want to leave!

PRACTICALITIES

1. Wood

Seal wood floors and cabinetry with a quality tung oil. When adding wood to a wall or floor, consider lining the wall with roofing felt first to protect from any water that might get through.

2. Water

Bathrooms account for around 25 per cent of household water usage. When replacing toilets and taps, ensure they comply with standards for conserving water. This will benefit the environment and save money on water bills.

3. Heating

If you're installing a new floor, consider underfloor heating from a company offering a lifetime guarantee. Consider installing a heated mirror to prevent fogging.

SLEEPING

In Chapter 4, we touched on Jay Appleton's prospect-refuge theory, which explains how we all have an inborn desire for opportunity (prospect) and safety (refuge). To make us feel safe and help us unwind so we can rest properly in our bedrooms, we really need a sense of refuge and a view – if not from a window, then of the room itself.

Before exploring the physical elements of creating refuge and prospect, let's consider the psychological implications. In many ways, our contemporary bedrooms are somewhat reminiscent of the Middle Ages when privacy didn't exist, and people did everything together in the great hall. Today, everyone wants to be able to reach us 24/7/365: our phones are forever on; we check social media, emails and messages compulsively; we work in bed, and even video-conference from it. Sometimes it feels as if there's no escape from the global community – even in our bedrooms!

In Chapter 7 we'll see why we're so ensnared in the digital world, and explore steps to help us disconnect. When we don't have refuge from the world in our bedrooms, our mental and physical health suffer because we can't completely relax, and so our sleep is affected. Not only does a call or text jar us awake in the middle of the night, but it's the anticipation that it *might* happen which can compound our stress and prevent us from sleeping deeply. In the US, a third of adults suffer from sleep deficiency.

Most adults need 7–9 hours of sleep a night in order for body and mind to rest and heal. Quality sleep balances hormones, relieves stress, helps us to concentrate and think clearly, and improves immune function. Studies have found that lack of sleep can lead to high blood pressure, heart disease, stroke, kidney disease, diabetes and mental health issues. Plus we all know how groggy and awful we feel when we haven't slept well!

Having good boundaries (turning off devices), a sleep routine (the same bedtime and a healing ritual to help us unwind) and a sanctuary (a comfortable and relaxing bedroom) can all help to improve the quantity and quality of our sleep. Bedtime becomes something to look forward to, rather than another must-do on our daily list.

FIRST IMPRESSIONS

We tend to design our bedrooms in daylight, completely forgetting that we spend most of our time there at night! How the space feels and functions once the sun sets should be our primary focus if we want to support our mental and physical wellbeing. It's very important to address the following issues.

Light

Our circadian rhythm (the 24-hour internal clock that regulates the sleep–wake cycle) responds to light and dark in our environment: bright light signals to the brain that it's time to wake up and be alert, while darkness tells it to sleep. While natural light gives our body reference points of when to stop or slow down, artificial light – especially blue light – interferes with our natural cycle. This can lead to health issues if we're exposed to it when we should be sleeping; it prevents the deeper stages of sleep in which healing and information processing occur. Studies have shown that too much light exposure at night can lead to depression and anxiety.

A dark bedroom is essential for quality sleep. As light is the most powerful cue for our circadian rhythm, blocking outdoor light sources with blackout blinds and curtains helps to create a suitably dark environment, but internal light sources can be just as harmful – especially bright LEDs on electronics.

> **Budget tip**
> Light filters and light blocking stickers come in a variety of shapes and sizes to deal with these glaring lights. They are inexpensive, easy to apply and remove, and bring instant relief. Use light filters for electronics with a remote, and light blockers for anything else.

Blue light emitted from screens suppresses the production of melatonin essential for sleep, and it's not good for eye health. Studies have shown that using a screen before bed can delay sleep by 1 hour, or more. Use night mode on all devices, and amber lights for reading in bed at night. You can download free apps like F.lux that automatically adjust your device display's colour temperature according to your location and time of day.

If watching television – or falling asleep with it on – is a part of your nightly ritual, remember that it emits blue light. This stimulates your brain, which reduces deep sleep, and – according to a 2019 study – increases the risk of obesity in women.[7] Try using a sound conditioner, or music to lull you to sleep instead. If you must have a television in your room, consider concealing it in a TV lift cabinet.

Be aware of all light sources in your bedroom, including light filtering under the door. Fitting a draught excluder along the bottom of the door addresses this – and helps with soundproofing too. If you get up in the night, avoid exposure to bright light in the bathroom, corridor or kitchen – the fridge is a serious culprit! Fit light filters on LEDs and make sure any other light source is a dim, amber light.

Research has found that the gradual disappearance of light in the evening is a powerful signal to the brain to rest and prepare for sleep, and dawn simulation enhances our wellbeing and mood, and can improve cognitive performance.[8] Smart lighting achieves this in your chosen style and on your preferred schedule; in the evening it changes to a softer, warmer light to signal when to start winding down for the day, and for your personalised dawn, it slowly brightens over a period of time, so that you're not jarred awake by an alarm.

Alternatively, try a wake-up light. There are wake-up lights to suit all needs: some simulate the colours of sunrise and sunset; some include sound options (coloured noise and nature sounds) and/or wind-down features like mediations and bedtime stories; some have a night mode so displays can be turned off.

> **Budget tip**
> If you don't want to invest in smart lighting or wake-up lights, try circadian light bulbs in your current bedroom lamps.

Try to avoid using your phone's alarm, especially if you're tempted to immediately check emails and messages when you wake up – which is likely to throw you into work/stress mode!

Sound

Addressing soundproofing in the bedroom is vital to relaxation and good sleep. Please see Chapter 1, page 16 and Resources for options.

While people living in cities aren't necessarily woken by sirens, horns and other loud sounds, their sleep stages are still affected. Studies have shown that environmental noise from planes and vehicles increases stage one (lighter sleep) and decreases stage two (slow wave/deep sleep) and stage three (REM sleep).[9] For optimal mental and physical health, we need to experience all three stages every night. Night-time noise is also associated with higher levels of the stress hormones adrenaline and cortisol, as well as elevated heart rate and blood pressure.

In *The Sleep Solution*, neurologist and sleep expert W. Chris Winter references research showing that people sleep better when they're adjacent to nature – hence why sound conditioners featuring sounds of rain, the ocean or a flowing river are so popular. They also help mask loud sounds that disrupt sleep with coloured noise.

- **White noise** – also known as broadband noise – contains all frequencies found in the spectrum of sounds that you can hear in equal parts. It's the steady, humming sound that a fan makes. Studies have shown that white noise improves sleep as it masks loud sounds that stimulate the brain.
- **Pink noise** – also known as ambient noise – produces a deep, flat sound. It's more even and less layered than white noise. Pink noise includes rushing water, steady rain, rustling leaves and wind. A Northwestern University study found that people who fell asleep listening to pink noise slept more deeply and their memories were boosted. Pink noise reduces brain waves, increasing deep sleep which supports memory.
- **Brown noise** – also known as red noise – is deeper than white and pink noise, and sounds like a heavy waterfall or thunder. Less research has been done on the effects of brown noise on sleep, but many swear by it.

Listening to music can help with sleep: studies have shown that the right kind of music improves the ability to fall asleep, and sleep quality. While classical music with tempos of 60–80 beats per minute, stable rhythms and low-pitched sounds does the trick, so do lullabies! You don't have to listen to *Twinkle, Twinkle, Little Star*: Spotify has compilations of lullabies for adults. Depending on your musical taste, there's bound to be a lullaby rendition.

A Harvard University study led by Dr Sam Mehr found that infants relax to lullabies even when they are from unfamiliar cultures and in unfamiliar languages.[10] Dr Mehr plans to investigate what the musical features really are that make lullabies work so well across all ages and cultures.

Smell

Studies have shown that smells affect our sleep quality. One study on people suffering from post-traumatic stress disorder (PTSD) – in which nightmares and sleep disturbance are common – found that exposure to pleasant smells improved participants' sleep quality.[11]

Everyone has different sensitivities to scent, but our sense of smell is typically strongest around 9pm, and diminishes throughout the night. A pleasant smell may help you relax and drift off, while an unpleasant one may keep you awake. Consider diffusing essential oils with an ultrasonic diffuser. It's all down to personal taste, but a combination of Roman chamomile, bergamot, frankincense, lavender, rose and vetiver can be relaxing and calming. Clean sheets are appealing to our noses, but be wary of fabric softeners with artificial, strong-smelling fragrance; they're neither healthy for us, nor relaxing!

Prospect

Even if your bedroom doesn't have a good view from the window, make the landscape of the room itself pleasing. Colours and textures found in nature work best as they have a soothing effect and make us feel safe – as do fractal patterns. As Oliver Heath points out: 'From our ancestors, we've inherited fractal fluency: a preference for natural fractal patterns. Research has found that viewing fractals can reduce stress by 60 per cent, and it can also have a restorative effect. Natural fractals are more appealing to us than man-made, exact fractals because they're less precise and occur naturally.' All the more reason to surround ourselves with natural materials rather than mass-produced!

As you craft your indoor view in the bedroom, use lots of plants that release oxygen at night. Easy-care varieties include peace lily, rubber plant, snake plant, Boston fern, English ivy, spider plant and pothos.

With light, sound, smell and prospect in mind, conduct both a daytime *and* night-time viewing of your property to decide if your current bedroom is in the best location. Primary bedrooms usually have more generous proportions, but size shouldn't be the determining factor. Where your bedroom is facing, and how sequestered it is from outside and household noise are essential considerations. East-facing bedrooms are ideal as they get the morning sun, which is invigorating, and are sheltered from midday heat, making them cooler for afternoon naps. Bedrooms at the back of properties have less street noise, while the further away from the kitchen and communal areas bedrooms are, the less household noise there'll be.

Wander from room to room, letting your intuition guide you. Where do you feel safe, and which view do you like best? If you cater to your need for refuge and prospect in your choice of bedroom, you'll relax and sleep better.

Authority on the spiritual side of Chinese medicine, Jean Haner, says: 'The bedroom needs to be peaceful and restful. Try to create a sedate, comforting, easy space – especially when it's shared by a couple. Chances are you're different personality types in Chinese medicine, and need different things. People tend to take things very personally, and to blame without understanding. The solution is to come to an agreement where everybody's needs are met. It can't be one, or the other. Remember, this isn't personal: it's just two different personality types with different ways of being and needs.'

Bed

Once you've settled on the ideal room, choose the ideal spot for your bed using the prospect-refuge criteria. It's often easier to clear the bedroom of all furniture apart from the bed, visualise the space with fresh eyes, and imagine new possibilities. Test different bed positions and lie and sit on it for a while in each to see how you feel, and where you're most comfortable.

Being able to see the bedroom door from where you're lying creates a feeling of safety. Try to avoid the door opening onto – or being located behind – the bed. Having the head of the bed against a wall –

or at least against something tall and solid – feels secure. To cater to prospect, can you position your bed so you feel safe *and* have a view? Sometimes this requires a cater-corner (diagonal) position – which is fine as long as you have a solid headboard and feel cosy.

Try to avoid working or arguing in bed! Soft surfaces absorb energy more than hard surfaces, and it builds up over time (especially if you're stressed while working) and can affect your sleep. Plus, as Jean Haner says: 'As we go into the dreaming state, we're off-gassing and processing a lot of unconscious stuff. This can soak into the mattress, or sit in an invisible cloud above the bed. Every night when you climb onto that mattress and lie back into that cloud, you're affected by the energy held there. Doing a clearing of the bed is ideal, but even just pounding the mattress can help release stuck energy.'

We spend around a third of our time in bed, so a quality mattress that's comfortable, supports the body and is free from VOCs is essential. The lifespan of a mattress depends on a number of factors, but the average is between 7–10 years.

Donating your old bed can help an individual or family through a tough time, and it's the ecologically responsible choice. If you're replacing your bedlinen and towels, donate them to large charities: anything that isn't good enough for their retail locations is usually sent to re-processors abroad to be turned into upholstery stuffing, insulation, paper, cleaning cloths, windscreen wipers etc. Alternatively, donate direct to homeless shelters, or animal shelters. Planet Aid collect and recycle over 90 million pounds of clothes and shoes every year, so keep them in mind when you declutter your wardrobe! The criteria for all charities and shelters is that all donations must be clean and dry.

For your health and the planet's, consider investing in an eco, organic, non-toxic mattress. There are lots of suppliers with great credentials to choose from, many of which support reforestation or donate to protect endangered wildlife with each purchase.

For the most relaxing and healthy experience, choose natural, 100 per cent organic materials for bedding and bedlinen. Cotton with a high thread count (600+) feels soft and luxurious, as does bamboo. Linen, silk and eucalyptus keep you cool in the summer. The best pillowcases for your hair and skin are made from silk – mulberry silk is known for its breathability, hypoallergenic and moisture retention qualities, plus mulberry trees need less water than cotton to grow, and aren't sprayed with pesticides. The natural fibres are biodegradable, and only take between one and five years to decompose – 50 times faster than synthetic materials.

For the best sleep, the optimal temperature for your bedroom should be between 15.6°C and 19.4°C (60–67°F). A hot room reduces REM sleep, which is essential for proper immune and cognitive function.

If falling asleep is still an issue once you've addressed light, sound, smell, prospect, and the position and quality of your bed, some natural sleep aids to consider include melatonin, valerian, magnesium, GABA, lavender essential oil, German chamomile and passionflower teas. And, as we'll see in Chapter 8, spending just 20 minutes a day in nature has immediate positive effects on our mental and physical health, including improving sleep.

EXPRESS YOURSELF

Explore some fun, creative ways to give yourself refuge and prospect in your bedroom. Here are three suggestions to get you started:

1. Cosy retreat
A four-poster bed is elegant, stylish and instantly transforms any bedroom. If you don't want the fuss of curtains, opt for a sleek contemporary design that won't make you feel hemmed in.

Budget tip

If your ceiling height is standard – or lower – create your own four-poster with metal extendable net curtain/café rods, large cup hooks to hang the rods from the ceiling and sheers to hang from the rods. If your ceiling is white, choose white or cream rods and cup hooks to blend seamlessly. A contrasting rod finish like black or metal also works, but draws the eye to the four-poster's proximity to the ceiling. (Please see the book's website for project details.)

2. Plant immersion

Surrounding your bed with plants and trees that produce oxygen at night is healthy and soothing as they filter toxins, add humidity to dry rooms, absorb sound, reduce stress and lower blood pressure.

Create a bed canopy with bamboo, which can easily be trained into interesting shapes. Having your bed in a cater-corner position is ideal as the plants fill the triangular void behind the bed nicely. Make sure you have easy access for watering – or have plant watering devices. Add smart lighting uplighters for mood lighting.

3. Fabric walls

If you like the idea of upholstering your bedroom walls, but can't justify the cost, consider unlined curtain panels hung from a flexible, ceiling-mounted track running around the entire room. It's a relatively easy DIY project, and not too expensive – depending on the curtain panels you choose. White or neutral cotton work well, especially if your ceiling and walls are a similar shade. Conceal smart lighting uplighters behind the panels in the corners of the room to change your wall colour at whim: it's a spectacular transformation! Add blackout panels to any pairs of curtains that pull across windows, or have blackout blinds. The installation adds soundproofing, creates intrigue by day and night, and is excellent for rooms with awkward shapes.

MAKING YOUR BEDROOM WORK

Studio room

While a pull-out wall bed (Murphy bed) or sofa bed will save on floor-space, they can be irritating – especially when you're tired at night, and don't want to rearrange the furniture.

A cost-effective solution is to place one side of your bed against a wall and have tall shelving units (with backs) at each end of the bed (please see Plans 12 to 14, pages 168–170). This instant alcove gives you refuge and prospect while providing additional storage for clothes, books, ornaments etc.

For a seamless look, upholster the entire back of the unit at the head of the bed as a luxurious headboard, and use the top of the unit for lamps or smart lighting to light both the bed and dressing area. If you can't live without a TV, install a flatscreen on the back of the unit at the foot of the bed. Plants on top of the units create high planting, and an additional sense of privacy. To make the bed alcove private, add ceiling-hung sheers that open against the sides of the two units. When you want to hide the bed, pull them across to create a sense of intrigue, especially when the lighting is on.

Small bedroom

Small bedrooms have the same issues as small living rooms, as we saw in Chapter 3 (please see page 62), where walls and the door dominate. Create the illusion of space with:

- White or neutral palette on walls and fabrics, with plenty of contrasting textures and the occasional pop of colour.
- Plants – especially high planting.
- Mirror: a vintage overmantle above the bed, painted to match the walls, is ideal for reflecting a view and adding character.
- Glass to reflect light: S-shaped, all-glass bedside tables look great.
- Translucent ceiling or light panels to create the illusion of an additional view.

- Changing your bedroom door to glazed isn't ideal, but glass doors work well for fitted wardrobes (closets). Add frosted window film to conceal clothes.
- If you need additional storage, consider having furniture that multitasks.

Large bedroom

If you don't enjoy sleeping in a king or super-king, don't feel obliged to fill a large bedroom with a large bed. To break the floorplan up, and turn your bedroom into a retreat, create a comfortable seating area facing a window with a combination of upholstered pieces and a coffee table. Add a fireplace if you can. Adapt an attractive piece of furniture with doors into a tea and coffee station: if you add a smart WiFi electric kettle and/or smart coffee/espresso maker, you don't have to leave the bedroom for your morning beverage! Make sure the unit accommodates everything you need (cups, spoons, mini fridge etc.).

As we saw with open-plan bathrooms (please see page 149), plants, tall trees, a curved bookcase or a movable partition are all good at dividing large rooms into more intimate spaces and are a good way to create a dressing area too.

Child's bedroom

Please see Chapter 9.

A FINAL NOTE

SONIA CHOQUETTE SUGGESTS

Chakras are energy centres in your body that help you experience life in a grounded, creative and productive way. The Secret chakra is one of the lesser known that, when activated daily, becomes a superpower station for attracting what you want!

To locate it, feel the back of your head at the base of your skull, and find the slight indentation. The Secret chakra is also called the Health, or Moon chakra as it's shaped like a crescent moon, and its associated colour is milky white.

Night-time practice If you're restless, anxious or troubled, massage the Moon Chakra in a gentle, circular motion for 1–2 minutes. Breathe deeply while massaging. It brings about a profound sense of inner calm, and relieves nervousness, depression, heavy heart and any emotions that might prevent you from sleeping well. Do this every night to induce deep, relaxing sleep.

Morning practice If you want to create something, close your eyes, and focus your intention in the greatest possible detail while massaging the Moon chakra in a gentle circular pattern. Do this for about 1–2 minutes, then take a deep breath, and relax.

For visualisation, and creating your heart's desire, it's best to massage the Moon chakra in the morning.

CHAPTER SUMMARY

BATHING

- Streamlined, rational bathrooms don't prioritise wellness because they're not conducive to lingering and relaxing, which affects sleep quality.
- *Ofuro*, the Japanese ritual of soaking in a deep tub of hot water daily relaxes body and mind.
- To be healing, bathrooms must engage all our senses with haptic invitations (pebbles, clay, wood, plants, natural fabrics and storage containers); scent (essential oils, soaps, candles, natural cleaning

products); sound (white noise, sound insulation, music, nature sounds).

- Maximise natural light with mirror and sun pipes.
- Camouflage straight lines and sharp corners with wave patterns, cylindrical containers and round accessories, curtain panels on a curved track, high planting.
- Have multiple sources of dimmable lighting (task, mood and feature). In windowless bathrooms, consider circadian lighting.
- Camouflage coloured sanitary ware by introducing harmonious colours, or highlight with complementary colours.
- Create your ideal healing bathroom with an escape to nature, a hammam or a reading room.
- Open-plan bathrooms are ideal for *ofuro* tubs, but may need to be screened with plants, a curved bookcase or a movable acoustic partition.
- In small bathrooms, replace pedestal or wall-mounted basins with a vanity unit. Create floor-to-ceiling storage to reduce clutter, and consider seamless shower screens and mirroring a wall.
- If you're renovating a large bathroom, position sanitary ware perpendicular to walls to break up the space. Create privacy walls around the toilet with plants or open bookshelves. Add comfortable seating.

SLEEPING

- A sense of refuge and a view (if not from a window, then of the bedroom itself) are essential to unwinding and sleeping well – especially as we tend to be connected to the global community 24/7.
- For body and mind to rest and heal, adults need 7–9 hours of sleep per night. Good boundaries, a sleep routine and a bedroom sanctuary will improve the quality and quantity of sleep.
- Blue light suppresses melatonin production, preventing the deeper stages of sleep as it interferes with our circadian rhythm. To adjust

your devices' displays, use night mode apps and amber reading lights.

- Cool, dark bedrooms are essential for quality sleep, so block outdoor and internal light sources.
- Smart lighting supports circadian rhythm with the gradual disappearance of light in the evening, and dawn simulation for gentle awakening. Or try a wake-up light.
- Address soundproofing (please see Chapter 1, page 16) and mask environmental and household noise with sound conditioners using white, pink or brown noise.
- Music – especially adult lullabies – helps many to fall asleep. Aromatherapy also works.
- Create prospect even if you don't have a good window view. Natural fractal patterns reduce stress by 60 per cent and are restorative.
- East-facing bedrooms at the rear of properties are ideal.
- If replacing your bed, donate the old one and choose an eco, organic, non-toxic mattress.
- For prospect and refuge, consider a four-poster bed, plant immersion or fabric walls.
- In a studio, a wall bed or sofa bed can be awkward. Try creating an alcove with two tall shelving units at the head and foot of the bed to give extra storage and create a dressing area.
- Conjure up the illusion of space in a small bedroom with a neutral palette, high planting, mirror, glass, glazed wardrobe doors and furniture that multitasks.
- Turn a large bedroom into a retreat with a comfortable seating arrangement and fireplace. Create a dressing area with plants, tall trees, a curved bookcase or a movable partition.

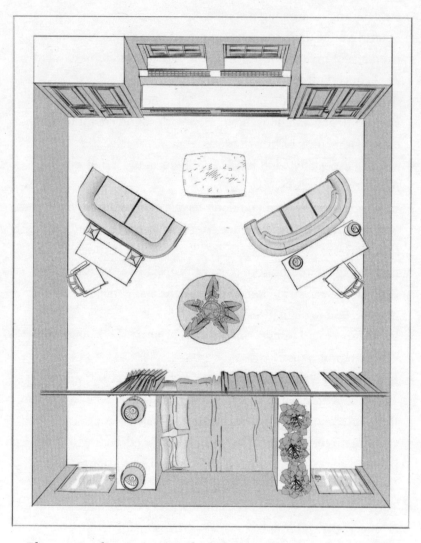

Plan 12: Studio – creating a bed alcove with maximum storage

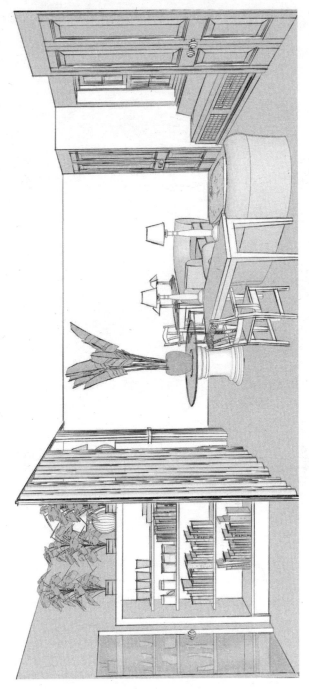

Plan 13: Studio – creating a bed alcove with maximum storage

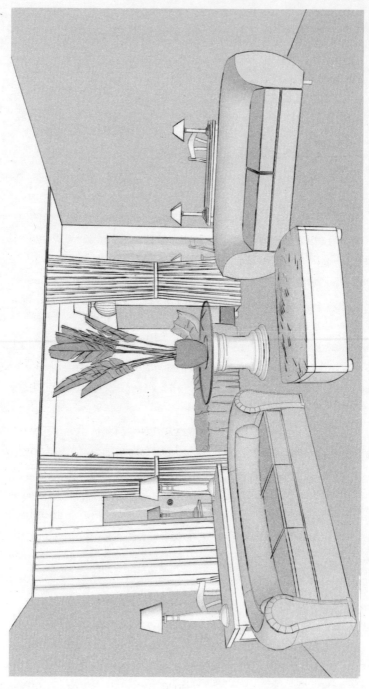

Plan 14: Studio – creating a bed alcove with maximum storage

WORKING

'The morality of routine has been pushed hard during the mechan-
isation of human culture and the drive for ever-greater "efficiency"
judged by external authorities. We have internalised this way of being
which is not natural to us as cyclical creatures of flesh and blood.'
—Lucy H. Pearce, *Creatrix: She Who Makes*

For most of us, our model of working is based on childhood and our
physical and emotional experience of school, where we sat on uncomfortable chairs at hard little desks and deferred to our teachers. As
adults, we sit at bigger – but equally hard – desks on slightly more
comfortable chairs and defer to our employer, or clients if we're self-
employed. Our desk and office have become our new classroom with
its pervading sense of control and captivity.

Stem cell biologist and author of *The Biology of Belief*, Dr Bruce
Lipton believes that our lives run on subconscious programming that
we downloaded as children from observing others when our brains
were still in theta wave. Essentially, we're sponges until the conscious
mind kicks in at the age of seven, and by then our subconscious
programming is already installed.

WORK BLUEPRINT

We all have a Work Blueprint whose foundations lie in our early
childhood experiences, and evolved as we became part of the working

world. Have you ever considered that the way you're currently working might be following a model prescribed by your teachers, parents
and bosses – and *doesn't* actually suit your personality or needs at all?

If this resonates, jot down any thoughts and impressions in your
Book of Inspiration. Think back to your classroom days, and where
you did homework. How did these environments make you feel?
Remember the sensations in your body, and how you behaved. Did
you rebel against – or go along with – the rules of the classroom and
home study? Did you feel hemmed in by your surroundings, or safe
and in control? When and where did you have a sense of mastery?
What made you unhappy? What gave you a sense of freedom and
creativity when you were at school? Was it in the playground? On
field trips? During art classes? When were you at your happiest and
most productive? The more detail you can access, the more familiar
you'll become with your Work Blueprint and subconscious programming, and how they're either helping or hindering your working life
today.

Next, think about your experiences in the working world. Which
settings have made you happiest and most inspired? Which set your
teeth on edge? Note any details that come – however silly. Becoming
aware of positive and negative impressions helps to clarify the
elements that inspire you, and trigger creativity and productivity –
which will make it easier to decide what you do and don't want in
your home office!

FIRST IMPRESSIONS

Location

Whether you already have a home office, or are deciding where to
locate one, conduct a 'viewing' to get started. The space should
ideally be somewhere you like and feel happy in. Unless you're a
creative requiring lots of space to work, size isn't the determining
factor: light levels, comfort and privacy take precedence. If you

suffer from SAD (Seasonal Affective Disorder) try to avoid north- or east-facing rooms, and opt for south- or west-facing to maximise sunlight throughout the day.

Try to forget the engrained office model of desk, chair, filing cabinet and storage; this belongs to an era that confined us to desks, weighed down by paperwork. In our digital age, most of us work primarily on our devices with cloud storage, giving us freedom and versatility in *where* we work, but this has some major issues in *how* we work.

Technology and the digital age should give us more free time, but most of us are working longer hours than ever. We're more stressed, and have less time and energy for our family, friends and leisure. What's behind this disturbing phenomena, and how do we overcome it?

The digital issue

Our working environments are now two-fold: the physical spaces where we work and the digital world in which we immerse ourselves for endless hours as we stare at screens.

If the digital world is consuming inordinate amounts of your time, I highly recommend watching the TED Talk 'How a Handful of Tech Companies Control Billions of Minds Every Day' by technology ethicist Tristan Harris. Regaining autonomy over our digital world is essential to our wellbeing according to Harris, who founded the Center for Humane Technology under the guiding principle that technology should serve us, not the tech companies who constantly hijack our attention in the name of profit. Try their Take Control Toolkit (humanetech.com/take-control) to detox your digital life. It covers how to turn off notifications, remove toxic apps, set boundaries and remove outrage from your diet. You'll reclaim your time and feel empowered in the digital world instead of sucked down endless rabbit holes. It really works, I promise!

If you're struggling with behavioural addiction to digital devices, understanding the problem is key. Adam Alter, a professor of psychology and marketing at New York University, explains the issue in *Irresistible*, and provides useful strategies to reverse-engineer it. If you're checking your inbox every few minutes, *A World Without Email* is an eye-opening read. Humans aren't wired for constant digital communication, and Alter suggests an alternative way to work that eliminates distractions that aren't productive – including the endless volley of back-and-forth emails.

To get a true sense of exactly how you're spending your time throughout the day, try Rescue Time (rescuetime.com), which gives detailed feedback on your behaviour, and helps improve your productivity.

Constant attention switching between tasks reduces our cognitive capacity. This is why we get so stressed and are generally less productive: every time we focus on a task and a device makes a sound, or a notification banner appears, it distracts us. The solution is to switch all devices to 'silent' or 'focus' mode for time periods that suit you. This lets you concentrate and get important work done uninterrupted. Both modes are highly customisable: you choose which people and apps are essential and hide notification badges for anything else.

Journalist and author Johann Hari believes we've lost our ability to pay attention – both individually and societally. In *Stolen Focus*, he investigates the 12 causes of our loss of focus and shows how to address them, including how technology and other aspects of modern life impact our ability to concentrate through no fault of our own. Unlike computers, the human brain isn't designed to multitask; when we focus completely on one task at a time that has meaning for us, we enter the flow state, and can easily and successfully complete it. Hari stresses the importance of rest, relaxation, getting enough sleep and allowing ourselves to mind-wander for at least an hour every day to regain our focus and ability to think deeply.

Experts all agree that taking a 24-hour digital break from all devices at least once a week is essential to our mental and physical health. Try it and see how much better you feel afterwards; 48 hours – formerly known as a weekend – is even better!

Proactive versus reactive mode

How you begin your working day sets the tone for what follows. Do you always start by checking your phone and opening your inbox? A barrage of emails and red notification badges is stressful and immediately puts your system into reactive mode, making you more inclined to head down paths you had no intention of travelling.

Instead, why not start each day with intention, spending a few moments to note the things you want to achieve, and deciding how you'd like to go about it. This puts you in a proactive and positive mindset where you are the one in charge of your actions and timeline. With a sense of control and clear direction, you'll make better decisions once you're ready to check your devices.

Decide what would help you start your working day with intention, and jot ideas down in your Book of Inspiration. Anything that engages your senses, and keeps you grounded in the real world is the antidote to digital overwhelm. A hot drink in your favourite mug. Flowers on your desk. Lighting a scented candle. Opening a leather organiser to discover what's planned for your day. Reaching for a notebook. If your personality type is the Nurturer, taking time to pause and think in an intentional way about what you need to accomplish creates a calm, cohesive energy to your day.

Engaging as many of your senses as possible is the goal. Screens only engage sight and sound in limited ways, so surround yourself with things that speak to multiple senses at once.

THE CALL-BACK

One of your home office's most important roles is to ground you in the real world and offer respite from the digital world. Ideally, it needs to *call you back* from the digital world.

When a shaman journeys, their soul is brought home by the call-back signal, a distinct change to the continuous drumming rhythm. A brief period of time follows, allowing them to readjust to ordinary consciousness and integrate the information gathered during their journey. It's not like flipping a switch but is more of a gradual transition.

Once we immerse ourselves in the digital world, we struggle to disconnect from it because it's currently designed to consistently grab our attention and time. Whenever we do manage to disconnect, we often experience a jolt because returning to the real world is sudden, and the two worlds are very different. Humans do best when we have a transition time – no matter how short – between different states. Transition phases are how we acclimate to change. Change, even when it's positive, is inherently stressful, and requires an adjustment.

The ideal transition from the digital to the real world is to go outside and be in nature for a moment: this grounds you and reminds you what's real. Standing barefoot on the ground does the trick, which is why working outdoors is ideal, as we'll explore later. But when going outside isn't possible, your home office has to provide your call-backs. Here are some options:

Sound

If you live in the country and can have your windows open to hear nature's sounds, this is a perfect call-back from the digital world.

If you live in a city, introducing a nature-inspired, biophilic sound-scape works well. These can includes wind in the trees, a babbling brook or flowing river, waves breaking on a shore or birdsong. The sounds of nature are deeply soothing to us, reducing stress levels and improving focus and concentration; they are part of our DNA. A study in 2019 found that participants who listened to nature sounds (crickets chirping, waves crashing) performed better on demanding cognitive tests than those who listened to urban sounds like traffic and the clatter of a busy café.[1]

Unfortunately, the soundscape in most home offices typically includes the constant drone of office equipment, intermittent alerts from devices, and general household noise. Sound conditioners mask background sounds with white, pink or brown noise (please see page 157) which is soothing to most, but it can be hard to find the sweet spot between loud enough to focus, but soft enough to not distract during calls. Sound conditioners loop, which is fine when we're sleeping but more unsettling when we're awake because a constant sound isn't natural to humans. In primitive times, we were highly attuned to the ever-changing sounds of nature, which alerted us to danger: if the birds fell silent, it meant a predator was approaching.

When I'm researching and writing indoors, I livestream Africam; the sounds of the African bush are invigorating (which helps my focus and concentration), deeply relaxing (which keeps my stress levels down), and some of the wildlife sounds really make me smile! Or for nature, wildlife and ocean life from around the world, try live-streaming Explore.

Studies have shown that listening to happy music stimulates divergent thinking: free-flowing, non-linear ways of generating creative ideas by exploring many possible solutions.[2] However, if you're problem solving, music can actually impair convergent thinking:[3] the logical process of deriving the single best answer to a problem.

A view of nature

Looking out at nature – whether trees, a body of water, tall grasses blowing in a breeze – is relaxing and stimulating. Nature is never static, and its non-rhythmic sensory stimuli (NRSS) intrigue us; our minds can't predict how the wind will move the branches of a tree or the surface of water, so we're mesmerised and engaged. The movement of living things is processed in our brains in a different place than mechanical objects. A 2015 study published in the *Journal of Environmental Psychology* found that green spaces are restorative and boost attention, while looking at concrete worsens attention during tasks![4]

Looking out of a window at the complexity of nature isn't just healing to our minds, but also to our eyes. When we stare at our screens, we forget to blink and our eyes become dry. Try the 20/20/20 rule to ease eye strain and reduce headaches and fatigue: shift your gaze away from devices every 20 minutes and focus on something 20 feet away for 20 seconds.

If you don't have a view of nature, have lots of plants in your home office as a call-back and consider a living desk with a trough-shaped base for planting herbs, succulents etc., and a removable, flat glass panel on top for easy watering and pruning. Research conducted by the University of Exeter found a significant increase in creativity, productivity and motivation among people who have live plants in their workplace.[5]

Animals

Animals are the perfect call-back from the digital world. Birds coming to a feeder outside your office window and/or honeybees at work in an indoor observation beehive on your wall (please see page 27) are fascinating to watch, and also inspiring in their work ethic. Cats, dogs and other furry friends increase our oxytocin levels when they engage with us or come for a snuggle. And observing them while they sleep often makes us smile or laugh because of the contorted positions they adopt!

Sensory-rich materials

Everything you perceive through your senses (sight, smell, touch, taste and sound) in your home office should have a positive effect on you. If you did your Sensory Signposts in Chapter 1 (please see page 14), refer back to them and decide which might be the best call-backs for you, and how you could introduce them. Have several call-backs in your workspace – the more, the better!

Beyond aesthetics and ergonomics, the chair and desk you work on are very important, especially if your personality type is the Nurturer. If they have a positive sensorial effect on you, you feel supported and are more easily called back from the digital world. If they don't, you're more likely to be sucked into the digital world because the real world – the one your body is in contact with – doesn't appeal to your senses.

Movement

Kinetic art and mobiles, wind chimes, suspended crystals refracting light (please see page 39) are all call-backs, especially when caught in a breeze or draft. They draw your attention and help you relax for a moment.

However, anything that gets *you* up and moving and helps to break your sedentary habit is a perfect call-back. Having multiple places to work entices you from one spot to another, especially if the promise of comfort is involved. If your personality type is the Free Spirit, you likely do best working in short spurts, so multiple workplaces are ideal.

A tea and coffee station may pull you back from the digital world more easily than the thought of trekking to the kitchen for refreshments (please see page 164).

An under-desk bike keeps you actively engaged with the real world. There are several types available: from an under-desk set of pedals to an all-in-one bike desk. The latter is perfect for both small work spaces and larger offices that can accommodate more than one desk. Whichever option you choose, make sure it's quiet and offers you the best resistance range.

Finally, an option to avoid tunnel vision and being sucked into the world of a small screen is to wirelessly mirror your desktop to a wall-mounted TV. Because the TV screen is further away and everything – especially text and numbers – appears much larger than on your devices, this option should prevent squinting and hunching over. Plus you're more aware of your surroundings in your peripheral vision, which keeps you grounded, and less myopically focused on the digital world.

LIFE–WORK BALANCE

Establishing a good life–work balance can be difficult when working from home. Identifying the potential issues and finding healthy ways to deal with them greatly reduces stress levels.

Overworking

The digital world encourages us to spend more hours on our devices than is healthy for us and the tendency to overwork is rife when working from home. We want to appear efficient, so we make ourselves constantly available, responding in record time to messages, texts and emails. Even when nothing is happening or expected of us, we're drawn to our devices out of habit, because we're afraid of missing something, or simply because we're bored. We linger in front of them, convincing ourselves that we're being productive when all we're doing is exhausting ourselves.

Before the days of constant connectivity, the old corporate model of working five days a week from nine to five created clear boundaries between work and life; we all had more leisure time and were less stressed – unless the boss had our home number!

In our digital age, we believe that we're not productive unless we're always on our devices and available to everyone on demand. It's like having a newborn baby, but with no end in sight. Becoming very clear about our goals and objectives and knowing how long they'll take is key to freeing us from perpetual overwork.

Entrepreneur and business innovator Andrew Barnes successfully proved that working fewer hours makes people happier, freer to pursue leisure, and more productive in their jobs. His fascinating experiment with his trust company, Perpetual Guardian, is documented in the book, *The 4 Day Week*.

'Work expands so as to fill the time available for its completion'. Understanding Parkinson's Law, an axiom based on Cyril Northcote Parkinson's 1955 essay in *The Economist*, makes us aware that the more time we allocate to a task, the more complex it becomes, and therefore the more time is needed to complete it. This leads to procrastination, stress and overwhelm, regardless of how simple the task might be.

Time management tools like Timeboxing help you plan your day and improve productivity by allocating fixed periods of time to specific activities. You stop when the time is up, and then ascertain whether you've achieved your goals. Taking more breaks throughout the day and rewarding yourself for achievements rather than constantly slave-driving yourself is important. Be a decent boss to yourself!

In the evening, to avoid disrupting your circadian rhythm, curtail screen time as it keeps your brain in beta wave. Don't be tempted to send a quick email, or add something to a document: use a pen and notebook instead and take action in the morning. You'll sleep better because your brain waves can drop into alpha, which facilitates relaxation and sleep.

Boundaries

There are far more distractions to manage at home, and establishing good boundaries is key to productivity and mental health. Just because you're at home shouldn't make you any more available to family or friends than if you were working in an office – where they'd think twice about dropping round uninvited! Terri Cole's *Boundary Boss* is worth reading – especially if you're an empath or HSP (highly sensitive person) and find it difficult to maintain appropriate boundaries with others.

You should also train yourself not to automatically answer the doorbell or phone every time it rings. Your time is precious and must be respected – by you as much as anyone else.

Compartmentalise

One of the hardest parts of working from home is the awareness of the number of things clamouring for your attention. If you leave home daily to work in an office, you can't worry about the washing-up (dishes) piled in the sink, or the overflowing laundry basket until you return home. In a home office setting, your focus can be inexorably drawn to domestic tasks – either because you need a sense of order to concentrate properly on your work, or because you're procrastinating. It's easy to become overwhelmed, slip into 'freeze mode' and not achieve anything concrete on the work front. This is where compart-mentalising comes into play: decide what needs your focus in priority order and deal with each task accordingly. You might want to try photographer and creativity coach Carla Coulson's method of divid-ing her week:

'Planning a clear visual of how you set up your time and week immediately brings a sense of calm and order,' says Carla. 'Creatives often think having a calendar is not creative, but being able to *see* your time helps you see where there may be "over packing", or not enough padding between tasks and appointments. Staking out your time allows you to create clear boundaries around it, gives you more time to create, and highlights what you need to say "yes" and "no" to.

'I break my week into theme days. I categorise them by gathering things on one day that are "inside" or "outside", and asking myself how I energetically feel on different days during the week. I like to stay in on Mondays to set up my week, do admin/marketing and goal setting. Wednesdays and Fridays are "creative" days when I create my own work, research projects, or have meetings relating to my creativ-ity. Other days may be devoted entirely to "coaching" so I'm at my desk, fully present for my clients, and not multi-tasking.'

Carla is a big fan of bringing as much fun and joy into her work as possible. 'When I'm procrastinating, I use Jon Acuff's mantra from *Finish*: "Make it fun and get it done". I'll change my location and go somewhere fabulous, do social media in a café, put a playlist on and try to finish my work by the end of the list. A key for me is working in 2-hour time blocks. You can get a lot done in 2 hours, and it's often more productive that devoting 8 hours to one task.'

Paying close attention to what you say 'yes' and 'no' to is important to Carla. 'Herein lies the magic: when you say "yes" and you feel angry and resentful, it's probably a "no". Ask yourself: "Am I building some-one else's dreams, or my own?" I make sure joy, downtime, self-care, fun, and time for friends and family are in my calendar *every* week. I value this time as much as a business meeting. Our lives need to be sustainable, and the way we use time is key to living a life we love with more grace and ease – and less anxiety and "crazy busy". This is when life becomes easier, and we bring more things we dream of to life.'

Vary your routine

As neuroscientist and researcher Dr Joe Dispenza points out, doing the same thing day in and day out only attracts more of the same – especially if your mindset isn't positive. Be willing to change things up; if you go for a walk or run before you begin your working day, change your route. You'll be amazed how variety, and noticing new and different things inspires and uplifts you. Be aware of your traffic patterns as you move around your work space, and alter them as much, and as often, as possible.

In your Book of Inspiration, write down everything you do on a daily basis in the order in which you do it. Beside each task or activity note the emotion you feel when you do it: is it positive, or negative? Then have a critical look at your list. Decide what's essential, and what can go. Make sure that everything which remains in your daily routine has a positive spin to it. If it's an essential activity with a nega-tive connotation, what can you do to transform the associated emotion?

Dress up

I don't mean wear formal office attire, which can be uncomfortable and restrictive, but don't be tempted to dress top-down, with your upper half Zoom-ready, but still wearing pyjama bottoms and fluffy slippers! Others may not see your lower half on camera, but you do. It can be demoralising because, on some level, you feel as if you're pretending. You're physically comfortable – but not psychologically. The duality is difficult to juggle and affects you subliminally.

What we wear influences our mood, even if nobody else sees us all day. We tend to think of dressing to impress others, but it has an effect on us too. Think about going on a first date with someone you fancy: would you feel your best if you wore washed-out, stained clothes, peppered with moth holes?

Each day, consider the mood you want to conjure, and dress accordingly. This could range from playful, outrageous and creative through to serious or understated, depending on the work tasks ahead and how you want to tackle them. Difficult tasks are sometimes best offset with a contrasting outfit: a prospective audio call with a cantankerous client might call for a silly hat or outfit that makes you grin.

Jo Glynn-Smith, transformation coach and dressing for confidence expert, suggests: 'Wear what makes you feel confident. Clothing is an incredibly powerful tool – I'm not talking about fashion, but what makes you *feel good* about yourself. Think back to an occasion when you had success. What were you wearing? How did it make you feel? Visualise what your best felt like. What about it made you feel amazing? Sometimes it's as simple as red lipstick, or a certain style of shirt that captures that feeling. Once you've clearly identified it, you can bring it into your home office wardrobe – whether you have video meetings, or not.'

Natural rhythm

Making yourself stick to a schedule that doesn't feel natural or doesn't allow you to get enough sleep is detrimental in the long run. If you're a night owl, forcing yourself to rise and shine early is counterproductive, as you likely get your best ideas later in the day or evening. Equally, if you get up very early, pushing yourself to keep going once your energy levels drop for the day is futile. Know your natural rhythm, and adapt your working schedule accordingly. This is especially important for difficult tasks: do these when your energy is highest and leave easy tasks for when your energy ebbs.

Power naps

Naps are good for your health. Consider emulating Arianna Huffington, author of *The Sleep Revolution,* who installed nap rooms at *The Huffington Post* to great effect. Have a daybed, sofa, hammock or floor cushions for when you need a power nap – even a deckchair by a sunny window. If space is tight, consider a chair that resembles a structured beanbag. The nap doesn't have to be long to be restorative. Cultures who routinely nap in the afternoons live longer and suffer less heart disease. But do have your Book of Inspiration close at hand when you nap: some of our best ideas come just before we drift off.

Energy

Energy can accumulate over time – particularly if you're under pressure daily. As Jean Haner points out: 'The chair you sit in to work holds stress and tension you've previously felt there in a big cloud around it. This builds up the more often you sit there and feel that way again. It can help to clear some of the old energy by thumping the chair, or clapping over it. Upholstered chairs hold onto energy more than wooden or metal ones.'

EXPRESS YOURSELF

While the space where you work has to be conducive to the type of work you do, it's essential to also discover and create your own ideal work spots and methods. This is where knowing and understanding your Work Blueprint comes in handy.

Shun traditional work set-ups, and be open to new possibilities that feel right to you. As Jean Haner says: 'This subtly helps you break out of an old mould. Creating this kind of space for yourself can literally change your future: all of a sudden, almost magically, you get an offer that allows you more freedom, or brings the kind of work you really want. As we manage our energy and the energy around us, it changes the energy that we broadcast, and this changes our lives.'

Start with you and your needs – don't try to fit yourself into an accepted working model. This is one of the greatest advantages of working from home: the ability to indulge the individual, without the requirement to blend into the homogenous surroundings of a corporate office. Artists have always been adept at picking exactly the right spot to work in, and conjuring an atmosphere around them that's conducive to creation. Light and practical working space dictate their choice of work area, and convention doesn't enter into the equation.

Unfortunately, corporate life and our unconscious Work Blueprints have deprived many of us of the instinctive sense of what our best working spot could be. The strict discipline of sitting at a desk has been reenforced to the point where many doubt they can be productive outside of this rigid setting. To the corporate worker, being home-based can often seem like an ideal they yearn for. But to the entrepreneur whose budget or family commitments tie them to working from home, this can feel like a prison sentence while they long for daily connection and meaningful interactions with work colleagues.

Flexibility, adaptability and inspiration are key factors in any successful working environment that helps us achieve our best. If space allows, having distinct areas for different types of work is conducive to success; focused work requires quiet and a lack of distractions, while informal, spontaneous work (including audio and video chats) needs more relaxed settings. Where you work in your home should be a comfortable, uplifting and inspiring space – one that you look forward to spending time in each day.

Have a theme

Children love themed rooms, so why not treat yourself to a themed home office?

As the American humourist Leo Calvin Rosten astutely wrote in his book, *Passions and Prejudices*: 'Most of us never really grow up or mature all that much – we simply grow taller. Oh, to be sure, we laugh less and play less and wear uncomfortable disguises like adults, but beneath the costume is the child we always are, whose needs are simple, whose daily life is still best described by fairy tales.'

Companies like Apple, LinkedIn, Google and Zillow understand this, and have redesigned their corporate offices in innovative, playful ways that now prioritise employees' mental and physical wellbeing over corporate identity and value-for-money furnishings. Google and Yahoo have organic vegetable gardens to reduce employee stress and boost morale. If big corporations can embrace flexibility, fun and sustainability in the office environment, so can all of us!

Your office's theme can be as subtle or overt as you like. It's all about creating an atmosphere that's enticing to you and doesn't feel staid. Excitement and adventure are the perfect antidotes if your work is dull. Here are some ideas to get you started:

1. Forest bathing

A forest theme is easy to create with tall trees and high planting and has many benefits: greenery makes the air you breathe healthier, reducing bacterial colonies by a staggering 60 per cent, headaches by 24 per cent and eye irritation by 52 per cent! Plants also increase indoor air's humidity, which is critically low when central heating or air conditioning are on. Plus caring for your forest office is a stress-reducer. Look for rugs made to look like the forest floor and add tree stump coffee table and stools as an alternative working spot to complete your forest theme.

2. Aviator

If flying is your passion or ambition, don't limit yourself to memorabilia on your walls and shelves. Aviator desks come in many guises, and are either made from, or inspired by, aircraft wings. You can also often find aviation parts in architectural salvage yards that – with a little creativity – can be adapted to all manner of uses in your home office. Paint the walls silver, or your preferred aircraft colour, but be wary of bright reds and oranges – a little goes a long way!

3. Dream destination

If you love to visit – or long to live – in a certain place, surrounding yourself with reminders of it helps manifest it in your life sooner. Be wary of mass-produced, kitsch representations, and get creative with more original interpretations that play to your senses. For example, for a Moroccan theme, make a version of the *sedari*, a deep, very low bench seat with plush cushioning on top in vibrant colours (perfect for power naps). Team it with carved low tables or a large, low table. Get the ergonomics right, and this could become an alternative desk area. For relaxing at the end of the working day, introduce a clash or contrasting bright colours, and metal lanterns with cut-away patterns to create mood lighting.

Vision board

Emma Jones, founder of Enterprise Nation (a small business community supporting founders to start and grow a business) says: 'Every day in business presents perplexing questions, challenges and opportunities. You're thinking about your product, team, finances and future. It's important therefore to have an inspiring space in which you can contemplate and work on these tasks. Having a vision board reminds you why you are doing what you do.'

Turn your vision board into wall art by getting your own images printed onto canvas, acrylic, wood or even brushed metal. You could also consider a self-adhesive wall mural, but be wary of scale and proportion in a small room so as not to be overwhelmed.

MAKING YOUR HOME OFFICE WORK

Each type of work space presents its unique challenges, so let's explore these, along with some of the many possible solutions.

No office

It can be stressful if you don't have a room or dedicated space to work at home. This makes the life–work divide harder to maintain as reminders of work (even if just paperwork and a few folders) are either ever-present, or need to be tidied away at the end of the working day when you're tired. If you don't live alone, household noise and distractions can impinge on your work, and vice versa, and you're probably often on the move in search of a quiet place to work. Hot-desking has become hot-rooming!

Psychologically, it's important to have a place to work – no matter how small – whether it's the corner of a table, a room or a broom cupboard (closet). Pick somewhere that feels good to you, that you'll look forward to spending time in daily, and stake your claim! Make sure your back isn't to a door or traffic corridor where others walk behind you as this creates a disconcerting feeling and affects concentration. Also, when you're on a video call, people walking behind you is distracting to anyone else on the call.

If your chosen workspace is part of another room, having flexible furniture that can multitask helps to create a good life–work balance. Chairs and furniture on castors are easy to move and reposition, but make sure the castors can be locked, especially on hard flooring. A contemporary-style, comfortable swivel chair can divide a room nicely and can face whichever direction you want.

A floating desk or wall-mounted worktop (countertop) is often suggested for limited floorspace. While some offer the versatility of folding away against the wall, I'm not a fan: working inches from a wall can be psychologically and metaphorically uncomfortable. You'll probably sit at an angle to the worktop rather than face on, which isn't good for your posture.

> **Budget tip**
> Consider a vintage telephone seat (also known as a gossip bench). Originally designed in the late nineteenth century as a hall seat with an attached table for the telephone, it became popular in the 1950s and 60s, so there are many styles to choose from. Make sure the seat is comfortable and the table has generous space for your laptop, phone etc. Most gossip benches include at least one drawer for storage. Have fun updating a vintage model with contemporary fabric and finishes, or find a modern version. For maximum seating flexibility, position it perpendicular to a wall, or freestanding in the room so you can sit astride the bench. Add additional back support if needed, and raise the level of the table to a comfortable working height – large coffee table books work well for this, and look attractive.

Another vintage option that's very versatile is an adjustable bed reading table. Popular with Victorians for doing their correspondence in bed, they're height-adjustable and are fitted with castors, and many models tilt and rotate too. Some have reading flaps, bookrests and candle stands that can all be put to new uses in a contemporary workspace. These sturdy hardwood tables are quite eye-catching in the right setting.

If you need lots of quiet time to concentrate, make calls, or record material away from the fray of the household, one of my favourite solutions is the soundproof pod, also known as an office telephone booth. Pods come in a wide range of colours, styles and sizes – handy if you occasionally need to accommodate more than one in the pod. You can customise the interior to suit your working needs, but consider having a height-adjustable standing desk to vary your working position from standing to sitting. A comfortable upholstered stool instead of a chair aids your posture, takes up less space and can multitask in the rest of the room when not in use in the pod.

While a pod certainly dominates a room, you can turn this to your advantage. Make it a focal point and statement piece that multitasks from a home office by day to an eye-catching display case by night. This can be achieved with clever lighting in the pod: a crystal pendant light that contrasts to the pod's contemporary feel, or concealed, colour-adjustable smart lighting. On the pod's desk surface, display a sculpture or stunning piece that's easy to move when you're working. Pods have either two solid and two clear sides, or three solid sides and one clear. Having two clear sides make a pod less bulky and more intriguing. When strategically positioned, a pod is a great room divider and can also be a source of mood lighting when other lighting is off (please see Plans 15 to 16, pages 204–5).

If a soundproof pod is too large for the room, consider acoustic upholstered seating with high back and sides to attenuate noise while comfortably cocooning you and giving a sense of privacy. Position the piece where nobody is likely to walk in front of you, and angle it away from doors and natural corridors. Siting it close to a window not only gives you a view, but creates the sense that you're in a separate space, your own mini world. Have a side table for devices, mug etc.

Small office

If you're stuck with a small office, create the optical illusion of space. Keep the walls white or neutral to reflect more light. Consider mirroring one wall from floor to ceiling to maximise light, add depth and make the room look larger. If your window is small, mirror the window wall for maximum effect. Use a professional glass company for the installation.

Budget tip

If you enjoy DIY, tile one wall with mirror tiles instead. While typically used in bathrooms and kitchens, there's no reason why mirror tiles can't make a statement wall in your office, especially if you create your own art piece using the many different sizes and shapes available. Polished edge mirror tiles give a cleaner, less busy look than bevelled tiles. They're also available in mosaic sheets.

An all-glass desk deceives the eye as to how much space it occupies, so you can have a much larger working surface without it dominating a small office. The glass reflects light – unlike wood which absorbs it. To create the exact size you want, team a bent glass console table with a toughened glass top available in different shapes. A bevelled-edge finish looks more sophisticated than a plain, polished edge. The toughened glass is heavy so it won't move easily, and is very strong. The only downside is fingermarks, which stand out in sunlight. Glass feels cold to the touch – a bonus in the summer, but not so pleasant in the winter if your arms are bare. An all-glass desk offers ample room underneath to add attractive storage to complement the style of your office.

Large office

Get creative with a large office and avoid a traditional layout of an executive L-shaped desk. Working in the same position every day can be monotonous, while movement and change keep the brain alert and ideas free flowing, so plan your office with distinct spaces for different activities. This encourages you to gravitate to other areas as the day progresses – but make sure you have practical worksurfaces in each activity corner (please see Plans 17 to 19, pages 206–8). If you have more than one window, be a sunflower and follow the sun as it moves across your office during the course of the day. Include fun elements like a deckchair by a window, a swing or hammock, or a sofa facing a living wall. Don't let furniture hug the walls, leaving a large, empty space in the middle.

Standing desks are proven to be better for our posture and health. Many are height-adjustable, so you can also sit at them. If contemporary styles don't appeal, look for a vintage architect or geometer's table. They're ideal if you need a large working surface with plenty of depth, and some tables also have a tilt mechanism. Height adjustment can be more fiddly with vintage models, but the character is worth it.

I like built-in work island units, positioned slightly off-centre to allow sufficient space elsewhere in the office for comfortable seating for relaxing and brainstorming. A well-designed work island with a generous sized worksurface and a base made up of maximum practical storage will give you plenty of flexibility. Your main working position can overlook a view, with the option to move to any of the other three sides, depending on what you're doing at the time. Include good leg room on all four sides of the work island, and ensure seating gives adequate back support and includes a foot rest. Work islands are perfect for crafts, and any kind of work requiring lots of storage and a large worksurface.

Shared office

Sharing a home office – especially if it's with an assistant – can be more distracting than working in an open-plan corporate office. A low ceiling and small footprint exacerbate noise, and you can be more easily distracted. It's worth measuring your office's environment with the Noise Exposure app.

To reduce echo and absorb sound waves, minimise the amount of hard surfaces and please also see Chapter 1, page 16 for soundproofing suggestions. If you opt for acoustic panels, aim to have 20–40 per cent of your home office's walls covered with them. Look into acoustic furniture which includes office chairs, desks, high-backed upholstered chairs and sofas. Consider installing sound absorbing material *under* the desks' tops too.

Budget tip

Make your own desk by creating an upholstered outer U-shaped shell (the taller, the better) that's either freestanding or fixed to a wall. Inside the U, install a worktop of your choice, and add a narrow shelf or two for storage. This helps with soundproofing and feels like a private cocoon. Place two U-shaped shells back to back, or one in each corner facing into the room so that each person's back is to a wall. To avoid a matched look, choose different colour fabrics for each shell. This project requires more advanced DIY skills.

Alternatively, have a sound absorbing table screen on each person's desk.

All of these soundproofing suggestions also apply if household noise is distracting you while you work, or if you're disturbing others by making calls etc. Do also check your office door. If it's hollow-core, replace it with a solid-core door. Adding weatherstrip around the doorframe prevents sound travelling through any gaps.

Introducing coloured noise (please see page 157) or biophilic sounds has been shown to decrease stress levels and increase concentration, whether you're working alone or in a shared home office. We tend to think that total silence helps us to focus, but research has proven that silence is actually distracting to humans!

Alternate office

If you have a garden (yard), there are many ways to create additional working space, including converting an existing shed or adding a Tiny House or Accessory Dwelling Unit (ADU) – planning permission may be required based on the unit's size, height and proposed location in relation to the main house.

- Repurposing a shed is often the most cost-effective solution. If the windows need enlarging, consider installing folding and sliding doors to open the space up in the summer, and let in maximum light in the winter. Opt for eco building materials (especially insulation) and alternative energy sources like solar panels. If the structure can support it, a living roof is attractive to wildlife, and offers good insulation in all seasons.

- A Tiny House is no larger than 37 sq/m (400 sq/ft) – excluding the sleeping loft – and is either on wheels (mobile) or placed on a poured foundation (fixed). Many Tiny Houses include a kitchen and a bathroom so can double as guest accommodation as well as an office, although this can be an issue if you have frequent guests as the sleeping area is open plan.
- At a minimum of 60.5 sq/m (650 sq/ft), an ADU is much larger than a Tiny House, and always includes living, eating and sleeping spaces along with a kitchen and a bathroom. Because of its larger footprint, an ADU can comfortably accommodate an office and guest accommodation/gym, or whatever you need.

Portable office

If you're hot-rooming around your home regularly in order to work uninterrupted, being able to quickly and easily gather everything you need – without dropping anything or making multiple trips back and forth – is essential. Some options include:

- Mobile office bags will help you transport everything – including your water bottle – in a cleverly designed case that opens up into a mini office space.
- A vintage lap/writing desk's hinged top lifts up to reveal ample space for devices, pens, folders, etc. and is slanted so it's ideal for writing and using your laptop on your knee.

Outdoor office

As we'll explore in the next chapter, being in nature is *so* much better for our mental and physical health than being stuck indoors.

If you have access to a green space, try working outdoors: it's a game-changer – for you and others. When I worked on my covered balcony and made calls, people always remarked on how relaxing and peaceful it was to hear birdsong and insects humming in the background. I loved working outside so much that I created an outdoor office under a gazebo in a sheltered part of the garden. Complete with sand underfoot, it offers total nature immersion but with the office essentials of a glass desk and comfortable chairs and a sofa to work on. (Please see the book's website for details.) Pop-up gazebos are cost-effective, waterproof and include sides for maximum shelter – but they won't always stand up to strong winds. That said, they're easy to take down, but a fixed gazebo is worth the additional investment.

Working outdoors is the most grounding and enjoyable experience; you're in your natural environment, surrounded by non-rhythmic sensory stimuli (NRSS), and you don't easily get stuck down virtual rabbit holes.

Budget tip

Instead of hiring an electrician, get power to your outdoor office with a rechargeable, portable power station.

- If your outdoor office is on a patio or balcony and has to multi-task, choose a desk that doubles as a dining table, or a folding desk or flip-top table that's easy to store when not in use.
- To minimise glare on your screen, and avoid eye strain, try a privacy screen: the anti-glare blocks 95 per cent of reflected and blue light, and 92 per cent of UV light. Or try a laptop sun hood; there are many options available, or you can make your own. Or adapt an attractive but sturdy container that can also carry work necessities.
- An outdoor space heater makes working outside during sunny winter days possible, especially if your work area is sheltered.

- In the summer, a ceiling fan or waterproof outdoor fan (standing, tabletop, or wall-mounted) will keep you comfortable. There are battery-operated and solar versions if you don't have power.
- If you're sitting under a tree or out in nature, Japanese zaisu or tatami chairs maintain your posture, and alleviate neck and back pain. They're portable, easy to store, and since they're legless and armless, you can sit comfortably with your legs crossed or outstretched.

Public office

If your work involves clients or patients coming to your home office regularly, health and safety regulations apply, and any upholstery fabrics have to comply with the fire code. Regulations aside, creating the right atmosphere in this type of office is as important for the people visiting as for you. Pay close attention to colours and their therapeutic value and sound absorption (please see Chapter 1, page 15) plus furniture arrangement. Configuring seating perpendicular to a window works well if you're sitting opposite each other, and it also puts everyone in proximity to essential daylight. If your home office's layout means that one person will have their back to a door, window or natural corridor, adding a screen, large plants or a bookcase behind the seating will make them feel more at ease.

Keeping the energy clear in a public home office is essential, especially if you're working with patients facing mental or physical health challenges. Palo Santo is excellent for energy cleansing: burn incense sticks, diffuse the essential oil or, if the scent is too strong, add several drops to a glass spray bottle, mix with purified water and spritz the space as needed. To alleviate mental and physical fatigue, and to sharpen your focus, try diffusing Scots pine.

SONIA CHOQUETTE SUGGESTS

You need to keep the energy of your office clear, calm and elevated for you to be at your creative best. Treat your office like a sacred sanctuary.

1. Have strong, delineated boundaries to establish an energetic working space that's respected by everyone. This is *your* workplace and isn't part of the Grand Central Station flow of the home!

2. Ring a small crystal bell each morning before starting work to clear the energy of the space and give you a fresh and uplifting start to your day.

3. Have refractive crystals in the window to catch the light. The rainbow patterns they create on walls throughout the day will cleanse your energy and inspire your creative mind.

4. Play spiritually uplifting music to keep the vibration and frequency elevated. Gregorian chants, New Age music, or Baroque composers like Telemann, Vivaldi, Bach and Mozart put your brain into alpha state or heightened creative thinking mode. This immediately soothes your nervous system and entrains your heart to beat in the same state as if you were in deep meditation. Playing beautiful music while you're away from your office creates a wonderful energy to greet you on your return.

5. Place big, bright crystals in the corners of your office, or on your desk. Crystals absorb negative energy while amplifying positive, creative energy. It's important to clear them regularly (ideally every 2–4 weeks); place them in a bowl of salt water (like Epsom salts), soak overnight, then dry in the sun.

6. Have fresh flowers as they're emotionally uplifting and keep your spirits up.

7. Don't have anything that isn't pertinent to work in your office.

8. Frequently open windows to bring in fresh air and rejuvenate the energy so it doesn't get stagnant.

9. Avoid working constantly: walk away from work at the end of the day. If you have a door, shut it and don't go back into your office until the next day. Having clear boundaries between home and work life is extremely important to keeping your spirit balanced. If you don't have the luxury of a door, set up a screen to hide your office space at the end of the day: it makes a huge difference to your overall well-being.

PRACTICALITIES

1. Desk chair

To avoid developing long-term musculo-skeletal issues, your desk chair should ideally be height-adjustable and have adjustable back support. It needs to be stable, but easy to move with castors or gliders. You may also need a footrest.

2. Lighting

Have both task and mood lighting in your workspace. Task lighting relieves strain on your eyes and helps with concentration, while mood lighting eases you into a more relaxed work mode when you're not staring at a screen. Smart lighting can help you separate your work and home life: your lights tell you when it's time to focus, and when it's time to take a break. It can be controlled through an app or by using voice-activated smart assistants.

Look for table, standing and hanging portable wireless lighting which is USB or solar charged – perfect for working outdoors in lower light conditions.

3. Conceal equipment

Unless office equipment is a statement piece, your printer, router, external hard drive and chargers are best concealed, as they tend to make a home office look and feel cluttered. Installing them in a cupboard or purpose-built unit with doors hides them and minimises light pollution at night when you're trying to relax – especially if your office is part of another living space. But do ensure that any unit has adequate ventilation as equipment can overheat and become a fire hazard in an enclosed space.

4. Cable management

Staring at a tangle of cables is distracting and looks untidy. There are countless cable management options including fabric sleeves and cord protector tubes; cable boxes; on-wall cord covers that adhere to the wall without screws (but make sure they're paintable to blend seamlessly with wall colour); under-desk trays for concealing power adaptors and extension bars; and cable protectors for floors (essential to avoid tripping, but they can stand out like a sore thumb). Wireless devices help reduce the number of cables in your office.

5. Charging devices

If you have several devices to charge at once, multiple-port USB stations offer a clutter-free solution. If you have a mix of wired and wirelessly charging devices, use a combination charger. It's still best to give yourself plenty of options around the house including wall chargers, single charging stations and wireless chargers.

A FINAL NOTE

Keeping your work area clutter-free reduces stress and keeps the energy of the space clear. Avoid an accumulation of mugs, plates and any items which don't pertain to your work: they aren't call-backs from the digital world – in fact, they're more likely to keep you immersed in it!

Prevent household members from putting non-work-related items (bills, receipts etc.) on your desk; have a container or drop-off box somewhere other than where you work. Try not to dump clean laundry on furniture in your office: a pile of clothes in need of folding is a distraction. Leave your desk tidy at the end of the day so you're not greeted with chaos the following morning.

Be wary of devices claiming to block the harmful effects of electromagnetic frequencies. As Jean Haner says: 'Special objects that supposedly protect you, or fix a problem come from a very superficial understanding of energy. They're based on a fear-based judgement that you have to protect yourself from something bad – but there's no good or bad energy. It's how we react to it that matters. When you clear the adverse effects of a device, it actually transforms how *your* system reacts to EMFs. You're simultaneously training your system to stay in balance, no matter what energy you encounter.'

Don't forget to pause for a few moments after you finish a task and allow yourself a sense of satisfaction that it's done before rushing on to the next. It's grounding and increases your sense of achievement and contentment.

Emma Jones of Enterprise Nation has a great piece of advice: 'Too many days at home can lead to a feeling of isolation, and small issues can appear as large ones. Working from home can lead to losing a sense of perspective. Re-connect with people, get out into the world, and re-gain perspective. Every problem has a solution – sometimes you just have to leave your home office to work out what that is!'

Research at the universities of Utah and Kansas[6] has proved that spending time in nature boosts problem-solving and creativity by 50 per cent, so leave your devices inside and head outdoors! We'll look into the therapeutic wonders of nature in depth in the next chapter.

CHAPTER SUMMARY

- To create an ideal home office, start by identifying your Work Blueprint based on your childhood experiences of school and homework, and in the working world.
- Site your home office in a space that makes you happy, feels comfortable and private. Avoid north- or east-facing rooms if you suffer from SAD.
- Regaining autonomy over the digital world is essential to well-being. Do a detox of your digital life.
- Constant attention switching between tasks reduces cognitive capacity and increases stress.
- Regain focus and the ability to think deeply by resting, relaxing, getting enough sleep and mind-wandering for at least 1 hour every day.
- Take a 24-hour digital break from all devices at least once a week.
- Be proactive, not reactive: avoid checking devices first thing in the morning. Set your intentions for the day in a stress-free manner that engages your senses and keeps you grounded.
- Get respite from the digital world with call-backs: sound; views of nature; animals; sensory-rich materials; movement.
- Create a good work–life balance: avoid overworking and being constantly available; use time-management tools; set boundaries; compartmentalise; vary your routine; dress up; follow your natural rhythm; take power naps; be energy aware.
- Forget traditional office set-ups: flexibility, adaptability and inspiration are key to a successful home office.
- Give your space a theme that inspires you.
- Turn a vision board into inspiring art.
- If you don't have a dedicated office, have flexible furniture that multitasks and is mobile. Consider a vintage gossip-bench or adjustable bed reading table; soundproof pod; acoustic upholstered seating.

- To reflect light and increase the sense of space in a small office, try a neutral colour palette; mirror; an all-glass desk.
- Have multiple worksurfaces in a large office including a standing desk or work island.
- Soundproof a shared office (please see Chapter 1, page 16)
- Create a garden office with a shed, Tiny House or ADU.
- A portable office or vintage lap/writing desk lets you work anywhere.
- A gazebo offers full nature immersion. It's the ultimate stress-buster with a portable power station; WiFi extender; privacy screen for glare; space heater; fan. Or try a balcony or covered patio.
- A home office visited by clients or patients must comply with health and safety regulations and include measures to deal with energy build-up. Use essential oils; plants and flowers; crystals; soothing music.
- Consider desk chair ergonomics to maintain the best posture.
- Have good task and mood lighting and use smart lighting to customise your lighting to energise, concentrate, read or relax.
- Conceal office equipment with fire safety in mind, and use cable management.

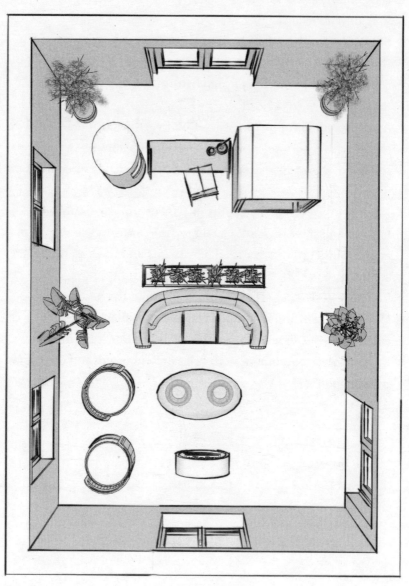

Plan 15: No office – integrating a soundproof pod into a living space

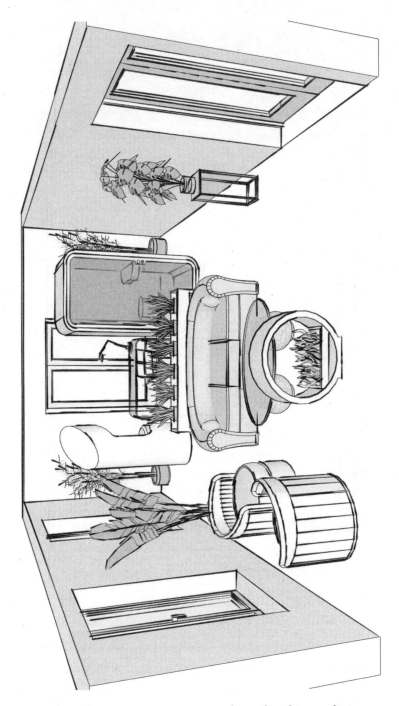

Plan 16: No office – integrating a soundproof pod into a living space

Plan 17: Large office – creating multiple working areas

Plan 18: Large office – creating multiple working areas

Plan 19: Large office – creating multiple working areas

8

OUTDOORS

'What is the use of a house if you don't have a decent planet to put it on?'
—Henry David Thoreau, *Walden*

Garden design over the centuries has always been about man's desire to tame nature and have dominion over her. The formal gardens of Louis XIV's Palace of Versailles, designed by landscape architect André Lè Nôtre, took this show of power and wealth to a whole new level and scale. Ornamental gardens were the privilege of the wealthy, and only became accessible to the masses after the Industrial Revolution. From then on, the perfectly mowed and maintained lawn became a status symbol of success.

We've resolutely stuck to this showy model, often thinking of our garden as an outdoor room maintained to the same standards as the other rooms in our home: vacuumed, dusted, neat and tidy. We worry about what our neighbours and guests think if we don't mow and weed and have flowerbeds full of pretty flowers – regardless of whether they're native species and support local wildlife essential to maintaining the web of life. Looks trump ethics – we use pesticides without thinking to kill anything that spoils this perfect picture – whether it's weeds, insects or small mammals.

THE THREAT TO HEALTH

There are two massive downsides to this approach to gardens: our physical and mental wellbeing and the health of the planet, which – as we know – is failing.

Our health

When we step into any manicured garden – whether it's Versailles, or a perfectly hardscaped or landscaped contemporary garden – we tend to experience a feeling of emptiness. We may even feel unsettled, wary and stressed. Why? Because nature and her magic are being constrained all around us. In contrast, a walk in a wood or forest lifts our spirits, reduces stress and puts us in a state of mindfulness.

Shinrin-yoku – commonly known as forest bathing – is the therapeutic Japanese practice of seeking a deeper connection with nature by spending intentional time surrounded by trees. It engages all our senses, and has extraordinary effects on health and happiness, including reduced stress; lower blood pressure; stronger immune system; improved mood and sleep; weight loss; and increased focus, energy and creativity. A 2019 study found that being exposed to natural environments improves working memory, cognitive flexibility and attentional-control tasks, while exposure to urban environments is linked to attention deficits.[1]

I highly recommend Dr Qing Li's *Forest Bathing*, which explains how to practise forest bathing in many settings (including your garden) and is full of fascinating insights, data from Dr Li's many years of research into forest medicine, and research from around the world. He found that people living in areas with fewer trees have significantly higher levels of stress and higher mortality rates than people living around good tree density. 'We are part of the natural world,' Dr Li says. 'Our rhythms are the rhythms of nature. As we walk slowly through the forest, seeing, listening, smelling, tasting and touching, we bring our rhythms into step with nature. *Shinrin-yoku* is like a bridge. By opening our senses, it bridges the gap between us and the natural world. And when we are in harmony with the natural world we can begin to heal. Our nervous system can reset itself, our bodies and minds can go back to how they ought to be.'

In the 1980s, the Japanese government endorsed *shinrin-yoku* as an antidote to 'technostress' by creating forest bathing clinics and protecting woodlands. Japanese doctors regularly prescribe forest bathing for patients suffering from stress and high blood pressure before resorting to drugs and other treatments. Forest bathing involves walking mindfully and slowly in nature, without a destination or goal, and paying close attention to your surroundings using all of your senses. Studies have found that spending at least 20 minutes per day (adding up to 2 hours per week) in nature produces the greatest noticeable improvements in wellbeing. Unfortunately, most of us spend the majority of our lives sequestered from nature: according to the US Environmental Protection Agency, the average American spends 93 per cent of their time indoors! That equates to only half a day per week spent outdoors.

Track your own time outdoors for 1 week and see if there's room for improvement: scheduling 20 minutes per day of forest bathing pays dividends, I promise! To find a forest bathing guide to help deepen your relationship with nature, and allow the natural world to promote your healing and wellbeing, visit the Association of Nature & Forest Therapy (natureandforesttherapy.earth). You can forest bathe in your own garden, especially if the land hasn't been suffocated just to look tidy.

The earth's health

Over two centuries of formal gardens filled with exotic, imported plants to beguile and impress are a legacy that we're still perpetuating today – especially in the US. While these non-native plants may look beautiful, they don't support the local insect and animal populations, and they have a tendency to become invasive, choking out native plants, which in turn jeopardises the survival of species dependent on them. The intricate web of life is a delicate balance between all species, and we're randomly unpicking it at an unprecedented pace.

Mary Reynolds is a leading expert on this issue, and a voice to heed at this crucial time. A reformed, internationally acclaimed landscape designer, and the founder of We Are the ARK (Act of Restorative Kindness), whose aim is to weave a patchwork of safe havens for nature globally in gardens, schools, public spaces and beyond, Mary believes that we are guardians *not* gardeners, and that real change has to come from each of us understanding the issues that nature is currently facing, and taking action.

'If you want to save the planet, start with your own patch of it. Don't wait for someone else to do it,' Mary says. 'If we each commit to restoring the land under our care – no matter how small, including a window box – to a native ecosystem that can become a pantry and habitat for our pollinators and wild creatures, we can restore the web of life, and the health of our planet. And in doing so, we also heal ourselves.

'There's some strange, magical shift that happens when you heal the land that you've been drawn into,' Mary says. 'We're drawn to land that has the same type of issues and damage that we have ourselves. For me, the land where I live does not trust anyone. It has major issues with abandonment and rejection. And it's very much like me. But it's slowly starting to recover as I keep maintaining my connection with it, and keep talking to it, walking it, and letting it know that I'm here, and I'm not going anywhere. And even if I go somewhere, that I'm not selling it on, and that it will be looked after. The energy has shifted and, interestingly, it's starting to shift in me as a result. The side effect of having a relationship with a piece of land is that, as you start to restore your patch of the planet and heal it, you heal yourself in the process. I don't understand why it happens, but it always does!'

In her two fascinating books, *The Garden Awakening* and *We Are the ARK*, Mary explains the importance of giving at least half of your garden or land back to nature (if not half, then as much as you can manage), and growing as much of your own organic food as possible in the other half. As you protect and guide your ARK to re-wild through nature's natural processes, it becomes a more and more complex ecosystem over time, supporting more species and diversity which are essential for the continuation of life on earth.

'It's about allowing the land to become what it wants to become,' Mary explains. 'That doesn't necessarily mean leaving it to go completely wild. You give it boundaries, like a parent. The land is like a child, because it's been ravaged back to a very immature system, and it's completely dependent on you as its guardian for guidance and direction. When you create an ARK, you're still designing your spaces – but you're asking different questions: How many habitats can I put in here? How many hedges? How many different systems? Everything has to be a habitat as well as to have a function. It's not about creating gardens for *our* visual pleasure. It's about asking: How can I be of help to all the other creatures that are *sharing* the space with me? You'll end up with a space full of all sorts of magical creatures, and you'll get excited about every dragonfly, firefly, butterfly, and whatever comes into your space because *you* were part of creating that home for them.

'An ARK is messier because it's alive, but it can still be structured and beautiful. You can create all the different layers of ecosystem maturity using design techniques within your space if you have enough land. All the life lies in the edges, so put an edge on different areas – like mowing a meandering path through a meadow. If you have symbols or shapes that have repeated themselves throughout your life, include them in the design of your ARK. There's a frequency in them, or something important which you may not understand.

'If you have the time, physical ability, and energy to grow as much of your own food as possible, you can replenish the land regeneratively by putting minerals and the microbiome back into the soil to feed the foods that you then eat. This restores your health beyond any level of organic diet – or any type of diet – because it's specific to you: when you walk barefoot on the earth, the enzymes in your skin interact with the bacteria in the soil, and a relationship begins because we came from the earth. When we're healthy, all the bacteria, fungi, parasites, and everything that's in the earth are present in our bodies. By restoring all the microbiome and soil in your land, you restore it in your own body by being out there, breathing it in, then eating it. So you're giving to the earth, and she's giving back to you.' Studies have found that bacteria that grow in healthy soil (specifically Mycobacterium vaccae, and Lactobacillus bulgaricus) can positively affect our immune systems, mental function and mood by increasing levels of serotonin and norepinephrine.

Davyd Farrell, quantum plant alchemist and co-founder of Quantum Plant Healing, says: 'One of the really interesting things I've learned about our gut flora and the microbiome in the soil is that whatever plants we need for our healing automatically grow in our immediate environment because we communicate. The intelligence in our gut communicates with the intelligence in the soil at a quantum level because we exist in the same energetic space. If you allow your grass and the weeds and plants that emerge to grow, you can go on an incredible journey of self-discovery. I can tell quite quickly what diseases a town has by the preponderance of certain plants that grow on the roundabouts.'

When you develop an ARK with as many layers of ecosystem as possible, nature comes back into balance, so you don't have to worry about your vegetables being eaten by insects and slugs because their natural predators are present in abundance.

If you live in the US, invasive plants are a major issue to contend with: the National Invasive Species Information Centre is a valuable resource, as is the Seed Savers Exchange who collect, store and regenerate the seeds of thousands of rare, heirloom and open-pollinated varieties, and sell them on their website. Do read entomologist, ecologist and conservationist, Douglas W. Tallamy's, two books: *Bringing Nature Home* and *Nature's Best Hope*.

Frequency and connection

As inventor and futurist Nikola Tesla said: 'Our entire biological system, the brain, and the earth itself work on the same frequencies.'

The Schumann Resonances (SR) are the earth's heartbeat, and its frequency is 7.83 Hz – which is also the alpha frequency in the human brain associated with relaxation, meditation and dreaming. In alpha, our cells can regenerate and our bodies heal. When we're in nature, we entrain to the earth's heartbeat, which explains why it's so healing for our bodies and minds. Conversely, when we're in cities, and indoors on our devices, we're surrounded by WiFi, radiofrequencies, electromagnetic fields and other frequencies that disrupt and cut us off from the earth's electromagnetic frequency. Professor R. Weaver of the Max Planck Institute conducted a fascinating experiment where volunteers (young, healthy students) were housed in an underground bunker that completely blocked out magnetic fields for four weeks. They began to suffer migraines and emotional distress, which were immediately alleviated when the Schumann frequency of 7.83 Hz was added back into the environment. Weaver concluded that the Schumann Resonances restore or improve health.

Extensive research has been done into the healing effects of earthing (or grounding) which is the practice of having direct skin contact with the earth by walking barefoot or sitting on the ground. This restores our electric connection with the earth, which is essential to our wellbeing. Earthing revitalises the body; reduces pain and stress; and improves health, sleep, mood and appearance. To learn more, I highly recommend reading Clinton Ober's *Earthing*, or watching the documentary *The Earthing Movie*. Unfortunately, 95 per cent of shoes have synthetic soles, which block the earth's electrons, and most people only go barefoot on the beach.

When we spend time immersed in nature, it becomes easier to feel truly connected to everything around us, and our Western dualistic view of the world recedes. As Dr Sharon Blackie points out in *The Enchanted Life*, this view is instilled in childhood when we begin to learn language: 'The English language in particular forces us to adopt a position of separation and distance from the rest of the world as soon as we begin to use it. Only humans may be properly given the pronoun "he" or "she". Everything else is an "it".'

Using the word 'it' separates us from the rest of the world – unlike indigenous cultures who have an animistic view of the world, and believe that everything is alive – including rivers, trees and rocks. As humans, we're part of this great web of life – not separate from, or above, it. People with a close affinity to their plants often refer to them as 'she' or 'he' (or maybe 'they' these days!) and treat them with respect – not as commodities to be bought, planted and then disposed of when they please. Having an animistic approach to your patch of land – and what grows and lives in and on it – pays dividends in terms of your joy and wellness.

FIRST IMPRESSIONS

Instead of starting with a visual inventory of your garden and what needs changing, try Mary Reynolds's method of first getting to know your land, however small. 'If you can just slow down and reintroduce yourself to the earth,' Mary says, 'a magical gate opens for you.' Here are her suggested steps:

1. Sit
Take off your shoes, and go and sit in the garden. Try to clear your mind by recalling a really powerful, happy memory. If you can't manage that, just appreciate your surroundings (a flower, the sky, a cloud) and feel gratitude. This brings your heart into an open space.

2. Walk
Walk around your land barefoot. As you're walking, say out loud (or in your head) that your intention is to release whatever's there, and to listen for anything else. You might feel nothing because the land may have nothing to release. Or you might feel upset, or angry, in which case just let the land know that you're sorry. Acknowledging its pain is enough for the land to release it. This is a type of listening cure that really works.

3. Wait

Do nothing for a while: slow down to 'tree time'. Nature's time is much slower than us, so we have to learn to really slow down and listen to her, and what she wants to become. Just get to know the land. If you rush to make changes, you might not know the land's characteristics: which part is really wet; where little oaks might be coming up; or where you feel most comfortable – at night as well as during the day.

Mary feels that it's very important for people to 'take back the night' and bring themselves out into the darkest part of their land – even though this can be a challenge in cities. In the dark, your senses are heightened because your sight is down and you start to sense what's around you. If you're lucky, you'll get to see the night-time creatures coming out, and this has a magic all of its own.

As you get to know your land in 'tree time', observe some of the typical elements found in our gardens today.

Trees

We live on a steady diet of fear thanks to the media, governments, institutions and the medical industry. We're always preparing for the next disaster to hit. This is particularly true when it comes to trees: we worry that a tree might fall on our home, car or our neighbour's property, so we avert catastrophe by removing it in advance. This is particularly true in the US where people cut down perfectly healthy, mature trees only because they're worried about the potential risks. A tree can be pruned: it doesn't have to be taken down!

Before you consider removing any trees, please remember their vital role in the web of life – especially given how much pollution humans are generating. Here are some of the wonderful things that trees do:

- Absorb carbon dioxide from the air and store it in their wood, shoots and roots through photosynthesis. Older trees store more than younger trees, so it's vital to preserve them.
- Filter particulate matter from fossil fuels (which is hazardous to our lungs and leads to asthma and heart disease) through their leaves. The silver birch is a master at this.
- Remove toxic chemicals from water by storing and filtering it through the water cycle/phytoremediation.
- Create shade and cool the surrounding environment, especially where there's hardscaping, which absorbs and retains heat in the summer.
- Shelter countless creatures and lifeforms. Oak trees support over 500 lifeforms when living, and thousands when decaying.
- Release phytoncides (the natural oils that protect trees from bacteria, insects and fungi) which research has shown reduce stress hormones; improve mood; lower blood pressure; increase hours of sleep; and increase anti-cancer proteins. Evergreens like cedar, pine, spruce and conifer produce the most phytoncides.
- Manage rain and surface water run-off, and minimise soil erosion, which helps to keep rivers, streams, lakes and oceans cleaner.

If you're still not convinced and want to remove trees, look into the research proving that when trees die, people die! The US Forestry Service found that when leafy neighbourhoods became treeless, mortality rates were higher. There are numerous studies – including one by the University of Exeter – proving that people are less anxious and depressed when they live around trees and green spaces. And remember that native trees and shrubs can be salvaged and relocated.

Before removing or relocating trees or shrubs, please check carefully for active nests and hives. While it's usually illegal to move native birds' nests – and can be inhumane if incorrectly done – hives can be successfully relocated.

Water

After native trees, installing a pond – no matter how small – is the second biggest support you can offer wildlife. Even a sunken bowl filled with rainwater provides a much-needed source of clean water – but avoid plastic containers at all costs. Repurpose metal cookware, but remember that their sides are steep and slippery, so add rocks or twigs as ramps to help creatures escape as they can struggle and drown. When digging a wildlife pond in your garden, make its shape curvy or sinuous to create the maximum amount of habitat. Keep the edges shallow so creatures can get in and out safely. If your pond is large, consider adding a small island in the centre as a safe place for birds to nest. Whether your pond is a bowl of water, a reclaimed cattle trough, a cast-iron boiler or a wildlife pond, add native oxygenating plants and a floating solar fountain or bubbler to keep the water oxygenated and attract birds. Wildlife Watch has detailed instructions on their website on how to build a pond, and how to repurpose various containers into mini ponds.

It's not just wildlife who benefit from a pond: we do too. As marine biologist Wallace J. Nichols explains in *Blue Mind*, proximity to water increases calm, diminishes anxiety, increases professional success and improves performance. 'Our oceans, waterways, and the life they contain are so much more than their ecological, economic and educational value. They have vast emotional benefits. They make life on earth possible, but also worth living. I like to imagine the world would be a better place if we all understood just how true that is. Water is medicine, for everyone, for life.'

Capturing rainwater in a rain barrel is easy, good for the environment and significantly reduces your water bill. Placed under a downspout, rain barrels prevent the environmental issues associated with water runoff. They're available in multiple styles and capacities – collapsible, portable rain barrels are the most cost-effective.

Ponds and birdbaths should be filled with rainwater as the chemicals used in treating tap water are not good for wildlife. Rainwater is also better for watering plants.

Plants and flowers

'We've been fed this narrative by the gardening industry to plant pollinator-friendly plants,' Mary Reynolds says, 'but it's basically to support the gardening industry – it's *not* to support nature! Depending on what part of the world you're in, you'll be given a list of plants that are good for pollinators – but if they're non-native, they're *not* good! The insects are attracted by their big showy flowers, and they get a great feed, but they *won't* pollinate the native plants. So the natives start to retract and they lose land. And then the insects have *nowhere* to lay their eggs, so they think they have nowhere to recreate a new generation of their own species. The whole system collapses because young birds and so many mammals depend on larvae and caterpillars for their main source of food.

'We need to work with the seed bank which is already in the ground and add in layers of diversity that aren't present. The 5,000 weed seeds in every square foot of soil are nature's healing mechanism, and *the* most important plants for pollinators!'

If you're accustomed to weeding and worry about the aesthetics of your garden if you allow the natural seed bank to flourish, please give it a try! I did, and it's so worth it: when allowed to grow naturally, they become beautiful over time, trees appear, and you'll be rewarded with the most amazing butterflies, dragonflies, and all manner of other fascinating life. The perfectly planted, mulched beds that felt so rigid and sterile to me when I moved in are now a flourishing haven that calms and soothes me when I'm stressed. As journalist and political activist Gloria Steinem says in *The Truth Will Set You Free, But First It Will Piss You Off!*: 'A weed is just a flower that no one loves.' For more on attracting and supporting butterflies, visit the National Wildlife Federation's 'Attracting Butterflies' page, and remember that butterflies need a place to 'puddle', where they can drink water and extract minerals from damp sand and soil.

Try to avoid the temptation to cut back and tidy up flower beds in the autumn as it's only for our benefit. Mary Reynolds suggests leaving everything until the fresh new growth appears in the spring. It may look untidy, but it's a sanctuary and pantry for countless creatures during the harsh winter months: lots of insects need the dead stems to complete their life cycle, and birds need the seed heads to survive. Also leave patches where growth falls on top of itself because this will form homes for bumblebees, shrews and all sorts of other little creatures. Ideally, work on a five-year cycle where some of it only gets cut back every five years, and the rest gets cut back in the spring.

The best fertiliser for plants, shrubs and trees comes from a compost pile, composter or wormery. There are countless models to choose from depending on your household's size and available space to house it. The Woodland Trust have a fun step-by-step guide for kids to make their own wormery, and get to know the vital role that worms play in maintaining healthy soil.

Lawns

In North America, lawns are the largest irrigated crop, and take up 16 million hectares (40 million acres). They're usually monocultures of non-native grasses. To keep them green and perfect, we mow and use pesticides, but what use do these vast, green carpets really serve? Most lawns never get used – at least not in their entirety. A good rule of thumb is to only mow where you go. It might also be worth examining why we're obsessed with mowing; Davyd Farrell suggests that mowing gives people a sense of control when so much in their lives feels out of control. It can become a bit of an obsession!

In the UK, the campaign 'No Mow May' encourages people to leave the mower in the shed for the whole month, to give pollinating insects a boost and encourage spring wildflowers to set seed and establish themselves in advance of summer. Mary recommends transforming lawns into short wild native grasses, with wild native herbs and clover. These look far more interesting than monoculture lawns, and you'll be amazed at the bees, butterflies, dragonflies etc. that come to visit. Mary also advocates the following maintenance practices to safeguard creatures:

- Never use robotic mowers as they're lethal for hedgehogs and small mammals. For exercise – or if you have help – consider a push mower or scythe. Begin mowing in the centre of the lawn and work out from there so creatures can easily escape. If you do use a power mower, leave the engine running for 1 minute to warn creatures before you start mowing.
- If using a strimmer, always check long grass before starting: strimmers cause major injuries to frogs, hedgehogs and other small mammals.

Fences

Fences and walled-in gardens isolate small wild mammals; these man-made structures cut them off from food and water sources, sanctuary and potential mates. Hedgehog territory can stretch from 4–20 hectares (10–50 acres) and they become very stressed when they can't move freely. Mary suggests – with the consent of your neighbours – creating 'hedgehog highways' by drilling one or two holes the size of a CD case in the base of each boundary fence. Better still, replace hard boundaries with living boundaries of hedges or native hedgerows that creatures can move freely through. If you're stuck with a hard boundary, bring it to life by growing a diverse range of native climbers and ivies, or create habitat by making a dry stone wall, or a dead hedge against the existing wall.

Outdoor lighting

Blue- and white-toned LED lighting causes major issues to the ecosystem, disrupting creatures' circadian rhythms, hormone levels and breeding cycles. It blinds insects and disorientates sea turtle hatchlings. Conservation biologist Jessica Deichmann's study in the Amazon rainforest found that disease-carrying insects were dispro-portionately attracted to white LED light, and that placing an amber-coloured filter over an LED bulb substantially reduced the amount and variety of insects drawn to the glow.[2]

Minimise nature's unnecessary exposure to blue- and white-toned LEDs by changing outdoor lighting to amber-toned bulbs, which will cast a soft and pleasing light. Have any outdoor lighting on a motion-sensor only. While it may look stunning to floodlight trees and your house at night, is it worth the stress that it's causing to the natural world? When you're dining outdoors, consider real candles in glass hurricane holders, or hurricane oil lamps: they give good illumination and the light levels are adjustable. Flames create a relaxing and convivial atmos-phere – unlike harsh LED lighting. If you must string fairy lights for Christmas and celebrations, make sure the bulbs are red-toned.

Help to reduce light pollution by turning off all unnecessary indoor lights and close your curtains at night to restore as much of the requi-site dark for the natural world as possible.

Green roofs

Consider bringing the cooling and soothing effects of nature to the exterior of your home and any outbuildings with a green roof planted with grasses, herbs, flowers and drought-resistant plants. Installation is more costly than traditional roofs, but grants are available as green roofs positively impact the environment – plus they last 80 years. They also provide natural insulation, keeping homes cooler in the summer and warmer in the winter, so utility bills are significantly reduced. They also give better sound absorption than hard roofing materials.

In Norway, turf roofs were the norm until the late nineteenth century, and are still very popular – The Scandinavian Green Roof Association holds an annual competition to determine the best green roof project in Scandinavia. Japanese architect Terunobu Fujimori is known for his eclectic designs embodying *shibamune*, the ancient art of fusing house and garden, with greenery planted on the roof and as an integral part of the structure itself. Fujimori's own home is covered in dandelions, and he has created fascinating tea houses with grass walls.

EXPRESS YOURSELF

As Mary Reynolds says, our job as guardians is not to tame the land under our care, but to support and guide it as it recovers; it will in turn support us. If you create an ARK, whether a window box or a large piece of land, it can be just as designed and shaped as a garden space, but the intention has to be different.

'People have for too long been looking at land as a blank palette for their own creative expressions,' Mary says. 'And that time has to stop. We have to build a new world. Gardens the way we've been designing them are a selfish imposition on nature, because we're not considering all the other creatures that we're sharing this planet with in those expressions.'

One of our primary concerns must be creating safe habitat for creatures. Planting native trees is top of the list, closely followed by adding a clean water source because so many rivers, streams and lakes are polluted.

Here are three fun habitat projects to do solo, or as a family. I've done all three and can vouch for how they lower stress levels, put you in a state of mindfulness, and bring joy – especially when you see the many wonders they attract!

1. Dead hedge

Dead hedges are stacks of branches, twigs and clippings tightly packed between two rows of wooden posts. You can also create a dead hedge against an existing wall or fence by securing wooden posts in front of it, and packing the material between the posts and wall. A dead hedge is an incredible foraging place for birds and mammals because fungi and insects love it. If you use pliable material like willow, the outer layers can be carefully woven and sculpted. This is a bit more time-consuming, but worth it if you're concerned about your hedge looking messy. There are many videos on making dead hedges, including one on the book's website.

Ask your neighbours or local landscape contractors if you can have their maintenance clippings to fill your dead hedge – or check local green waste sites. If branches are being trimmed, or a tree taken down, it's so much better to put the material into a dead hedge than a wood-chipper because dead or dying trees support thousands of species of life.

2. Bug hotel

One of the most satisfying, fun and easy projects is building a bug hotel. It can be as small and simple, or large and elaborate, as you like – although the RSPB recommend not exceeding 1 metre (3 feet 4 inches) in height. They have an excellent, step-by-step guide using old wooden pallets, terracotta pots, roofing tiles, bricks and other salvage materials. Your garden waste (dry leaves, bark, pine cones, soil etc.) provides cosy shelter within the structure for all manner of creatures, including solitary bees, bumblebees, ladybirds, woodlice, spiders, hedgehogs, frogs and toads. Depending on where you site your bug hotel, you'll attract different visitors; bees prefer warm, sunny spots, whereas frogs and toads like shady, damp conditions. A bug hotel offers creatures a safe place to shelter in the winter, lay eggs, raise their young – or just rest on a long journey, or seek refuge when you mow the lawn.

3. Mushroom farm on a wall

A wall or fence in the shade is perfect for creating a cordwood wall to grow mushrooms on. Not only are you creating habitat and food for creatures (and you!), but it can be an eye-catching work of art if you let your imagination run wild with shapes, patterns and pictures. You'll need natural wood slices in varying sizes. It's best to have a wood backing on to which you can fix the wood slices with tacks. Conventional glues are toxic, but an alternative is natural pine pitch resin glue. Next, fix the board to a wall. Depending on how thick they are, drill holes in the slices, and plug them with fungi spores. Alternatively, create several mini tableaux using round vintage baker's boards as your backing, and fix small wood slices close together. Hang the boards like art on your outside wall. (Please see the book's website for an example.)

MAKING YOUR OUTDOOR SPACE WORK

No outdoor space

'Even if you don't have any land at your home, you can still support nature and your own wellbeing in many ways,' says Mary Reynolds. 'By partaking in community allotments to grow some food, and sharing the land with wildlife. Even the smallest habitats are important. Connecting with the creatures under your guardianship will build your open heart and warrior spirit. If you know an older person with a garden they cannot care for, you could always ask them if you could grow food and build an ARK on their land, in return for sharing the produce and giving them the joy of seeing the wild creatures return there too. The company and interest you give them could change their lives, as older people are so often alone.'

WINDOW BOXES

Bring nature to your windowsill by filling a window box with organic, peat-free compost or soil mixes, and locally sourced, native weed seeds. Nettles attract Red Admiral butterflies, and milkweed is the only larval food source for the endangered Monarch butterfly in the US. If you're lucky, you may get to watch their eggs turn into caterpillars, and pupate into butterflies. Mary Reynolds likens window boxes to garages or service stations on a very long motorway for insects; if they spot one, they may lay an egg, or stop to rest and shelter, get a drink, and then move on. Having their larval food sources attracts them, but do have a clean water source which is almost impossible for creatures to find in cities.

BIRD FEEDERS AND BATHS

Bring the wonderful, magical world of birds into your life by hanging a bird feeder and bird bath outside your window. Buying from bird conservancies like the RSPB or the National Audubon Society is cheaper, supports their vital work and the materials won't have toxic glues and chemicals.

Place feeders and baths either at least 9 metres (30 feet) away from windows, or very close to them to minimise deadly collisions as any position in between can cause reflections from windows which confuses the birds. Better still, treat your windows to make them more visible with fly screens, window decals, and other suggestions from The American Bird Conservancy. Their advice applies wherever you're based in the world, and they have separate sections for individuals, companies, architects and planners.

Budget tip

A zen wind curtain – parachute cord hung outside a window and spaced 10cm (4 inches) apart – is one of the most effective, inexpensive, and least obtrusive methods of preventing bird strikes.

BUG HOTELS AND NEST BOXES

A small bug hotel, that either fixes to a wall, or hangs, provides a habitat for insects and offers shelter and an environment for nesting, which is vital during the winter months when insects need more protection from adverse weather conditions. Your guests will include solitary bees and wasps, ladybirds, butterflies and spiders. Convert an old, waterproof boot, or an enamel teapot for birds. Angle it slightly downwards so it won't take in water, and secure it firmly so it won't move around in the wind, or when the birds land. And a small wooden chest can even become a hedgehog house!

Budget tip

Get to know a little bit about different creatures and their needs, then get creative about what can be repurposed into a nest for them – just be sure there are no nasty chemicals in whatever you choose.

Balcony, patio or terrace

All of the suggestions above for windowsills apply to balconies, patios and terraces. Use walls to create vertical ARKs or living walls with native climbers as they have a cooling effect and are refreshing to look at, especially when butterflies visit.

To give your space character, consider adapting architectural salvage and vintage pieces as planters. Copper stock pots, urns, couscoussiers etc. have the necessary depth for planting and are very eye-catching; hotel cooking vessels are much larger and make quite a statement. Cast-iron boilers are often easier to find as they were a feature in most homes for family ablutions. Old metal buckets are inexpensive and have character and rusted ones won't even need drainage holes drilled! Old clay pipes and chimney pots look great as planters, and a glass display cabinet with shelves makes a perfect greenhouse. If you're hankering after a lawn on your balcony, create a mini version on top of an old coffee table: you need at least 10cm (4 inches) of compacted soil to sew native seeds in. It won't be a practical table for you, but wildlife will love it! Avoid placing planters around the balcony's edges with an empty gap in the centre. Positioning containers at angles and perpendicular to walls creates intrigue and the illusion of space, plus it's far more convivial. (For photographs of a terrace using architectural salvage, please see the book's website.)

Small garden

Many contemporary outdoor spaces – especially in cities – have a lot of hardscaping: manmade elements such as patios, paths, steps, walls etc. When hardscaping takes up a large proportion of the outdoor space, it feels austere and uninviting. Also, the materials used tend to retain heat and can feel oppressive during the hot summer months – whereas plants, trees and vegetation have a natural cooling effect. Look at ways to reduce hardscaping and give your patch of the earth a chance to breathe and regenerate. The 5,000 weed seeds that exist in every square foot of soil are nature's healing mechanism. Take up as much hardscaping as you can – especially if it's non-permeable (like concrete) because water can't get through into the ground. Put down pebbles or gravel where necessary to allow water to flow through.

Choose reclaimed or recycled materials whenever possible; architectural salvage yards are a great source for reclaimed stone and brick, and local landfills often sell usable materials. Avoid new concrete as it isn't environmentally friendly.

Add as many layers of ecosystem as you can to a small garden, remembering that trees support the most life, closely followed by water. Even if your garden is tiny, consider a water feature of some kind – even a hole dug in the ground with a bowl filled with rainwater, lots of stones and a floating solar fountain supports creatures, and makes you feel refreshed as moving water is very soothing and relaxing. If you can't plant a natural hedgerow, consider a dead hedge, rock pile or dry stone wall as they offer great habitat and can be made into interesting focal points.

Relax in bespoke rocking deckchairs handmade from sustainably sourced ash and organic cotton. All-glass tables work very well in small gardens as they're seamless but offer generous space. For a stunning contemporary dining table, team a bent glass console table with a glass top. Glass is quick and easy to clean and won't weather like so many other materials. Bent glass coffee tables and side tables also look stunning.

Large garden

A large garden is ideal for an ARK. To support as much life as possible, Mary Reynolds recommends creating as many layers of maturity as possible. These layers include:

- Woodland
- Scrub and shrubs
- Tall meadow with native wildflowers and herbs, with a meandering mown path cut through it
- Short native grass

The preferred habitat of solitary bees are bare earth or sand humps, so try to create some in warm, sunny spots. And don't forget a wildlife pond for creatures to drink, bathe or create a home.

Budget tip

The easiest and cheapest way to create an ARK in a large garden is to let nature do her thing, and then gradually shape the layers as they emerge. Granted, it can look a bit untidy for a year or two, but it's more than worth it. First, the grasses and weeds grow, but mowing paths through them makes all the difference visually. Next, the scrub and brambles appear. And, finally, trees emerge. It's like watching a child grow and develop; each stage is so different and fascinating. I did this on my land, and I can't tell you the joy of seeing trees rising up where there were just weeds before! It's very life-affirming.

It's best to have the woodland layer at the furthest point from the house, and then layer inwards in the following descending order: scrub, meadow and then short grass around the house. Avoid creating straight lines between the layers: flowing curves are easier on the eye and create far more habitat.

When you want shade or a retreat in a large garden, skip umbrellas and man-made structures in favour of willow sculpting. Willow is easily trained into eye-catching structures and offers shade on a hot day, and habitat for creatures – willows are next in line to oaks in terms of the amount of life they support. You can make a willow tunnel, dome, hide, hut, folly or serpentine wall – or anything that takes your fancy – there are plenty of videos online to guide you. The process is simple and straightforward: live willow stakes (cut sections of native willow branches) are placed directly into the soil at regular intervals and tied together into the desired shape. When the leaves come out in the spring and they start to grow, you'll have a breathtaking living structure. Make yourself a secret hideaway of willow in the darkest part of your garden to spot nocturnal creatures when they come out.

Live willow stakes are sold in inexpensive bundles – typically between 61–152cm (2–5 feet) long – and should be planted between the late autumn and the early spring. Site them at least 8 metres (26 feet) away from your house as they grow voraciously and have shallow roots that can damage foundations and pipes – especially if they're not getting enough water. Pruning your live willow sculpture provides a great source of wood every year for dead hedges, and mulch for paths.

If you have a swimming pool, consider switching to an oxygen-based water treatment. Given how much our skins absorb, chlorinated pools aren't healthy for us – and they certainly aren't good for wildlife. There are many oxygen-based water treatment systems available.

For ultimate summer relaxation in a large garden, string up some hammocks. At night, gather around a fire – but avoid the temptation to hardscape around your firepit. Keeping everything as natural as possible is like being on holiday rather than sitting in yet another man-made structure. Experiment with cooking over an open fire with *Food from the Fire* by Niklas Ekstedt and *Outside* by Gill Meller. If you're new to this lost art, find a day or weekend bushcrafting course, where you can hone wilderness living skills, nature connection and woodland crafts.

PRACTICALITIES

1. Lawn

Keep the area immediately around your house clear by mowing it. This discourages any little creatures from moving in uninvited!

2. Native trees and plants

It's essential to identify native versus invasive plants and trees on your land, and when purchasing from a local nursery. Use a combination of books, plant identification apps and regional databases to help you.

There are a number of apps that help you identify and care for your indoor and outdoor plants and trees. Take a snap of any plant or tree and the app will identify it, give its origins, advise on best care and troubleshoot any issues. I use Picture This.

3. Insect repellent

Chemical bug repellents aren't good for you or the environment. Consider alternatives using a combination of essential oils. By far the best way to repel bugs is to create a sanctuary for birds and bats in your garden: they'll keep the insect population in check, and restore balance.

If deer visit your garden and you're worried about Lyme disease, keep guinea fowl and/or chickens as they eat deer ticks which carry the disease – plus you'll get fresh eggs, and plenty of entertainment!

4. Cats and dogs

Cats are responsible for killing 500 million birds a year in the US, as well as lizards and other wild creatures. Pets who chase and hunt wildlife are an issue when you have an ARK. Try to keep them indoors, or under your control when they're out in the garden. Make sure they have collars with tags that jingle to alert wildlife of their presence, as cats in particular are very stealthful.

SONIA CHOQUETTE SUGGESTS

Try this meditation either outdoors or indoors to reconnect with the earth and the wonders of nature. Trees are sentient beings, so try becoming one for a while!

Sit comfortably with your back straight and your feet flat on the ground. Close your eyes, and allow your breathing to fall into a smooth, natural rhythm.

Imagine that the bottoms of your feet are turning into roots, travelling deep into the ground. Imagine with each breath you exhale that you're becoming a beautiful, strong tree.

As you inhale, imagine yourself deeply rooted to the earth. See and feel yourself solidly supported by the earth's loving energy. Imagine drawing this energy up through your body, starting with your feet, and travelling through your legs and trunk, flowing through your arms to your heart, and continuing up to the top of your head, and out into the limitless universe.

As you exhale, imagine all your personal anxieties and efforts draining out of your body through your roots, and flowing into the earth.

With each breath you inhale, feel the limitless support available to you. Make no effort to support yourself through your personal will. Know that you are part of the universe, and that you and your dreams are lovingly being cared for.

Relax as you deeply inhale and exhale for a few more breaths.

When you're ready, slowly open your eyes. Notice how you feel. How connected you are to all that's around you. To the web of life.

A FINAL NOTE

As Mary Reynolds says: 'The time for gardens as disconnected creative expressions has come to an end. Those gardens are mementos of the old world, and we need to build a new, simple and kind world as quickly as possible. We do not need our garden enclosures to protect us from the wilderness anymore, we need to turn right around and embrace it. The wild creatures need as much space as possible to survive, and we need them to be safe, to be well, to thrive, so that we may live.' *Our Wild Calling* by Richard Louv addresses our relationship with the wild in depth.

If you're worried about 'kerb appeal' in the early stages of restoring as much habitat and sanctuary as possible on your land, declare your intentions by putting up a sign to share what you're doing: 'This is an ARK – an Act of Restorative Kindness to the Earth', or 'Managed for wildlife'. It makes you proud, and will arouse the interest and curiosity of neighbours and passers-by, and may hopefully inspire them to create ARKs of their own. Add www.wearetheark.org to broaden people's knowledge and understanding of the important work you're doing. Having an information panel listing the species who have made your ARK their home helps people grasp the importance and necessity of a more messy native plant ecosystem. You'll be amazed at the buzz it creates – especially when people see how alive and vibrant your patch of land is by comparison to others! It starts conversations and creates meaningful connections.

If your ARK is a window box, give it a sign too. These mini ARKS are *so* important – especially in cities – as they provide sanctuary, food and resting places for insects who really need it.

Throughout this book, I've advised you to allow your own intuition to decide what's best for you but, when it comes to outdoor spaces, please allow nature to follow her intuition. She knows how to heal, so please let her do it and support her in her recovery. It's in our own best interests! And, as much as you can, go barefoot on your land: you'll get a powerful dose of the earth's healing electrons which ground and centre you, and help your body to function correctly. Aim for 20 minutes a day for maximum benefits.

One of the biggest issues for the environment is that humans tend to suffer from Shifting Baseline Syndrome (SBS): what we perceive as a healthy, natural environment today, previous generations would see as degraded; and what we consider degraded now, the next generations will see as normal. SBS increases our tolerance of environmental degradation, including wildlife population decline, increased pollution and loss of natural habitats. In 2018, Masashi Soga and Kevin Gaston investigated the causes, consequences, and implications of SBS and published their findings in a fascinating article in the journal *Frontiers in Ecology and the Environment*.[3] To help lessen the impact of SBS, they suggest environmental restoration; reducing the 'extinction of experience' (the decline of people interacting with nature) and education, as we'll explore in the next chapter. A night vision wildlife camera is a great way to pique kids' interest in nature; the motion-sensor captures nocturnal creatures visiting your garden. They're fascinating to watch and plentiful if you've created an ARK.

CHAPTER SUMMARY

- Seeing gardens as status symbols or outdoor rooms is bad for the planet's health and ours.
- For optimal mental and physical wellness, try forest bathing (20 minutes a day or 2 hours a week).
- Don't have exotic, imported plants in your garden: non-natives are often invasive, don't support local insect and animal populations, and break down the native ecosystem.
- To save the planet, start with your own patch (even a window box) and create an ARK: a native ecosystem that's a pantry and habitat for pollinators and wild creatures.
- Give as much of your land back to nature (ideally half) and use the other half to grow your own organic food which replenishes the land and restores your health.

- We're not gardeners creating gardens for our visual pleasure. We're guardians asking how we can help all the creatures sharing the space with us.
- ARKs can be structured and beautiful: you can create all the layers of ecosystem maturity using design techniques – but use flowing lines, not straight ones.
- In nature, we entrain to the Schumann Resonances – the earth's heartbeat – and our cells regenerate and bodies heal.
- Before removing native trees, consider their vital role in your health and the planet's. Before taking down any tree or shrub, check for nests and hives.
- After trees, installing a pond (no matter how small) or providing a clean water source is the second biggest support for wildlife. Proximity to blue space is also beneficial to our health.
- Use rainwater barrels to fill ponds and water plants. They also mitigate rainwater run-off issues.
- For fertiliser, have a compost pile, composter or wormery.
- Lawns are usually monocultures. Transform them into short, wild native grasses, with wild native herbs and clover to attract bees, butterflies, dragonflies etc.
- Only mow where you go! Try a push mower or scythe. Strimmers and robotic mowers can be deadly to small mammals and frogs.
- Fences isolate small mammals. Create hedgehog highways, or consider hedgerows, dead hedges and dry stone walls instead.
- Blue and white LED lighting causes major issues to the ecosystem, disrupting creatures' circadian rhythms, hormone levels and breeding cycles. Change garden lighting to red or amber tones, ideally on motion-sensor only.
- If you don't have an outdoor space, turn your windowsills into ARKs with window boxes planted with native seeds. Add bird feeders and baths, bug hotels and nest boxes.
- The above applies to balconies, patios and terraces. For interesting planters, use architectural salvage.

- In small gardens, reduce non-permeable hardscaping – especially concrete.
- In large ARKs, have the woodland layer at the furthest point, and layer inwards with scrub, meadow and short grass around the house.
- Consider oxygen-based water treatments for swimming pools.
- Be aware of Shifting Baseline Syndrome (SBS) and its potential impact.

9

CHILDREN & PETS

'No one will protect what they don't care about, and no one will care about what they have never experienced.'

—Sir David Attenborough[1]

CHILDREN

Nature sustains children in ways that indoor life just can't match. Being outdoors helps their mental and physical health and development, they learn better, and – most importantly – they're happier. Child psychologist Dr Sam Wass, who studies how stress and emotional arousal influence concentration and learning capacities during early childhood at the University of East London, has found that being outside encourages kids to play in a different way, one that makes them use their imagination and creativity more than when they're indoors on computers and watching television. The American Medical Association goes as far as to state: 'Children will be smarter, better able to get along with each other, healthier and happier when they have regular opportunities for free and unstructured play in the out-of-doors.' And according to the Norwegian government, the Nordic custom of *friluftsliv* – loosely translated to open-air life – 'offers the possibility of recreation, rejuvenation, and restoring balance among living things.' Linda Åkeson McGurk's wonderful illustrated guide, *The Open-Air Life*, shows how being out in nature combats stress, anxiety disorders and depression, and builds strong cross-generational family ties. Denmark introduced the first known forest school (*Naturbørnehavens*) in 1952, and outdoor education has spread across the world ever since. The Forest School Association has information and lists of accredited forest schools and kindergartens in the UK.

Wherever you live in the world, The National Trust's '50 things to do before you're 11¾' is a great way to inspire kids to get outside and have fun in nature, in all seasons. Activities include getting to know a tree, making mud creations and wild art, going cloud watching and helping a wild animal. Another excellent guide and resource is Richard Louv's *Vitamin N* with 500 activities for children and adults, from belly hiking, following a scent trail and building a snow fort, to making nesting bags of yarn and seed bombs, and planting a moon garden. To get you started, try a family bushcrafting course where you will learn to light a campfire (and bake bread over it), build a den or shelter and whittle wood. Or help nature to re-wild during an ecosystem restoration camp.

In his bestselling book, *Last Child in the Woods*, Richard Louv raised the alarm about nature deficit disorder and its detrimental effects on the mental and physical health of our children. Studies have shown that when children spend the majority of their time indoors, this can lead to vitamin D deficiency (essential for good bone health, metabolic and cognitive functioning) and myopia. In the US, 20 per cent of 12-year-olds suffer with short-sightedness, and in Asian metropolitan areas it's a staggering 30–50 per cent! Scientists attribute this in part to children being indoors so much, and focusing only on nearby objects, so their eyes aren't trained to see distant objects as they would outdoors.

The majority of children spend more than 7 hours a day on devices, which can lead to all sorts of issues, including obesity, irregular sleep, behavioural problems, anxiety and stress, and impaired academic performance. The American Academy of Pediatrics discourages media use by kids younger than two, and recommends limiting older children's screen time to no more than 1–2 hours a day. It states that 60 minutes of daily unstructured free play is essential to children's physical and mental health.

Limiting kids' screen time isn't the only way to disconnect them from the digital world. As we explored in Chapter 7 (page 175), callbacks are highly effective at bringing us back to the real world.

Call-backs can easily be incorporated into the design of a child's room, from adding views of nature to using sensory-rich materials and non-rhythmic sensory stimuli (NRSS).

BRINGING THE OUTDOORS IN

While tastes vary, the one universal design language that all humans can relate to in a positive way is nature and natural elements, so bringing these into the design of a child's room is soothing to them, and reminds them of the fun just waiting outdoors.

As biophilic architectural and interior designer, Oliver Heath, says: 'Creating natural reference points indoors that children can relate to elicits the positive emotional responses they've already experienced when they were out in nature. Creating a sense of an environment that's thriving and flourishing indoors is essential to wellbeing.'

Here are three options to consider:

1. Plants
Encouraging your child to grow and care for plants in their room entices their curiosity and awe of the natural world. Growing a bean plant is an easy and fun starting point for connecting with nature indoors. Window boxes, bird feeders, bird baths and bug hotels are great for drawing a child's attention and deepening their understanding of the cycles of nature right outside their window. (Please see Chapter 8, page 226.)

2. Natural colours
As Oliver Heath points out: 'Colour is a natural analogue that references nature or natural things without being the real thing. Using natural colours that complement each other and follow a similar pattern to natural scenes evokes a sense of a nature connection. Use colours in the same proportions as you might find them in nature, remembering that no colour is ever seen in isolation in a natural

setting. Aim for a harmony and contrasts.' (Please see Chapter 1, page 15.)

3. Natural textures and patterns

Haptic invitations (which we explored in Chapter 6, page 137) are very important to children, and affect their wellbeing. Like us, they can experience tactile deprivation and 'touch hunger' if their bedroom lacks texture. This is especially true of kids who are hyposensitive.

Choose natural materials like real wood, 100 per cent organic cotton, linen, bamboo and wool over man-made and synthetic materials. Not only do they look and feel better, but they don't off-gas.

As we saw in Chapter 6, seeing natural fractals (patterns in nature repeating infinitely at different scales) can reduce stress by 60 per cent, and has a restorative effect. A study in 2020 at the University of Oregon found that, by the age of three, children show a preference for visual fractal patterns commonly seen in nature.[2] Dr Richard Taylor, co-author of the study, says: 'The aesthetic experience of viewing nature's fractals holds huge potential benefits, ranging from stress-reduction to refreshing mental fatigue. Nature provides these benefits for free, but we increasingly find ourselves surrounded by urban landscapes devoid of fractals. This study shows that incorporating fractals into urban environments can begin providing benefits from a very early age.'

Budget tip

Create a natural fractal mobile for your child with a tree branch, and suspend different types of pine cones from it at varying heights.

FIRST IMPRESSIONS

Children's rooms don't have to blend in with the rest of your home, and they really shouldn't be cold, utilitarian or neutral. These types of spaces don't stimulate a child, arouse their curiosity or invite them to explore their environment. Instead, indulge their need for wonder and joy, sensory experience, and emotional comfort.

We're so used to seeing spaces from our adult height that we can forget what they feel like from a much smaller vantage point. Start by viewing your child's bedroom from their physical perspective: get down to their level and see everything as they do. Notice how vast and far away the ceiling appears to a baby or small child. How certain objects loom ominously when looked up at. Consider making the ceiling seem more accessible and intriguing to them by filling the void and turning it into another creative display surface with acoustic cubes in different sizes and colours, kinetic mobiles or your child's artwork. Hang them from a fishing line – so they appear suspended mid-air – in interesting configurations and varying heights. Or use the ceiling as a teaching zone by suspending brightly coloured, stuffed felt animals, planets, letters or numbers.

Identify areas of their room that feel cosy and safe, and are therefore ideal for sleeping, relaxing or focused activities. Are there certain areas that your child gravitates to naturally? Or others that they avoid? Make notes in your Book of Inspiration and then start to consider the following:

Comfort

Given the amount of sleep that children need (up to 17 hours for newborns; 14 for toddlers; 11 for school-age; 10 for teens) a bedroom that's comfortable, quiet and peaceful with minimal distractions supports their sleep hygiene and physical and emotional health.

Like adults, children need a dark bedroom for quality sleep. As light is the most powerful cue for circadian rhythm, use blackout blinds and curtains to block outdoor light sources, and address internal light sources like bright LEDs on electronics, and light filtering under the door (please see Chapter 6, page 155). If they need a nightlight to fall asleep, turn it off when you go to bed. A 2018 study at the University of Colorado Boulder found that exposing pre-schoolers to 1 hour of bright light before bedtime disrupts their sleep patterns and almost completely shuts down their production of melatonin (the sleep hormone), keeping it suppressed for at least 50 minutes after light's out![3]

Beyond having the right mattress for each stage of a child's development, sleeping in an area where they have a sense of refuge and prospect (please see page 80) decreases their stress levels. Being able to see the bedroom door from where they're lying is ideal. If possible, avoid putting their bed where the door is behind, or opens onto, it. Having walls on two sides usually gives kids a better sense of security. If that's impossible, place the head of the bed against a wall – preferably not under a window.

Most children do better in uncluttered environments where they don't feel overwhelmed by too many choices or activities. Creating a sense of separation between sleeping, playing and studying using clever furniture arrangement, a bookcase, or an acoustic screen to divide activity specific areas really helps – along with plenty of storage options.

Creating safe, cosy spaces encourages children to unwind and relax. Indoor tents are perfect as they offer a sense of privacy and adventure (cotton and natural canvas feel and look the nicest). Tents come in many sizes and guises, from teepees and playhouses to spaceship tents, ice cream stands and playpens with crawling tunnels and ball pits. Or let them create their own hideaway with a foldable play frame. For older children, a cotton bed canopy hung from the ceiling and teamed with a comfy chair creates a private reading nook.

Sound

Household noise can disrupt children's sleep, as well as their concentration when studying – especially if they're hypersensitive, have a strong reaction to sensory input, and startle easily at loud noises or unexpected touch. Introducing sound absorption with fun acoustic objects and wall panels (please see Chapter 1, page 17) will help – especially in a shared bedroom. A sound conditioner playing coloured noise (please see page 157), or live-streaming nature sounds attenuates other sounds, and can be calming and relaxing.

Natural light

Having as much daylight as possible is important to a child's mood and wellbeing so make sure that, when curtains and blinds are open, they don't block light by hanging over any part of the window. Lighter colours reflect light, whereas dark colours absorb it. If their room is dark, you might consider sun pipes (please see page 39).

If you can, create a window seat to give them a sense of prospect. This will also maximise their exposure to natural light and help their circadian rhythm.

Shape

With the shapes in your child's room, bear in mind that curves dispel irritability, depression and brain fatigue (please see page 48). A 2011 eye-tracking study found that five-month-old babies already show a distinct preference for contoured lines over straight ones.[4] On a practical level, furniture with curved lines creates a safer environment with no sharp edges to bump into.

Budget tip

Create wavy, circular or spiral shapes on walls by hanging pictures in these formations instead of straight lines. Or use floating shelves that become invisible behind a stack of books to create curved shapes.

Introducing biomorphic forms which resemble or suggest the forms of living organisms is restful and fun for children. Honeycomb-shaped cubbies, floating shelves and seating; pebble-shaped mirrors, pebble floor and scatter cushions (pillows); and branch-shaped coat hooks are all great ways to introduce natural shapes to their room.

Energy

Babies and young children seem to be especially sensitive to the energy of people, spaces and objects. They pick up everything in the world around them, from their caretakers' emotions to the energy of their crib.

Energy clearing expert Jean Haner suggests: 'If you notice that your baby keeps being fussy when all their physical needs have been met, and they're not responding to soothing, try moving their crib to a different part of the room. Someone might have experienced something stressful in that spot. It doesn't have to be anything terrible – a difficult phone call while standing in that spot ten years ago – but the energy can linger like invisible house dust and affect anyone who sits or sleeps there. Because it's invisible, we don't know it's happening. We vastly underestimate how much we're affected by the energy around us – whether it's the energy of people, or the energy held in a space.'

Toddlers are known for picking up the presence of ghosts or feeling uncomfortable in certain places. 'Parents often deny these out of a desire to make things better for the child,' Jean says. 'I recommend that parents respect their child's feelings around energy, listen and validate them. Don't tell them they're not feeling what they are. Just being receptive can bring relief to your child.'

KIDS EXPRESSING

It seems even pre-schoolers have very clear likes and dislikes when it comes to colours and furniture for their rooms! Including their wish list helps create an environment that feels safe and nurturing to them, plus it fosters exploration and creativity when they're directly involved in the process. If they're enthralled with a particular book, film or series, don't be tempted to go overboard, just include token elements. Kids get easily bored with themed rooms, or when they're surrounded by the same elements for too long – unless it relates to nature. Creating an Alchemy Box together (please see below) is a great way to discover their wishes and dreams which you can then bring to life in their bedroom.

SONIA CHOQUETTE SUGGESTS

Your child's dreams and desires – just like your own – arise from their most authentic self, their soul. Help them commit to their dreams by making an Alchemy Box.

Alchemy means transformation, and this magical box helps transform their energy into reality. Kids under eight take to it immediately because it's tactile, experiential and fun. It's a mysterious quest that works because of the focus required to create a collage of images, feelings, words and impressions that represent what they truly want to create in their life.

The process takes time and preparation, each act a decision to support their dreams in a kinaesthetic way. The entire activity can be accomplished by spending 10–15 minutes a day for a week. I highly recommend that you make your own Alchemy Box alongside them.

Phase 1: Gathering

Find a box with a lid or cover that you can close, like a shoebox, cookie tin or hatbox (but not a shirt box or flat gift box).

Gather scissors, découpage glue, sheets of coloured tissue or craft paper, stickers – anything to decorate your box and place inside to create a magical energy. Look out for special items that represent your dream. Once you commit to creating your box, the universe offers up all manner of ideas and unexpected materials!

Cut pictures from magazines or draw and colour in your own.

Make a collage of words to glue across your box.

Allow at least one week to collect all your materials and save them in a special place. Take your time; there's value in creating a sense of anticipation as you prepare for the work.

Phase 2: Making your Alchemy Box

This usually takes an uninterrupted 2–3 hours. Avoid all distractions: turn off the TV and your phone and listen to soothing music.

In making an Alchemy Box, you're creating a three-dimensional, symbolic representation of what your soul is working to create in your life. Notice your emotions as you work on your dream. Feel yourself empowering that dream. Let making your Alchemy Box soothe your soul, engage your creative spirit and celebrate your dreams as they move closer to manifestation.

Phase 3: Inscribe your heart's desires

Cut a sheet of beautiful paper into four pieces. On each, write what your heart desires. Then, one at a time, place each heart's desire into your box and close the lid.

Put your Alchemy Box in a prominent place where you'll see it daily. But don't open your box! Trust that – like a seed planted in the ground – things are happening and you'll soon see the proof! I'm amazed when I make an Alchemy Box how everything always manifests in my life. (For more details, please watch Sonia's two-part 'How to create an Alchemy Box' on YouTube.)

Here are three fun ideas to get you started on your child's room:

1. Camping indoors

Get them a tent bed to remind them of outdoor adventures and add a folding camp chair to create a fun campsite vibe. A stool, bookends or other furniture made from tree stumps are more intriguing and engaging to young minds than mass-produced furniture. For toddlers, add a handmade, stuffed cotton campfire set to play around.

> **Budget tip**
>
> Recreate the look and feel of a forest floor with bodhi or rubber tree skeleton leaves: real leaves harvested and processed by hand in Thailand. Sold in bags of 100 or 200, in a range of sizes and colours (including autumn and spring colours), they're inexpensive, lightweight, transparent and have a magical quality. Add a few of the world's oldest toy – the endlessly versatile stick – and some stones found on nature adventures, and kids will amuse themselves for hours.

2. On the beach

If your child loves the sea, create an indoor beach in a corner with a sandbox filled with play sand. Add a colourful bucket and spade (pail and shovel), pebbles, shells and driftwood. To enhance the experience, have a self-adhesive wall mural of a beach scene on two walls surrounding the sandbox. Suspend a sea bird mobile and add the soothing sound of waves breaking on the shore with a sound conditioner.

3. Making music

If you want to encourage your child's inner musician – and you love making things – take inspiration from Child's Play Music, the brainchild of early childhood educator Alec Duncan, who has designed his

60 musical instruments made from recycled materials to foster a love of music in kids through hands-on, self-directed play.

Go on a treasure hunt with your child – outdoors and in – testing the sounds of different things as potential instruments. Create an instant shaker with beans and rice inside a paper towel or toilet roll taped closed, or try playing an old oven rack with different utensils. It's a fun and highly immersive experience for the whole family and encourages everyone's creativity and lateral thinking – especially when it comes to making the newly created instruments look appealing.

Music therapist Brooke Sinang says: 'Music can help a child express themselves in a non-verbal way that can be less threatening than responding with words. Music therapy can address a variety of mental health goals like promoting wellness and relaxation, managing stress, alleviating pain, helping express and identify feelings, enhancing memory, and improving communication and socialisation.'[5]

If your child loves plants and trees, it's also worth reading *The Music of the Plants* by Silvia Buffagni Esperide Ananas, and potentially investing in a device that translates the electromagnetic impulse of plants into melodies. This can help us to understand the language of plants through music and kids love it!

MAKING A KID'S ROOM WORK

No room

Sometimes the nursery has to be part of the primary bedroom. To make space, some furniture may have to go, or adapt to a new use – like a chest of drawers multitasking as a changing table. To avoid having baby paraphernalia scattered around your bedroom, try to create a cosy corner away from radiators: ceiling-mounted muslin panels hung across or around the nursery area help to create visual separation. A suspended cradle with a canopy makes the baby feel snug and saves on floorspace.

When choosing the right spot, be aware that there's evidence to suggest that having the television or radio on near babies can adversely affect their language development because they can't distinguish background noise from important voices.

Nursery room

Larger rooms don't make the best nurseries: they can feel vast and empty to an adult – let alone a baby. Opt for smaller furniture – Granny's wardrobe is only fascinating when they read C.S. Lewis! Avoid placing everything against the walls and break the space up into smaller areas instead. Divide a large nursery with a two-seater sofa and small chest of drawers placed back to back in the centre: one side of the room for sleeping, changing and dressing; the other for feeding and playing. Add a fun nursery rug to each area to accentuate the separation.

Bring the ceiling down with mobiles and create stimulating focal points above the different areas. Instead of framed prints, try brightly coloured fabric wallhangings to attract their attention. Neutral, simple backdrops work well with off-white or cream walls – although the slightest hint of a warm, soft colour also works.

Opt for soft, warm-toned lighting – a dimmer switch is ideal. Central light fittings need a shade that covers the bulb's glare. Fun table lamps with cut-outs cast a magical, soothing light, and night-lights are practical for night feeds. Try to avoid LEDs – white in particular. Amber is easier on young eyes, and supports their circadian rhythm – as well as yours.

Toddler's room

Famous child educator, Dr Maria Montessori, showed how young children thrive when they have freedom of movement, independence and control over daily activities and decisions. Toddlers love when everything is at their height and within reach – without needing adult assistance. A floor bed to crawl in and out of when they want makes them happier and more independent. Hanging pictures at their eye level engages them more than having to crane their neck to see. Books facing forwards on open shelves arouse their curiosity, where book spines won't.

The Montessori Toddler by Simone Davies is a great introduction to the Montessori method. Montessori furniture is child-sized, made from natural materials, and includes tables, chairs, open toy shelves and wardrobes, bookshelves, floor beds and learning towers.

Try to include an open area for them to move freely and safely, and develop their gross motor skills with play furniture like balance boards and stepping stones. Have a bean bag for them to curl up on when they're tired. And consider a 'wonder bowl' for gathering all of their found treasures in one place.

Budget tip

Instead of a freestanding blackboard taking up floorspace, or a wall-mounted one with limited drawing space, you might paint the lower half of a wall with blackboard paint. Instead of a straight edge, finish it with a fun skyline of a mountain range, waves or treetops slightly above the child's head height. Or turn an alcove into a panoramic mini world on three sides.

Shared room

Giving each child a sense of their own space to retreat to for rest, solo play and daydreaming can be a challenge – especially in a small space. Ideally, divide the room into three distinct spaces: a separate area for each child, and a communal area blending elements of both. If space allows, try open bookcases fixed perpendicular to a wall to divide the room: they won't block light or box areas in, but create a feeling of separation and cosiness. Alternatively, consider ceiling-hung wall tidies, acoustic panels or tall plants.

For bed positions, try to avoid the dormitory look: side by side, or foot ends facing. Consider ladder beds with a snug space below, complete with work surfaces for creative time and comfy seating for reading. If space is really tight, and bunk beds are the only solution, choose something fun and original (please see Resources).

At study time, folding felt desk screens help each child concentrate. They come in bright colours and, when not in use, can hang on the wall to multitask as acoustic panels. Floor standing screens also give a sense of privacy, and help kids focus. For effective sound absorption, they need a porous, continuous core at least 40mm (1½ inches) thick.

Teenager's room

Indulge their need for self-expression and independence and let them choose their own colours, furnishings and artwork for their room – but try to dissuade them from painting walls bright red or orange as it's over-stimulating. Introduce good sound absorption (please see Chapter 1, page 16).

Having a comfortable space to study with good task lighting, and preferably a view for call-backs and to ease eye strain (please see Chapter 7, page 178) is important. Ideally, they shouldn't have their back to the door. A rise-and-fall workstation is handy for banishing reminders of study at the touch of a button.

If you have a garden, give them a sense of privacy – while having them in proximity – with a comfortable chill-out zone to relax and hang out with friends. A converted shed, Tiny House, or ADU are ideal (please see Chapter 7, page 194).

Playroom

Apart from having fun, there are six major developmental benefits children get from playtime: creativity, social skill development, cognitive development, physical development (balance, coordination etc.), communication skills and emotional development.

Kids need unstructured playtime and although this should ideally be outdoors, an indoor playroom is another option. Finished basements and insulated lofts (attics) offer maximum space, but if your home is small, don't overlook places like under the stairs, and unused cupboards (closets). Young children are drawn to them as they're cosy and fun, but replace doors with curtains or leave the spaces open as a safety precaution.

PRACTICALITIES

1. Breathing
Airing your child's room daily removes stale air and changes the energy of the space. Having an air purifier helps with seasonal allergies but doesn't address the root cause. With asthma, autoimmune diseases and scoliosis on the rise, making sure kids are actually breathing correctly is key to optimal health. James Nestor's *Breath* is an eye-opening read. For a quick introduction, watch *5 Ways To Improve Your Breathing with James Nestor* on YouTube. It will not only improve your child's health (and your own) but can save a fortune in orthodontic bills!

2. Temperature
For babies, toddlers and small children, the National Sleep Foundation recommends a room temperature of 18.3–21.1°C (65–70°F). Their crib or bed should be away from radiators, windows and direct air from fans.

3. Adult furniture
If budget is an issue, adapt adult-size furniture for young children as long as it's proportionally small enough, and painted with child-safe paint. Change handles to large, fun children's knobs. Free standing furniture must be sturdy as kids often use drawers as a ladder, and a piece can easily topple. Install good drawer runners for ease of movement and ensure the drawers can't be pulled out onto your child. Sandpaper any sharp edges.

4. Built-in furniture
Ensure that all built-in bed units and dividing bookcases are sturdy and rigidly fixed to walls.

PETS

Pets give us so much but ask for so little in return.

It's worth taking the time to see our homes from their perspective. While they're domesticated, being stuck indoors for most of the day isn't good for pets. If we spend an average of 93 per cent of our time indoors – and we're facing mental and physical health challenges as a consequence – imagine what it's like for animals! Like us, they become habituated to their environment and routines, but it doesn't mean it's good for them.

GROUNDING

We saw in the previous chapter how as humans we are negatively affected when we're disconnected from the Schumann Resonances (the earth's heartbeat) and aren't grounded (in direct contact with the earth's electrons). Being in nature is essential to our mental and physical wellbeing, and our pets are no different.

As holistic veterinarian Stephen R. Blake says: 'A very common example of an animal trying to ground himself is when they dig down into the carpeting or flooring of your home, when they're stressed or ill. They are trying to get closer to the earth. If you let them outside, they will do the same in the earth. Many times when a cat or dog is ill, you'll find them outside under a bush where they have dug a hole to rest in. My feeling is they are tapping into the energy field of the earth.'[6]

Dr Blake has seen animals who lived permanently indoors suffer health and behavioural issues that resolved when they were taken outside regularly. If you can't take your pet outside, Dr Blake advises providing a grounding surface for them with an earthing product. 'I suggest placing it in their bed, so they get maximum contact time with the earth throughout the day and night.' Or try a grounding pet bed.

SLEEP

Like us, cats and dogs need sleep in order to survive, but their sleep pattern is polyphasic. Dogs sleep for between 9–14 hours a day, usually in 45-minute stretches. Cats sleep for 12–18 hours, in periods of 50–113 minutes, 8 hours of which are in REM sleep. While we're diurnal, cats are crepuscular with one peak of activity before sunrise, and another around sunset. As they age, cats and dogs need more sleep.

Like us, their circadian rhythm is influenced by light, so dark and quiet in their sleeping zone at night is important. If your household is busy during the day with lots of visitors, make sure they get enough sleep and relaxation. Like us, dogs can suffer from REM sleep behaviour disorder, narcolepsy and obstructive sleep apnoea. A study on sleep patterns in dogs in a shelter found that, while they adapt to busy environments, dogs who sleep more during the day are more relaxed and appear happier. Lack of sleep in dogs can account for more intense reactions to stressful stimuli, irritability, mood disturbance and poor memory.

A pet's bed must be comfortable, and offer adequate support for their size and weight. Think carefully about where to site it: find cosy spots where they feel secure and can sleep undisturbed. Corner beds are a good option. If space allows, have more than one bed as pets like to have options, and be where you are. Dog teepee beds can help ease anxiety during thunderstorms or fireworks as they offer a place to hide.

NATURAL LIGHT

Scientists believe that Light Responsive Alopecia in dogs results from lack of sunlight exposure to the pineal gland in the winter. No one is sure if pets suffer from Seasonal Affective Disorder (SAD) like us, but their brain chemistry is similar to ours, so it's entirely possible. Have their bed in a sunny position in the winter (especially indoor cats), and ensure all curtains and blinds are open as pets' brain chemistry is positively affected when more light enters their pupils.

STIMULATING ENVIRONMENTS

Confining pets in cramped, gated spaces – or crating them at night or when we're out – may solve potential issues from our point of view, but pets can easily get bored and distressed.

Cats

Indoor cats are highly intelligent and need lots to keep them entertained:

- Vertical space (like cat trees, cat shelves and catwalks to climb, exercise and play) is essential to cat happiness as they feel safer and more comfortable looking down.
- Safe places to hide, like cat caves and cocoons.
- A cat perch with a window view.
- Scratching posts (ideally with horizontal, vertical and inclined positions) sited in areas where you and your feline spend most time. Cats scratch to mark territory, stretch, play, stay peaceful and calm, and keep their claws manicured.
- Food devices hidden around the home promote cats' foraging instincts.
- Rotate cat toys and have plenty of them with lots of diversity.

Dogs

With more than 100 million sensory receptor sites in the nasal cavity, dogs rely heavily on olfactory information. They use smell like a compass and can tell when humans or other animals are afraid, stressed or ill because they can smell the hormones secreted.

Allowing dogs to play, chase, chew and scavenge keeps them physically, mentally and emotionally satisfied. Unwanted behaviours usually mean that a dog is bored and attempting to enrich their experience. Keep their environment stimulating with:

- Dog puzzles. They're fun and easy to make: hide kibble under tennis balls, in a cupcake tin or conceal treats in a folded toilet roll.
- Obstacle courses. These don't need to be elaborate: a blanket over a line of chairs gets them going.
- Hide treats around the home for them to scavenge.
- Make meal times fun with kibble dispensing balls or puzzles.
- Interactive dog board games are excellent for stimulating dogs' brains – especially seniors. Studies have found that dogs who have a daily mental challenge to look forward to have less cognitive dysfunction and memory loss.

It's important not to leave dogs alone for long stretches of time, and to stick to a fixed routine. They can get stressed and misbehave when their day is unpredictable and they're unsure when to expect their next walk or meal. Another animal can provide company and ease loneliness. Proper exercise is essential to dogs' health and minimises behavioural problems, but vary your route so they have different smells and things to discover each time. Playing with them indoors and out is fun for you both and relieves your stress as much as theirs.

FOOD AND WATER

Dogs and cats are creatures of habit, and like their meals at regular times in the same place – although foraging for food keeps things fun for them. Make sure their bowls aren't in the middle of a thorough-fare as this can create anxiety.

Try to use filtered water: chlorine and chemicals in tap water aren't good for animals. Have more than one water source around your home. For dogs, have one bowl by their food and one by their preferred night-time bed so they can drink easily at night and have sufficient water if you're out and they accidentally knock their bowl over. Don't have water by a cat's food, but offer several sources around your home – including a drinking fountain.

ENERGY

Energy authority Jean Haner says: 'People underestimate how affected pets are by everyone's energy. If someone is going through a stressful time, pets – like children – can act out, so watch for the signs. When I do space clearings where someone in the home is ill, I often find that the pet has either the same or a highly similar illness. The pet is trying to transmute the illness for their human.'

To help prevent this, Jean suggests: 'Anytime you have a feeling, you have three choices:

1. Resist and suppress it – which only makes it intensify.
2. Get lost in it and have a big upset while your dog cowers in a corner.
3. Allow it and recognise that it's just a feeling. It will pass if you neither push it down, nor dive in and wallow, but instead respect and allow the feeling.

This is healthier for you and all around you – especially pets.'

EASING STRESS

Animals' senses are much sharper than ours – especially smell and sound. Be wary of strong odours (artificial air fresheners, disinfectant etc.), and make changes based on their reactions. Thunderstorms, fireworks and loud sounds can frighten them, and they're particularly attuned to human stress and conflict.

Moving is distressing to animals, and they need lots of attention and reassurance – which can be hard if you're already stressed yourself! Even rearranging the furniture can upset them, especially if whole sections of the home are in chaos. Try to keep pets segregated in an undisturbed room for the duration. Pay close attention to their body language as it's their way of communicating their distress. To help alleviate it, try:

1. An anxiety jacket should help most dogs feel more secure and calm. It's ideal for stress-related barking, loud noises, being left at home alone, travelling, vet visits and training sessions.
2. If your vet okays it, try Bach Rescue Remedy, a tincture of natural flower essences to calm and reassure.
3. Dog-appeasing pheromones can be sprayed onto a bandana and tied around the pet's neck and are widely used by veterinary practices to calm anxious puppies and dogs.

SENIOR YEARS

As they age, pets are much like people. As their mobility decreases, so does their confidence and independence, and they'll rely more heavily on you. As their sight, hearing and joints become impaired or fail, it's essential to adapt your home to their needs.

Hard flooring is a problem as they tend to slip and fall easily on surfaces that have no grip. Runners and large area rugs are a great solution, but keep them firmly in place with a non-slip rug gripper.

Carpet your stairs or have a stair runner that's carefully secured so they can't trip. Carrying them up and down stairs eases strain on their joints, and putting up a barrier at night prevents any potential tumbles in the dark.

If their eyesight is failing, make sure there's adequate light for them to move around at night without bumping into things.

An orthopaedic bed with plenty of support for ageing joints is essential as they spend a lot of time sleeping in their twilight years. In the winter, a heated bed can ease joint pain, but ensure they don't get too hot.

Raised feeding and drinking bowls are easier for seniors to reach comfortably.

Bladder issues and incontinence can be dealt with by training your senior to use artificial dog grass indoors whenever you're not available to let them out.

Affection, reassurance and proximity to you help older pets navigate life changes and maintain quality of life. Mental stimulation and treats are vital, especially if dogs can't go for long walks anymore.

OTHER CREATURES

Stress is a major issue for creatures forced to live out of their natural habitat. Please look at their living environment carefully, and ensure they have what they need to feel safe and appropriately stimulated.

To live comfortably, goldfish need at least 76 litres (20 gallons) of water at 20–25.5°C (68–78°F), with neither too much light nor noise near their tank. They also need places to hide.

Rabbits get very stressed if their cage is too small, doesn't offer somewhere to hide, and isn't in a quiet location away from cats and dogs. Rabbits need at least 1 hour of exercise a day (preferably outdoors) to stay healthy. They do best with the companionship of another rabbit, or lots of time with their humans – but without too much handling, as being picked up and held is perceived as a threat.

Domestic birds are very sensitive, and need a stable, safe

environment. Any change signals danger to them, including loud noises, change of routine or cage position, furniture rearrangement, moving house, change of guardian, and presence of cats and other predators. Caged birds need stimulation or they get easily bored, so make sure they have activities and toys, time with you, and time out of their cage. Having a mate, multi-level perches, visual barriers to hide from threats, nesting areas and birdbaths all improve their quality of life.

A FINAL NOTE

Reading aloud to a pet can help young children develop greater self-confidence – often the critical element in overcoming reading and learning difficulties. Dogs and cats empower young learners to enjoy reading out loud – sometimes for the first time – because they're non-judgemental. It's worth watching 'Therapy Dog Helps Kids Read And He Can Read Too!' on YouTube, and looking into therapy dog programmes that teach dogs to help kids read. Or consider Book Buddies, where children can go in to shelters and read to cats waiting to be adopted. It's a win-win where kids practise reading and felines are soothed by all the affection and attention.

CHAPTER SUMMARY

CHILDREN

- Being outdoors helps kids' mental and physical health and development. They learn better and are happier. They play in a different way and use their imagination and creativity more than when indoors with computers and TV.
- Try the Nordic custom of *friluftsliv* (open-air life) for stress, anxiety disorders, depression and building family ties. And look into forest kindergartens and schools.

- Too much time indoors leads to mental and physical health issues and nature-deficit disorder.
- Help kids' wellbeing by bringing the outdoors in with plants, natural colours, textures and patterns.
- View your child's room from their physical perspective.
- To avoid circadian rhythm disruption, keep their bedroom dark at night.
- Having a sense of refuge and prospect eases kids' stress.
- Uncluttered environments with separation between sleeping, playing and studying is ideal.
- Sound attenuation and natural light are important.
- Kids favour curved shapes over straight lines. Introduce biomorphic forms reminiscent of nature.
- Creating an Alchemy Box helps kids express dreams and desires which can be brought to life in their room.
- If the nursery is part of your bedroom, consider a separate screened area with a suspended cradle. TV sound can adversely affect language development.
- Divide a large nursery to create separate activity areas and make it cosy. Keep furniture small and have warm-toned lighting.
- Montessori furniture gives toddlers freedom of movement, independence and control over daily activities and decisions.
- Divide shared rooms into three distinct areas (one for each child, one communal) with open bookcases, acoustic panels, plants. Consider ladder beds and acoustic desk screens.
- Give teenagers good task lighting, sound absorption and views of nature for call-backs. Offer privacy while still in proximity with a chill-out zone in the garden.
- Insulated lofts and basements make ideal playrooms. Young kids love playing under the stairs and in underused cupboards.
- To ensure correct breathing and minimise orthodontic issues, read James Nestor's *Breath*.

PETS

- See your home from your pet's perspective. Being stuck indoors isn't natural for them!
- Grounding outdoors is best for pets, or try a grounding product or bed.
- Pets' circadian rhythm is influenced by light: night-time sleeping areas should be dark and quiet. Position beds in cosy spots where they feel safe and can relax. Teepee beds offer dogs a hiding place.
- Cats need vertical space, a cat cave, window perch, scratching posts near you, food devices and varied toys.
- Dogs need dog puzzles, obstacle courses, hidden treats, food-dispensing balls and interactive board games.
- Try to give pets filtered water.
- Pets are very sensitive to our energy and can become stressed. Pay close attention to their body language.
- Stressors include unpredictable routines, moving (even furniture), fireworks and thunderstorms.
- In senior years, cover hard flooring with rugs and stair runners. Have sufficient night-time light, orthopaedic beds, raised feeding bowls and artificial dog grass, and provide lots of affection and mental stimulation.
- Ensure other creatures have what they need to feel safe and appropriately stimulated.

FINAL THOUGHTS

If you're living in a property or country that doesn't feel like home to you, Jean Haner suggests thinking about other ways to create a sense of home until you can move. 'In Chinese Medicine, the theme of home expands out beyond the dwelling itself and centres around a sense of connection to friends who feel like family. Enjoy a meal together, help a neighbour or get involved in your community on a larger scale.'

Jean's advice dovetails with that of spiritual teacher and psychologist, Ram Dass: 'Each time we drop our masks and meet heart-to-heart, reassuring one another simply by the quality of our presence, we experience a profound bond, which we intuitively understand as nourishing everyone. Each time we quiet our mind, our listening becomes sharper and clearer, deep and perceptive. We realise that we know more than we thought we knew and can reach out and hear, as if from inside the heart of someone's pain. Each time we are able to remain open to suffering, despite our fear and defensiveness, we sense a love in us, which becomes increasingly unconditional.'[1]

Research has discovered that humans have a basic need for awe hardwired into our brains and bodies. Dacher Keltner, psychology professor at UC Berkeley who researches the biological and evolutionary origins of human emotion, has found that what brings us a sense of worth and belonging, and strengthens the people and natural environments around us, is to find awe. In his book *Awe*, he says that finding awe is easy for humans, and only takes 2 minutes per day to yield meaningful results: 'All of us, no matter what our background, can find our own meaningful path to awe,' he writes. 'Because brief moments of awe are as good for your mind and body as anything you might do.' If you ever struggle to find awe in daily life, look to nature: a butterfly alighting at your window box, fireflies lighting up the dark like mini fireworks, a squirrel's gymnastic leaps from one tree branch to another.

On your journey to creating your healing home and garden, I hope you find awe!

RESOURCES

RESOURCES BY CHAPTER

All products are listed in the order in which they appear in the book.

Additional international resources can be downloaded on the book's website (www.thehealinghomeandgarden.com). If you're a DIY enthusiast, there are also PDF guides to the projects mentioned.

CHAPTER 1: GETTING STARTED

Notebooks for your Book of Inspiration
Anya Sushko (www.anyasushko.com)
Refillable, handmade leather-bound notepads, available in 17 colours and can be personalised. The hardback refill notepads are stylish enough to use without the leather covers and come in 10 colours.

Space clearing
Jean Haner (www.jeanhaner.com)

Personal energy cleaning
Bruce Peters (www.clearliving.me)

CHAPTER 2: ENTERING

Smart lighting
Philips Hue smart lighting (www.philips-hue.com/en-us)
Comes in light strips, bulbs and recessed lights, all automated and controlled from your devices.

Indoor observation beehives
BEEcosystem (www.beecosystem.eu)
Indoor modular beehives that keep you and your bees safe.

Architectural salvage
Salvo (www.salvoweb.com)
For vintage cinema or theatre seating.

Felt pebble rug
Fluss Design (www.flussdesign.com)
Soft underfoot and hand-made in Austria from machine washable wool.

Whiteboard/blackboard paint
ScribbleWall (www.scribblewall.co.uk)
Whiteboard paint and wallpaper; magnetic paint and wallpaper; glow
paint; and blackboard paint in seven colours.

Sketchbooks for Mindfulness Book
Baileys (www.baileyshome.com)
An excellent selection of hand-made sketchbooks with pages made from
linen or recycled cotton rags – the indigo pages are eye-catching.

Macrosuede
Warwick Fabric (www.warwick.com.au)
A cost-effective but hard-wearing faux suede available in a variety of
colours.

Non-toxic, environmentally friendly paints
Ecos Paints (www.ecospaints.net)

Starlight ceiling lighting
Stellar Lighting (www.stellarlighting.co.uk/star-ceilings)

Robot vacuums and mops
• Neato Robotics (www.neatorobotics.com)
• iRobot (www.irobot.com)

CHAPTER 3: LIVING

Concealing TVs
Future Automation (www.futureautomation.co.uk)
TV-lift cabinets, motorised moving panels and an extensive range of auto-
mated ceiling, floor and wall retractable mountings.

Wireless speakers and home sound systems
Sonos (www.sonos.com)
Play music, podcasts and other audio entertainment (including any radio station worldwide) throughout your home, or in specific rooms. Controlled by your voice with voice-enabled speakers, or through any smart device.

Ball castors for sofas and furniture
Ross Castors (www.rosscastors.co.uk)
Offer an extensive range from antique to contemporary styles, in designer and budget ranges.

Bean bag chairs
Bean Bag Bazaar (www.beanbagbazaar.co.uk)
Available in a wide range of styles, colours and fabrics including leather, velvet and fleece.

Sofas with curved lines
• Soho Home (www.sohohome.com)
Emet, Cartmel, Clovelly and Luciana are all good options.
• Fatboy (www.fatboy.com)
Sofas that look more like inviting, very plump floor cushions. Made from recycled foam with washable and interchangeable covers.

Poofs and footstools
Noo.ma (www.noo.ma)
Sustainably made in many different sizes, heights and colours. The eye-catching Ü Pouf has a U-shape that multitasks as seating, footstool and rocker. It's also sold in bundles so you can create your own geometric pattern.

Cushions (pillows) in unusual shapes and styles
• EverydayProductArt (www.etsy.com)
Handmade cushions shaped like knots, waves, donuts, cashews, clouds, balls, flowers, cacti.
• Rock Cushion (www.rockcushion.com)
Cushions that look like real stones and pebbles and can double as seating.

All-glass coffee table
Glass Tops Direct (www.glasstopsdirect.com)
The Cocktail Table consists of a tempered glass top in multiple shapes and sizes, and two bent glass bases that can be configured into multiple shapes.

Indoor fire tables and burners
• Firepit (www.firepit.co.uk)

For a good range of fire tables which double as coffee tables.
• Bio Fires (www.biofires.com)
Their retro-inspired White Globe Fireplace is an 80cm (32 inch) high sculptural sphere, perfect for gathering around.

Wood smoke incense sticks
HazelFern Scents (www.etsy.com)

Portable dance floors
Dot2Dance (www.amazon.com)
Round and portable, Dot2Dance is made from Marley, comes in four sizes – from 41cm (16 inches) to 122cm (48 inches) – and can be placed on any floor surface without damaging it.

African furniture
Phases Africa (www.phasesafrica.com)
Excellent selection, including woollen poufs, a stylish wooden slatted bench, contemporary chaise and pebble side tables polished to resemble tree stumps that rhinos have rubbed themselves against!

Moveable acoustic partitions
• Blokaloks (www.blokaloks.com)
Modular wall system of stackable blocks that you can build to any width, height or shape within minutes. It's easy to disassemble and reconfigure in a different position, making it ideal for seasonal changes.
• Molo (www.molodesign.com)
Their freestanding Textile Softwall is made from sustainably sourced paper and can be shaped into any configuration. It absorbs sound and is available in a variety of colours, including white. When not in use, it folds away to the width of a book. Molo also make flexible LED ribbons to transform the textile Softwall into luminous space partitions at night. Their Benchwall offers high-backed seating integrated into the partition itself.
• Späh (www.spaeh-da.com/en/)
Acoustic panels made from recycled PET bottles.

Ceiling-hung tracks for curtains and panels
Silent Gliss (www.silentgliss.co.uk)
The Panel Glide System offers discreet curved or straight tracks, hand or rod drawn, corded or electric.

Smart glass wall partitioning
Gauzy (www.gauzy.com)
Switchable smart glass which changes from transparent to varying degrees of opaque on demand.

Window garden mirrors
Gardenesque (www.gardenesque.com)
Available in a variety of shapes, styles and sizes, in wood and metal.

3D stretch ceilings
Easy Ceiling (www.easyceiling.co.uk)
Translucent ceilings and light panels that are cost-effective and recyclable.
They come in different shapes, textures and colours, or can be printed to
look like a sky – or any other effect you choose.

Luminous wireless furniture
Slide Designs (www.slide.it)
Excellent range of luminous pieces including the Cubo stool which can
multitask as seating, side table and lighting. Its variation of three bright-
nesses and 15 colour settings are quick to adjust with the remote control.

Majlis floor sofas
LorientalaHD (www.etsy.com)
A hand-made range of stylish, customisable floor sofas at very reasonable
prices. Available as single sofas or sets in various shape configurations. The
covers are removable and washable, and come in shades of white or various
colours of velvet and linen.

Upholstered walls and ceilings
Fabritrak (www.fabritrak.co.uk)
The system is ideal for irregular shapes and uneven or curved surfaces. The
range includes everything from contemporary to traditional styles.

Forest floor rugs
Alexandra Kehayoglou (www.alexandrakehayoglou.com)
Made from carpet scraps to look like a forest floor.

CHAPTER 4: RELAXING & WELLNESS

Soundproof pods
Furnify (www.furnify.co.uk)
Available in a wide range of colours, styles and sizes.

Wireless, portable lights
Philips Hue (www.philips-hue.com)
Hue Go is dimmable, colour-changing and provides a diffused lighting
effect.

Wireless portable speaker
Sonos (www.sonos.com)
Roam SL has a 10-hour battery life and excellent sound.

Labyrinth rugs
Portable Labyrinth (www.etsy.com)
Their 5-circuit cloth circle in the style of Chartres Cathedral's Labyrinth is
ideal for walking meditations. Rugs come in multiple sizes, designs and
colours, and are machine-washable.

Acoustic privacy chairs
Furnify (www.furnify.co.uk)
Comfortable upholstered seating with high backs and sides to attenuate
noise, especially the Cega High Back Chair (tubular cocoon on a swivel
base) and Mango Privacy Chair.

Moveable acoustic partitions
(Please see Chapter 3 Resources)

CHAPTER 5: COOKING & DINING

COOKING

Donating your old kitchen
• Habitat for Humanity ReStore (www.habitat.org)
• Buy Nothing (www.buynothingproject.org)

Floating, wave-patterned wood shelves
Ewartwoods (www.etsy.com)

Environmentally friendly splashbacks and worktops
• Smile Plastics (www.smile-plastics.com)
Their panels are hand-made in Wales from 100 per cent recycled and recyclable waste plastic, have no VOC off-gassing, are waterproof, mould-
resistant, and easy to work with and maintain.
• Foresso (www.foresso.co.uk)
Their worktops (countertops), tables and furniture are all zero-waste products and look stunning. There are two ranges: Timber Terrazzo made of
waste wood from trees felled in Britain, and No-Chip made from Foresso's
sanding dust.

Mirror splashbacks
Mirrorworld (www.mirrorworld.co.uk)

Splashbacks with a curved shape
• Designer Tile Company (www.designertile.com.au)
For round mosaic tiles, like Penny Round Bianco Carrara.
• Fireclay Tile (www.fireclaytile.com)
For sustainable, zero-waste, made-to-order tiles in non-traditional shapes, like Wave or Picket-Braid.

Plug-in under cabinet lights
Lights.co.uk (www.lights.co.uk)

Environmentally friendly finishing products for wood, terracotta and stone
Osmo (www.osmocolorusa.com)

Tiles that look like real wood and stone
• Flaviker (www.flavikerpisa.it)
Their Dakota tiles even have realistic wormwood holes, stains and scratches.
• Ariana (www.desvresariana.com/it)
Elegant parquet flooring style tiles.
• Mogu (www.mogu.bio)
100 per cent plastic-free floor tiles that resemble natural stone, made from corn crops, rice straw, coffee grounds, discarded seaweed and clam shells.

Traditional-style wooden sieves
Baileys (www.baileyhome.com)

Hydroponic living walls and towers
• AeroGarden (www.aerogarden.com)
Grow up to nine different herbs and vegetables in their Bounty Basic.
• Lettuce Grow (www.lettucegrow.com)
Their Farmstand comes in five sizes, ranging from growing between 12–36 vegetables, fruits and leafy greens at once. Glow Rings (LED indoor grow lamps) integrate seamlessly with the Farmstand.
• Modern Sprout (www.modernsprout.com)
Their stylish and cost-effective Smart Growhouse sits on the worktop and is made from brass.

Kitchen waste disposal and composter
Cavdle (www.cavdlelife.com)
WasteCycler is odourless and breaks down degradable plastics, paper products, fruit peels, vegetable leaves, meat scraps, fish bones, fallen leaves, twigs, coffee grounds, eggshells, pasta and rice, turning them into fertiliser for your indoor plants or garden.

Blackboard paint
(Please see Chapter 2 Resources)

Freestanding kitchen
FRAMA (www.framacph.com)
The Studio Collection of custom, metal-framed pieces is available in painted and timber finishes that don't need to be wall- or floor-mounted. The only downside is they still have a more uniform, utilitarian look.

Tea towels and mugs
Arthouse Unlimited (www.arthouseunlimited.org)
Brightly coloured and fun, their products are made by artists living with complex neuro-diverse and physical support needs.

Ceiling-hung tracks for curtains and panels
(Please see Chapter 3 Resources)

Coloured glass splashbacks
Optidek (www.optidek.com)

Quiet extractors and appliances
Quiet Mark (www.quietmark.com)

DINING

Upholstered dining chairs
World Market (www.worldmarket.com)
Elena dining armchairs upholstered in cream linen are stylish, comfortable, lightweight and on ball castors.

Living dining tables
Forge (www.forgecreative.co)
The handmade Forage dining table seats four, has a solid ash top, silver birch branch legs (with bark!) and a central sunken container for growing herbs.

Industrial drafting tables
ZinHome (www.zinhome)
Available in a good range of sizes, shapes and styles.

Reclaimed church pews
Antique Church Furnishings (www.churchantiques.com)
An impressive range of antique church pews. They also makes bespoke (custom) pews, and L-shaped and corner pews from reclaimed timber.

Folding bistro sets
Fermob (www.fermob.com)
French nineteenth century style tables and chairs in wood and metal.

Indoor fire tables and burner
(Please see Chapter 3 Resources)

Tablecloths
Ecualama (www.ecualama.com)
Colourful, organic, fair trade tablecloths handmade by Ecuadorian artisans.

Hurricane lamps
Baileys (www.baileyshome.com)

Stoneware
Camphill Village Trust (camphillvillagetrust.org.uk)
Handmade by adults with learning difficulties.

All-glass tables
(Please see Chapter 3 Resources)

Frosted/opaque window films
The Window Film Company (www.windowfilm.co.uk)

Living walls and towers
(Please see Cooking Resources above)

CHAPTER 6: BATHING & SLEEPING

BATHING

Glass tiles
Oasis Tile (oasistile.com)
An excellent selection that look exactly like pebbles. I like their Riverbed Pebbly Shore White Pebble.

Clay plasters
Tierrafino (www.tierrafino.com)
Available in a variety of wonderful textures and colours. They're non-toxic, have zero emissions, are heat- and moisture-regulating, anti-fungal and environmentally friendly.

Eco 'concrete'
Senso (www.sensofloors.co.uk)
Plant-derived resin floor and wall coverings to give you the concrete look
without the environmental impact.

Sustainable flooring including bamboo
Woodpecker Flooring (www.woodpeckerflooring.co.uk)
This family-run business is also planting a forest of 50,000 oak saplings
over 200 acres in south Wales.

Living wall system
Florafelt (www.florafelt.com)
Pocket panel system made from recycled plastic water bottles.

Living moss bath mat
Art of Gaia (www.etsy.com)

Wood and bamboo accessories
Bali Mystique (www.balimystique.com.au)
Ladder towel rails and mirrors in a wide choice of styles, sizes and finishes
all handmade in Bali. The Fruitwood River mirror is eye-catching and
original.

Japanese bath products, accessories and oil diffusers
Amayori (www.amayori.com)
Inspired by Japan's bathing traditions, using ingredients that include
Japanese essential oils, green teas, herbs, botanicals, sea vegetables, salts
and minerals.

Fair trade soaps
• Niugini Organic (www.niuginiorganics.com)
Made with organic virgin coconut oil by a community of independent
farmers wild harvesting in Papua New Guinea.
• Baileys (www.baileyshome.com)
Handmade soaps that look like pebbles.

Plant wax candles
Arthouse Unlimited (www.arthouseunlimited.org)
Handmade by a collective of artists living with complex neuro-diverse and
physical support needs. They also make triple-milled, paraben-free soaps.

Wireless bathroom speakers
Sonos (www.sonos.com)

Donating bathroom fittings
(Please see Chapter 5, Cooking Resources)

Tile recycling
Crossville (www.crossvilleinc.com)
This family-run business recycles not only tiles, but porcelain toilets and
other cast-off products.

Sun pipes
Solatube Daylighting Systems (www.solatubescotland.co.uk)

Ceiling-hung tracks for curtains and panels
(Please see Chapter 3 Resources)

Moroccan kessa gloves and black soap
Little Moroccan Things (www.littlemoroccanthings.com)

Hammam installation
Effe (www.effe.it)
Steam generator, insulation kit, door and range of accessories, including
benches, seats, water springs, colour therapy and sound system.

Tadelakt hammam finish
Tierrafino (www.tierrafino.com)
Environmentally friendly, extremely hard wearing, water resistant, heat and
moisture regulating and anti-fungal. Pigments from a range of six colours
get mixed into the plaster.

Traditional peshtemals (foutas)
The Turkish Towel Company (www.turkishtowelcompany.com)

Acoustic moveable partitions
(Please see Chapter 3 Resources)

Ofuro Japanese soaking tubs
• Zen Bathworks (www.zenbathworks.com)
Make two models in several sizes, and also do bespoke (custom).
• Aquatica (www.aquatica.eu)
Have a stylish range of ofuros with built-in seat. Their True Ofuro Mini is
compact and ideal for smaller spaces.

Portable, inflatable bathtub
Tubble (www.tubble.com)
Rectangular tubs in three colours and two sizes that can be set up in one

minute with their electric air pump and auto-inflator. They also sell accessories and repair kits. Their packaging is sustainable and shipping carbon-neutral. They partner with Justdiggit, and used Tubbles are upcycled.

Quality tung oil for sealing wood floors and cabinetry
• Waterlox (www.waterlox.com)
• Rubio Monocoat (www.rubiomonocoatusa.com)

Underfloor heating
The Floor Warming Company (www.floorwarmingcompany.co.uk)
Offers a lifetime guarantee.

SLEEPING

Light filtering and blocking stickers
Light Dims (www.lightdims.com)
Six types of stickers in a variety of shapes, sizes and colours to conceal LEDs on electronics.

Wake-up lights
• Philips Hue smart lighting (www.philips-hue.com/en-us)
• Loftie (www.byloftie.com)
• Casper (www.casper.com)
Glow Light is minimalist, stylish and portable: if you get up in the night and need light, shake Glow and take it with you.

Upholstered walls
(Please see Chapter 3 Resources)

Donating unwanted mattresses
In the UK
• Collect Your Old Bed (www.collectyouroldbed.com)
• The Mattress Recycling People (www.themattressrecyclingpeople.co.uk)
In the US
Donation Town (www. donationtown.org)
In Australia
Mattress Recycle (www.mattressrecycle.com.au)

Eco, organic, non-toxic mattresses and bedlinen
• Avocado (www.avocadogreenmattress.com)
• Birch (www.birchliving.com)
They donate one percent of all sales to The National Forest Foundation to support reforestation.

• Koala (www.koala.com)
Australia's highest rated mattress. Koala also donate to protect threatened and endangered wildlife with each purchase.

Mulberry silk bedlinen and eye masks
Lilysilk (www.lilysilk.com)
Partnered with TerraCycle's no-waste recycling programme.

Contemporary four-poster beds
Noo.ma (www.noo.ma)
Their Eton bed is minimalist and sleek.

Ceiling-hung tracks for curtains and panels
(Please see Chapter 3 Resources)

Frosted/opaque window films
(Please see Chapter 5 Cooking Resources)

CHAPTER 7: WORKING

Living desks
Blooming Table (www.bloomingtables.com)
Come in white or black with a waterproof, trough-shaped base for planting herbs, succulents etc. and a removable, flat glass panel on top for easy watering and pruning.

Indoor modular beehives
(Please see Chapter 2 Resources)

Desk bikes
FlexiSpot (www.flexispot.com/desks/desk-bike)
Desk Bike V9 has eight resistance settings, an adjustable desktop surface and seat height, and is available in white, making it less prominent.

Armchairs
Fatboy (www.fatboy.com)
BonBaron resembles a structured beanbag.

Forest floor rugs
(Please see Chapter 3 Resources)

Aviator desks and industrial drafting tables
Zinhome (www.zinhome.com)

Vision board wall art
Pictorem (www.pictorem.com)
Produce art-quality prints on canvas, acrylic, brushed metal and wood, with a good selection of varnishes including Knife Varnish (oil painting finish) and Epoxy (high gloss). They also make multi-panels and self-adhesive wall murals.

Contemporary-style, comfortable swivel chairs
Soho Home (www.sohohome.com)
To divide a room, try Garrett Armchair or Rolland Chair.

Soundproof pods and acoustic furniture
(Please see Chapter 4 Resources)

Sound-absorbing panels, hanging room dividers and table screens
Wobedo Designs (www.eng.wobedo.com)

Saddle leather desk
Zanotta (www.zanotta.it)
Tucano is stylish, contemporary, absorbs sound and feels luxurious to work on.

ADU (Accessory Dwelling Unit)
Azure (azureprintedhomes.com)
They 3D print their ADUs in one day using recycled materials. They also offer an 11 sq/m (120 sq/ft) Backyard Studio which is light-filled, stylish, sustainable and worth the investment.

Mobile office laptop bags
Rovingwork (www.rovingwork.com.au)
Cleverly designed case which opens up into a mini office space that helps you avoid poor posture and ensures eye-level video conferencing.

Advice on correct working posture
Bennett Workplace (www.bennett-workplace.co.uk/ergonomics/chair-set-up.php)

Portable wireless lighting
Made in Design (www.madeindesign.co.uk)

CHAPTER 8: OUTDOORS

To find a forest bathing guide

Nature & Forest Therapy (www.natureandforesttherapy.earth)

Advice on invasive plant species in the US
National Invasive Species Information Center (www.invasivespeciesinfo.gov)

Native seed sourcing
Seed Savers Exchange (www.seedsavers.org)
The database helps you find thousands of rare, heirloom and open-pollinated varieties.

Relocating native shrubs and trees
Native Resources International (www.nativeresources.com)

Pond building advice
Wildlife Watch (www.wildlifewatch.org.uk)

Attracting butterflies
National Wildlife Federation (www.nwf.org)

Hurricane lamps
Baileys (www.baileyshome.com)

Guide to building a bug hotel
RSPB (www.rspb.org.uk)

Sustainably sourced wood slices
Rustikwoodwork (www.etsy.com)
Ideal for making a cordwood wall to grow mushrooms on.

Eco-friendly bird feeders and birdbaths
· RSPB (www.rspb.org.co.uk)
· The National Audubon Society (www.audubon.org)

Preventing bird strikes
· American Bird Conservancy (www.abcbirds.org)
· Acopian Bird Savers (www.birdsavers.com)

Nest boxes
NestBox Company (www.nestbox.co.uk)
Boxes and easy-to-assemble box kits for insects, birds, bats and small mammals.

Glass outdoor dining tables
Glass Tops Direct (www.glasstopsdirect.com)

Information about bees
The Natural Beekeeping Trust (www.naturalbeekeepingtrust.org)

Oxygen pool systems
Oxygen Pools (www.oxygenpools.com)
For oxygen-based water treatment to safeguard you and wildlife.

Hammocks
Ecualama (www.ecualama.com)
Organic cotton double hammocks handmade by artisans in Ecuador in a range of colours and patterns.

Bushcrafting
David Willis Bushcraft (www.davidwillis.info)
For day or weekend bushcrafting courses.

Advice on native plant species
PlantNative (www.plantnative.org)

Growing trees from seed
National Forest Gardening Scheme (www.nationalforestgardening.org)
Their Forest Garden in a Box scheme is worth looking into.

Organic bug sprays
Sky Organic (www.skyorganics.com)

CHAPTER 9: CHILDREN & PETS

CHILDREN

Accredited forest schools and kindergartens in the UK
The Forest School Association (www.forestschoolassociation.org)

Bushcrafting and re-wilding courses
• David Willis (www.davidwillis.info)
• Ecosystem Restoration Camp (www.ecosystemrestorationcamps.org)

Acoustic panels and desk screens
(Please see Chapter 7 Resources)

Sun pipes
(Please see Chapter 6 Resources)

Floating shelves
Umbra (www.umbra.com)
These become invisible behind a stack of books.

Tent beds
Mathy by Bols (www.mathy-by-bols.be/en/)
They also make fun Treehouse Bunkbeds & Slides and Wagon Beds.

Folding camp chairs
Strongback (www.strongback.com)
Ergonomically designed for kids.

Cotton campfire sets
Chimera Custom Quilts (www.etsy.com)

Skeleton leaves
Skeleton Leaf (www.skeleton-leaf.com)
Sold in bags of 100 or 200, bodhi or rubber tree skeleton leaves are
harvested and processed by hand in Thailand.

Self-adhesive wall mural
(Please see Chapter 7 Resources)

Seabird mobile sculptures
John Perry Studio (www.johnperrystudio.com)

Music of the plants devices
Music of the Plants (www.musicoftheplants.com)
Can translate the electromagnetic impulse of plants into melodies, helping
kids to understand the language of plants through music.

Play support
• Piccalio (www.piccalio.com)
Make the Pikler triangle, Stepping Stones and Reversible Rockwall that
help develop kids' gross motor skills.
• TodGym (www.etsy.com)
For a hand-made indoor playground.

Beanbags for toddlers
Fatboy (www.fatboy.com)
Their oversized cuddly rabbit, CO9 XS Velvet, is very cosy.

Cost-effective and original art frames for teenagers
Runner Frames (www.runnerframes.com)

Child-safe paints
Earthborn Paints (www.earthbornpaints.co.uk)

PETS

Pet beds
Pet Beds Direct (www.petbedsdirect.com)
Hand-made in a wide variety of styles and fabrics, including waterproof.

Cat caves and cocoons
Distinctly Himalayan (www.distinctlyhimalayan.com)
Handcrafted by women's collectives in Nepal using a blend of Tibetan and New Zealand wools.

Cat scratchers
Smartykat (www.smartykat.com)

Anxiety jackets
ThunderShirt (www.thundershirt.co.uk)

Dog appeasing pheromones
Adaptil (www.adaptil.com)

Artificial grass
Top Dog Turf (www.topdogturf.co.uk)

Training programmes for dogs and cats to help kids overcome reading anxiety
• Zoom Room Ruff Reading Therapy Dog Program (www.zoomroom.com)
• Certa Pet (www.certapet.com/therapy-cat/)

GENERAL RESOURCES

Architectural salvage yards
• Antique Church Furnishings (www.churchantiques.com)
• Cox's Architectural Salvage Yard (www.coxsarchitectural.co.uk)
• Lassco (www.lassco.co.uk)
• SALVO (www.salvoweb.com)

Architects and designers
• ARK designer
Mary Reynolds (www.marymary.ie)

- Biophilic architectural and interior designer
Oliver Heath (www.oliverheath.com)
- Eco-sustainable architecture
Giancarlo Zema Design Group (www.giancarlozema.com)
- Intuitive interior designer
Paula Robinson (www.paularobinson.com)

Donations and recycling
In the UK
- British Heart Foundation (www.bhf.org.uk/shop/donating-goods/
book-furniture-collection-near-me)
- DEBRA (www.debra.org.uk/furniture-collection)
- Furniture Donation Network (www.furnituredonationnetwork.org)
- NewStarts (www.newstarts.org.uk/donate/)
- Reuse (www.reuse-network.org.uk/donate-items/#/)

Local councils often recycle household waste and organise collections. To find out more, please visit: www.gov.uk/recycling-collections

In the US
- Donation Town (www.donationtown.org)
- Earth911 (www.earth911.com)
- Habitat for Humanity ReStore (www.habitat.org)
- Planet Aid (www.planetaid.org)

In Australia
- Sustainable Choice (www.sustainablechoice.com)

International
- Buy Nothing (www.buynothingproject.org)
- Recyclers World (www.recycle.net)
- Repair Café (www.repaircafe.org)
- TerraCycle (www.terracycle.com)
- Zillch (www.au.zillch.com)]

Coaching
- Confidence coach
Gaëlle Deschamps (www.gforceco.co.uk)
- Creativity coach
Carla Coulson (www.carlacoulson.com)
- Transformation coach and dressing for confidence expert
Jo Glynn-Smith (www.joglynnsmith.com)

Intuitive intelligence consultants
• Sonia Choquette (www.soniachoquette.com)
• Bernadette Pleasant, The Emotional Institute (www.theemotionalinstitute.com)
• Sonia Tully (www.soniatully.com)

Visualisation tools (2D and 3D apps for room visualisation)
• On Point Designs (www.onpointdesigns.co.uk)
• Room Sketcher (www.roomsketcher.com/blog/visualize-your-interior-design-ideas)
• Roomstyler 3D Home Planner (roomstyler.com/3dplanner)
• Planner 5D (planner5d.com)
• Housecraft (apps.apple.com/us/app/housecraft/id1261483849)

RECOMMENDED READING

BIOPHILIA

Biophilia: A Handbook for Bringing the Natural World Into Your Life by Sally Coulthard (Kyle Books, 2020)

Design a Healthy Home: 100 Ways to Transform Your Space for Physical and Mental Wellbeing by Oliver Heath (DK, 2021)

BOUNDARIES

A World Without Email: Reimagining Work in an Age of Communication Overload by Cal Newport (Portfolio, 2021)

Boundary Boss: The Essential Guide to Talk True, Be Seen, and (Finally) Live Free by Terri Cole (Sounds True, 2023)

Digital Minimalism, Choosing a Focused Life in a Noisy World by Cal Newport (Portfolio, 2019)

Dodging Energy Vampires: An Empath's Guide to Evading Relationships that Drain You and Restoring Your Health and Power by Christiane Northrup, M.D. (Hay House, 2019)

How to Do Nothing: Resisting the Attention Economy by Jenny Odell (Melville House, 2020)

Irresistible: The Rise of Addictive Technology and the Business of Keeping Us Hooked by Adam Alter (Penguin Books, 2018)

CHILDREN

Balanced and Barefoot: How Unrestricted Outdoor Play Makes for Strong, Confident, and Capable Children by Angela J. Hanscom (New Harbinger Publications, 2016)

Home for Dinner: Mixing Food, Fun, and Conversation for a Happier Family

and Healthier Kids by Anne Fishel, Ph.D. (American Management
Association, 2015)

*I Love My World: Stories, Games, Activities and Skills to Help Us All Care for
the Planet We Call Home* by Chris Holland (Wholeland Nature Connection,
2020)

Last Child in the Woods: Saving Our Children From Nature-Deficit Disorder by
Richard Louv (Algonquin Books, 2008)

Messy Maths: A Playful, Outdoor Approach for Early Years by Juliet Robertson
(Independent Thinking Press, 2017)

*The Montessori Baby: A Parent's Guide to Nurturing Your Baby with Love,
Respect, and Understanding* by Simone Davies (Workman, 2021)

*The Montessori Toddler: A Parent's Guide to Raising a Curious and Responsible
Human Being* by Simone Davies (Workman, 2019)

*There's No Such Thing as Bad Weather: A Scandinavian Mom's Secrets for
Raising Healthy, Resilient, and Confident Kids (from Friluftsliv to Hygge)*
by Linda Åkeson McGurk (Touchstone, 2018)

CREATIVITY

Almost Lost Arts: Traditional Crafts and the Artisans Keeping Them Alive by
Emily Freidenrich (Chronicle Books, 2019)

Creativity: A Short and Cheerful Guide by John Cleese (Crown, 2020)

Creatrix: She Who Makes by Lucy H. Pearce (Womancraft Publishing,
2019)

Handmade Home: Living with Art and Craft by Mark Bailey and Sally Bailey
(Ryland, Peters & Small, 2017)

The Book of Symbols: Reflections on Archetypal Images by Archive for
Research in Archetypal Symbolism (ARAS) (Taschen, 2010)

HEALTH & WELLNESS

8 Steps to a Pain-Free Back by Esther Gokhale and Susan Adams (Pendo
Press, 2008)

*Atomic Habits: An Easy and Proven Way to Build Good Habits and Break Bad
Ones* by James Clear (Random House Business Books, 2015)

*Awe: The New Science of Everyday Wonder and How It Can Transform Your
Life* by Dacher Keltner (Penguin Press, 2023)

*Breaking the Habit of Being Yourself: How to Lose Your Mind and Create a
New One* by Dr Joe Dispenza (Hay House, 2013)

Breath: The New Science of a Lost Art by James Nestor (Riverhead Books,
2021). Or for a quicker read, try James Nestor's *Breath: The New Science of
a Lost Art: Get the Key Ideas from Breath in Minutes, Not Hours*

Clear Home, Clear Heart: Learn to Clear the Energy of People & Places by Jean Haner (Hay House, 2017)

Earthing: The Most Important Health Discovery Ever! by Clinton Ober (Basic Health Publications, 2014)

Human Heart, Cosmic Heart: A Doctor's Quest to Understand, Treat and Prevent Cardiovascular Disease by Thomas Cowan, M.D. (Chelsea Green Publishing, 2016)

Hungry Woman: Eating for Good Health, Happiness and Hormones by Pauline Cox (Ebury Press, 2023)

It's Grief: The Dance of Self-Discovery Through Trauma and Loss by Edy Nathan (AS I AM Press, 2018)

Mirror Work: 21 Days to Heal Your Life by Louise Hay (Hay House, 2016)

Pause, Rest, Be: Stillness Practices for Courage in Times of Change by Octavia F. Raheem (Shambhala, 2022)

Pussy: A Reclamation by Regena Thomashauer (Hay House 2018)

Sensehacking: How to Use the Power of Your Senses for Happier, Healthier Living by Charles Spence (Penguin, 2022)

Stolen Focus: Why You Can't Pay Attention -- and How to Think Deeply Again by Johann Hari (Crown, 2023)

The Big Leap: Conquer Your Hidden Fear and Take Life to the Next level by Gay Hendricks (HarperOne, 2010)

The Body Keeps the Score: Brain, Mind, and Body in the Healing of Trauma by Bessel van der Kolk (Penguin, 2015)

The Five-Element Solution: Discover the Spiritual Side of Chinese Medicine to Release Stress, Clear Anxiety, and Reclaim Your Life by Jean Haner (Hay House, 2020)

The Good Life: Lessons from the World's Longest Scientific Study of Happiness by Robert Waldinger, M.D. (Simon & Schuster, 2023)

The Healing Power of Essential Oils by Eric Zielinski (Harmony, 2018)

The Pleasure Prescription: To Love, to Work, to Play – Life in the Balance by David Pearsall, PhD. (Hunter House Publishers, 1996)

The Power of Vulnerability: Teachings on Authenticity, Connection and Courage by Brené Brown (audiobook: Sounds True, 2013)

The Sleep Revolution: Transforming Your Life One Night at a Time by Arianna Huffington (Harmony, 2017)

The Sleep Solution: Why Your Sleep is Broken and How to Fix It by W. Chris Winter, M.D. (Berkley, 2018)

The Untethered Soul: The Journey Beyond Yourself by Michael A. Singer (New Harbinger Publications, 2007)

The Wild Woman's Way: Reconnect to your Body's Wisdom by Michaela Boehm (Enliven Books, 2021)

Unbound: A Woman's Guide to Power by Kasia Urbaniak (TarcherPerigee, 2021)

INTUITION

If Women Rose Rooted by Sharon Blackie (September Publishing, 2019)
Psychic Powers: Unlock Your Natural Intuition by Sahar Huneidi-Palmer (Sirius, 2022)
Sensitive is the New Strong: The Power of Empaths in an Increasingly Harsh World by Anita Moorjani (Enliven Books, 2022)
The Intuitive Way: The Definitive Guide to Increasing Your Awareness by Penney Peirce (Beyond Words, 2009)
Trust Your Vibes: Live an Extraordinary Life by Using your Intuitive Intelligence by Sonia Choquette (Hay House, 2022)
You Are Amazing: A Help-Yourself Guide for Trusting Your Vibes + Reclaiming Your Magic by Sonia and Sabrina Tully (Hay House, 2017)

NATURE

Blue Mind: The Surprising Science That Shows How Being Near, In, On, or Under Water Can Make You Happier, Healthier, More Connected, and Better at What You Do by Wallace J. Nichols (Back Bay Books, 2015)
Bringing Nature Home: How You Can Sustain Wildlife with Native Plants by Douglas W. Tallamy (Timber Press, 2009)
Finding the Mother Tree: Discovering the Wisdom of the Forest by Suzanne Simard (Vintage, 2022)
Floriography: An Illustrated Guide to the Victorian Language of Flowers by Jessica Roux (Andrews McMeel Publishing, 2020)
Food from the Fire: The Scandinavian Flavours of Open-Fire Cooking by Niklas Ekstedt (Pavilion Books, 2017)
Forest Bathing: How Trees Can Help You Find Health and Happiness by Dr Qing Li (Penguin, 2019)
Home Hydroponics: Small-Space DIY Growing by Tyler Baras (Cool Springs Press, 2021)
Ikebana: The Art of Arranging Flowers by Shozo Sato (Tuttle Publishing, 2013)
Messages from Water and the Universe by Dr Masaru Emoto (Hay House, 2010)
Nature's Best Hope: A New Approach to Conservation That Starts in Your Yard by Douglas W. Tallamy (Timber Press, 2020)
Our Wild Calling: How Connecting with Animals Can Transform Our Lives – and Save Theirs by Richard Louv (Algonquin Books, 2020)
Outside: Recipes for a Wilder Way of Eating by Gill Meller (Quadrille, 2022)
Regeneration: Ending the Climate Crisis in One Generation by Paul Hawken (Penguin, 2021)

Shinrin-Yoku: The Japanese Art of Forest Bathing by Yoshifumi Miyazaki (Timber Press, 2018)

The Enchanted Life: Reclaiming the Magic and Wisdom of the Natural World by Sharon Blackie (September Publishing, 2021)

The Garden Awakening: Designs to Nurture Our Land and Ourselves by Mary Reynolds (Green Books, 2016)

The Great Animal Orchestra: Finding the Origins of Music in the World's Wild Places by Bernie Krause (Back Bay Books, 2013)

The Modern Preserver's Kitchen: Cooking with Jam, Chutney, Pickles and Ferments by Kylee Newton (Quadrille, 2021)

The Music of the Plants by Silvia Buffagni Esperide Ananas (Dhora, 2014)

The Nature Fix: Why Nature Makes Us Happier, Healthier, and More Creative by Florence Williams (Norton & Co, 2018)

The Nature of Play: A Handbook of Nature-based Activities for all Seasons by Delphina Aguilar (Fanny & Alexander, 2019)

The Nature Principle: Reconnecting with Life in a Virtual Age by Richard Louv (Algonquin Books, 2012)

The Open-Air Life: Discover the Nordic Art of Friluftsliv and Embrace Nature Every Day by Linda Åkeson McGurk (TarcherPerigee, 2022)

The Self-Sufficient Garden by Klaus Laitenberger (Milkwood Publishing, 2021)

Vitamin N: The Essential Guide to a Nature-Rich Life by Richard Louv (Algonquin Books, 2016)

We Are the ARK: Returning Our Gardens to Their True Nature Through Acts of Restorative Kindness by Mary Reynolds (Timber Press, 2022)

PHILOSOPHY

The Book of Circles: Visualizing Spheres of Knowledge by Manuel Lima (Princeton Architectural Press, 2017)

The Poetics of Space by Gaston Bachelard (Penguin Classics, 2014)

SPIRITUALITY

Black Elk Speaks: Being the Life Story of a Holy Man of the Oglala Sioux by John G. Neihardt (University of Nebraska Press, 1988)

Singing the Soul Back Home: Shamanic Wisdom for Every Day by Caitlín Matthews (Eddison Books, 2003)

Solomon Speaks on Reconnecting Your Life by Dr Eric Pearl and Fred Ponzlov (Hay House, 2014)

The Power of Now: A Guide to Spiritual Enlightenment by Eckhart Tolle (New World Library, 2004)

QUANTUM PHYSICS

The Biology of Belief: Unleashing the Power of Consciousness, Matter &
Miracles by Bruce H. Lipton, Ph.D. (Hay House, 2016)
The Field: The Quest for the Secret Force of the Universe by Lynne McTaggart
(Harper Perennial, 2008)

NOTES

CHAPTER 1: GETTING STARTED

1 www.saturdayeveningpost.com/2010/03/imagination-important-knowledge/
2 Ibid.
3 https://doi.org/10.1073/pnas.0906172107

CHAPTER 2: ENTERING

1 https://www.sciencedirect.com/science/article/abs/pii/S0958259207000533
2 https://blog.ted.com/vulnerability-is-the-birthplace-of-innovation-creativity-and-change-brene-brown-at-ted2012/

CHAPTER 3: LIVING

1 https://www.ncbi.nlm.nih.gov/pmc/articles/PMC6395805/
2 www.nbcnews.com/better/health/what-happens-your-brain-when-you-binge-watch-tv-series-ncna816991
3 https://doi.org/10.1037/h0072647
4 https://pubmed.ncbi.nlm.nih.gov/17462678/
5 https://pubmed.ncbi.nlm.nih.gov/25387270/
6 https://www.sciencedirect.com/science/article/abs/pii/S1744388121001390?via=ihub

CHAPTER 4: RELAXING & WELLNESS

1 https://edynathan.com/grief-its-not-just-about-the-death-of-a-loved-one/
2 https://www.terricole.com/the-art-of-self-soothing/

3 https://www.michaelaboehm.com/the-non-linear-movement-method-2/
4 https://www.saturdayeveningpost.com/2010/03/imagination-i important-knowledge/
5 https://www.nature.com/articles/nn.2726; https://www.ncbi.nlm.nih.gov /pmc/articles/PMC3734071/
6 https://pubmed.ncbi.nlm.nih.gov/30947484/

CHAPTER 5: COOKING & DINING

1 https://twitter.com/DrJoeDispenza/status/1253393348817154048
2 https://link.springer.com/article/10.1007/s40750-017-0061-4

CHAPTER 6: BATHING & SLEEPING

1 https://www.sciencedirect.com/science/article/abs/pii/S1087079218301552 ?via=ihub
2 https://www.sciencedaily.com/releases/2005/06/050630055256.htm
3 https://www.sciencedirect.com/science/article/pii/S0944711319303411
4 https://onlinelibrary.wiley.com/doi/abs/10.1002/ptr.5163
5 https://karger.com/cmr/article/22/1/43/356771/Effects-of-Bergamot-Citrus-bergamia-Risso-Wright
6 https://www.scielo.br/j/reeusp/a/pxVJcRwHMzPQmNkcKdYJGLn/?lang=en
7 https://jamanetwork.com/journals/jamainternalmedicine/fullarticle/2735446
8 https://www.ncbi.nlm.nih.gov/pmc/articles/PMC5299389/
9 https://pubmed.ncbi.nlm.nih.gov/21203365/
10 https://www.nature.com/articles/s41562-020-00963-z
11 https://onlinelibrary.wiley.com/doi/10.1002/jts.22359

CHAPTER 7: WORKING

1 https://link.springer.com/article/10.3758/s13423-018-1539-1
2 https://journals.plos.org/plosone/article?id=10.1371/journal.pone.0182210
3 https://onlinelibrary.wiley.com/doi/full/10.1002/acp.3532
4 https://www.sciencedirect.com/science/article/abs/pii/S0272494415000328
5 https://news-archive.exeter.ac.uk/featurednews/title_409094_en.html .
6 https://www.sciencedaily.com/releases/2012/12/121212204826.htm

CHAPTER 8: OUTDOORS

1 https://journals.sagepub.com/doi/full/10.1177/0963721419854100

2 https://resjournals.onlinelibrary.wiley.com/doi/full/10.1111/icad.12479

3 https://esajournals.onlinelibrary.wiley.com/doi/abs/10.1002/fee.1794

CHAPTER 9: CHILDREN & PETS

1 https://www.bbcwildlife.org.uk/everyone-connected

2 https://www.nature.com/articles/s41599-020-00648-y

3 https://www.sciencedaily.com/releases/2018/03/180305160151.htm

4 https://onlinelibrary.wiley.com/doi/10.1111/j.1532-7078.2011.00107.x

5 https://health.choc.org/how-music-can-benefit-your-childs-mental-health/

6 https://earthinginstitute.net/a-veterinarian-perspective-on-grounding/

FINAL THOUGHTS

1 https://www.ramdass.org/making-every-act-an-offering-of-service/

ACKNOWLEDGEMENTS

Researching and writing this book has been such a fun and enriching journey, full of many unexpected discoveries along the way!

Thank you Sonia Choquette for all your support and generously sharing your wealth of knowledge about intuition in your 'Sonia Suggests' boxes in each chapter.

I also had the great privilege of interviewing some amazing experts: Jean Haner, Mary Reynolds, Richard Louv, Oliver Heath, Carla Coulson, Bernadette Pleasant, Davyd Farrell, Emma Jones, Bruce Peters and Jo Glynn-Smith. Talking to each of you was such a pleasure and broadened my thinking for this book immeasurably. Thank you all for your time and enthusiasm – especially Jean and Mary: your input was truly invaluable!

I am so grateful for the love and support from my family and friends throughout: Leon Rossouw, John Thomas, Dr David MacDonald, Awais Khan, Sophia Claire Thompson (who also introduced me to Jean Haner's work), Nita Davis and Sarah Mellish.

My deepest thanks to the team at Yellow Kite – especially Carolyn Thorne, Lindsay Davies, Clare Sayer and Jo Myler – and to three people who always go above and beyond: my agent Rob Shreeve; Phil Robinson, the architectural illustrator who produced the book's plans and 3D visualisations; and photographer Darren Setlow who took the cover photograph for the book.

ABOUT THE AUTHOR

Credit: Darren Setlow

PAULA ROBINSON

As an intuitive interior designer, Paula Robinson understands the profound effect that the spaces where we live and work have on our health, happiness and success in life. Often called the 'space whisperer', she helps people to create living and working environments that transform their lives on all levels. Paula has been an interiors columnist for *The Sunday Times*, the *Sunday Telegraph* and *Move or Improve?* magazine, and is the author of *The Room Planner: Over 100 Practical Plans for Your Home*. Paula is happiest in nature – especially by the sea – and loves designing outdoor spaces. She is passionate about the environment, sustainable design, re-purposing furniture and objects, and supporting craftspeople over mass-producers.

To learn more please visit: www.paularobinson.com.

INDEX

Page numbers in *italics* refer to illustrations

F
fabrics: fabric walls 17, 36, 66, 162
  furniture 68
  natural fabrics 140
fans 197
Farrell, Davyd 76, 214, 221
fences 222
fertilisers 221
fight, flight or freeze mode 76, 82
fire: bioethanol fires 67
  entrance areas 36
  fire circles 57, 121
  fire pits 231
  fireplaces 45, 66
  fire tables 58
fish 24, 263
Fishel, Anne 114
flats (apartments), small entrances 35
flea markets, kitchens 106
flooring: bathrooms 137
  carpet 16, 262–3
  clean floors 40
  hard floorings 16, 262
  kitchens 100–1
flowers 24, 40, 84, 120, 199, 220–1
focal points: in bathrooms 139
  in home offices 191
  in kitchens 103, 108
  in living areas 45, 63
FOMO (fear of missing out) 30
food, pets 261, 263
foot health 25
forest bathing 187, 210–11
forest schools 241
fractals 158, 244
Frederick, Christine 95
The Free Spirit 9
  bathrooms 146
  dining areas 114
  home offices 179
  kitchens 97, 104, 107
  personal sanctuaries 86, 88
frequency 96–7, 214–16
friluftsliv 241
Fujimori, Terunobu 223–4
fun entrance areas 28
furniture: ball castors 52, 62, 67, 104, 112, 121
  children's rooms 254, 256
  dividing space with 34
  entrance areas 37
  furniture poverty 54
  home offices 179, 185, 189, 190, 197, 199

kitchens 105, 112
layout of 68
living areas 45, 47–8, 52–3, 65, 68
Montessori 254
moving 52–3, 105, 112
nurseries 252–3
upholstered 16

G
gardens: alternate offices 194
  balconies, patio or terrace 228
  children's spaces 255
  expressing yourself 224–6
  fences 222
  first impressions 216–24
  garden design 209
  giving back to nature 212–13
  indoor gardens 66–7, 69, 102–3, 109, 124
  large gardens 230–1
  lawns 221–2
  living tables 119
  making outdoor space work 226–31
  non-native plants 211
  practicalities 232
  small gardens 229
  threat to health 210–16
  water 219
  see also flowers; plants
Gaston, Kevin 235
Gibran, Kahlil 2, 93
glazing: doors 36, 63, 98, 109, 111
  walls 67–8, 108
Glynn-Smith, Jo 184
green colours 15, 23
green roofs 223–4
grief 75, 76
grounding 25, 82, 175, 196, 201, 215, 257–8
  grounding cable visualisation 115
Gullah Geechee 38
gut flora 214

H
Haint Blue 38
hammam 147–8
hammocks 231
hand scrolls 12–13
Haner, Jean 5, 6, 7–8, 10, 96, 159, 160, 185
  children's rooms 248
  creating a sense of home 267
  downtime 73–4
  electromagnetic frequencies 201
  home offices 186
  pets 261